Southern Literary Studies

Southern Literary Studies

LOUIS D. RUBIN, JR.
Editor

A Season of Dreams: The Fiction of Eudora Welty
Alfred Appel, Jr.

The Hero with the Private Parts
Andrew Lytle

Hunting in the Old South: Original Narratives of the Hunters
Clarence Ghodes, Editor

Joel Chandler Harris: A Biography
Paul M. Cousins

John Crowe Ransom: Critical Essays and a Bibliography
Thomas Daniel Young, Editor

A Bibliographical Guide to the Study of Southern Literature
Louis D. Rubin, Jr., Editor

Poe: Journalist and Critic
Robert D. Jacobs

Love, Boy: The Letters of Mac Hyman
William Blackburn, Editor

The Complete Works of Kate Chopin
Per Seyersted, Editor

Kate Chopin: A Critical Biography
Per Seyersted

Without Shelter: The Early Career of Ellen Glasgow
J. R. Raper

Without Shelter

The Early Career of Ellen Glasgow

Without Shelter

The Early Career of Ellen Glasgow

J. R. RAPER

Louisiana State University Press · Baton Rouge

ISBN 0–8071–0904–5
Library of Congress Catalog Card Number 74–142337
Copyright © 1971 by Louisiana State University Press
Manufactured in the United States of America
Printed by The TJM Corporation, Baton Rouge, Louisiana
Designed by J. Barney McKee

To A. B. R. and E. H. R.

Preface

The central drama of Ellen Glasgow's early career is the struggle to unmask an ideology within which her contemporaries took shelter. Throughout her life she fought to free herself from the concept that there is an inescapable essence called Southern-ness, or that as a consequence of heredity and childhood environment she was condemned for life to the attitudes and closed patterns of behavior which mark the "Southerner" and the "Southern Lady." Man is condemned to be free, our philosophers say; yet on every side he still tries to escape into the old slaveries of religion, patriotism, militarism, racial nationalism, and puritanical revolutionary fervor, as in the past he has sought the alibis of Providence, biology, and environment. Although Ellen Glasgow never achieved the radical freedom that man must live with today, she was undoubtedly the most critically aware important southern novelist of her generation, and without question her ability to resist the enslaving forces of her conceptual environment, the southern world view, was the primary strength of her mind.

The central concern of the present study is to follow Ellen Glasgow's use of the complex realism associated with Darwin as a critical tool to strip away the veneers of southern ideology. Since absolutism did not characterize her mind, we must also acknowledge aspects of the regional outlook she chose to salvage: specifically, a highly idiosyncratic form of Jeffersonian agrarianism and the stub-

born fortitude of the southern Scotch-Irish, which she called a vein
of iron.

In addition, I have tried to correct several erroneous opinions
which have been spread about under the guise of criticism or schol-
arship. First, there is Joan Foster Santas' conclusion in *Ellen Glasgow's American Dream* (Charlottesville, 1965) that "we have Ellen
Glasgow's novels to support her revolutionary faith in the possibility of broadening an old Southern path to glory into a durable
public thoroughfare to heaven" (234). This is true only if in our
search for a trustworthy path we go back beyond Calhoun and his
period to the era of Jefferson, at which point it is impossible to
separate, in any significant way, the southern dream from the American, for the Bill of Rights and popular election of the House of
Representatives guarantee the southern dream, embodied in Jefferson's faith in free men, a lasting place in the national way of
life. Second, all I have written should help correct Blair Rouse's
comment in *Ellen Glasgow* (New York, 1962) that Miss Glasgow's
"reaction to her reading of Darwin was more emotional than philosophical" (29), if that implies that her use of Darwinian ideas
was too muddled to merit careful attention. Third, at the same
time I will defend Miss Glasgow against charges similar to Barbara
Giles's—in "Character and Fate: The Novels of Ellen Glasgow,"
Mainstream, IX (September, 1956)—that Miss Glasgow throughout
her career inclined toward a belief "that human beings are 'born'
with noble or ignoble character, . . . basically a belief in 'good
blood' or 'bad' " (30–31); for Miss Glasgow, the interaction of blood,
environment, and free will is a good deal more complex than Barbara Giles suspects. The reason for such mistaken views is that, in
general, critics, taking Miss Glasgow in the tradition of the novelist
of manners, dwell upon the "general outer envelope" of her writing, the social history materials, and neglect the "inner substance,"
which she believed to be "universal human nature"; to appreciate
her distinction we must go deep into Darwinian philosophy.

Finally, I have attempted to answer the question that puzzled
historian C. Vann Woodward when, in his *Origins of the New
South, 1877–1913* (Baton Rouge, 1951), he praised Miss Glasgow

as the forerunner of all literature of the New South. Woodward
put the riddle thus: "The rebellion of Ellen Glasgow [a sheltered
daughter in a Richmond rose garden] can, as yet, only be recorded,
not explained, for of all the strange mutations in this age of the
South's transition hers was the most unaccountable" (434). The
time has come perhaps when by careful interpolation of and extrap-
olation from old and new biographical materials, we can indicate
the scattered factors which in accumulation prepared this remarkable young lady to accept the critical attitudes of Darwinian science
and also the event which probably triggered her amazing revolt.

By 1906 Miss Glasgow had completed her initial sortie under the
banner of southern realism, and although she was temporarily in
retreat she had already established the major themes and positions
which her later works would develop. In addition, she had by 1906
survived several of the most traumatic experiences of her life, painful episodes to which her imagination would return, time and again,
to collect tragic materials for her novels. From both biographical
and literary points of view, she had completed an important phase
of her career.

The study which follows has then two general themes. Of central interest will be the critical analysis of Miss Glasgow's early
novels, while woven throughout this analysis will be interludes of
intellectual and psychological biography. For I (citing William
James, Weber, Mannheim, and many others for authority) am of
the opinion that a man (or a woman) accepts an idea as much
because it satisfies an emotional need or personal prejudice as for
its probable truth. I believe also that this element of emotion in
no way diminishes the historical importance of the idea—once accepted. Such, at least, was the case with Ellen Glasgow, although,
for her, personal need and probable truth more often than not ran
hand in hand.

I wish to acknowledge my great indebtedness to the Council of
Southern Universities, Inc., for the funds on which this research
was begun, and to the Research Committees of Northwestern University and the University of North Carolina at Chapel Hill for
travel grants. I thank First Merchants National Bank of Richmond,

Virginia, for permission to quote from the Ellen Glasgow Collection of Alderman Library, University of Virginia; William W. Kelly for permission to quote from his dissertation, "Struggle for Recognition: A Study of the Literary Reputation of Ellen Glasgow"; the staff of Alderman Library for permission to quote from the Mary Johnston and James Branch Cabell Collections; and Harcourt, Brace & Jovanovich, Inc., for permission to quote from *The Woman Within* and *Letters of Ellen Glasgow*.

I thank also Professors Ernest Samuels and Harrison Hayford of Northwestern University for their patient assistance. More recently, I have benefited from conversations with and the editorial assistance of Professor Louis D. Rubin, Jr., of the University of North Carolina; many of the insights into southern letters found here grew from some clue or hint given by Professor Rubin in casual conversation. Others who have responded to my requests with helpfulness are Miss Marjorie Carpenter and the staff of Deering Library, Northwestern University, Miss Anne Freudenberg and Mr. Harold Eads of Alderman Library, Mr. Mark P. Stumpf of the Joseph Collins Foundation, and Mr. Richard B. Duane, a relative of Dr. Collins. To Anne Raper, my lasting appreciation for her private assistance at all times and all levels.

J. R. R.

Contents

Without Shelter

The Early Career of Ellen Glasgow

Chapter I

The Other Garden, 1607–1892

PLOWS AND ROSES

In the opening pages of Ellen Glasgow's first Virginia novel, *The Voice of the People*, there is a description of a garden, a square enclosure "laid out in straight vegetable rows, marked off by variegated borders of flowering plants." It extends from the brick wall of a graveyard to "the large white pillars of the square front porch" adorning the home of a judge. Nearer the end of that novel, at which time the judge is bedridden with paralysis, the garden itself, which was first transformed by the plow to grow vegetables and mint for juleps, has finally been allowed to lie in ruin.

From her earliest works Ellen Glasgow used formal gardens to symbolize qualities of the social order associated with the Virginia aristocracy. Intentionally or not, this garden stands between man's individual destiny, which is the grave, and his dream of social justice, represented by the judge's columned mansion. In later novels, Miss Glasgow came to use such gardens as metaphors for qualities of the mind of her region. It is a commonplace of psychological theory that social structures are often internalized as psychic structures. This is what happens, in Freudian theory, to a male child who develops an intolerable conscience from growing up under an autocratic father. Or, in existential analysis, a black man who grows up in a colonial society comes, as Frantz Fanon has shown, to see himself and other blacks as inherently inferior because he unconsciously

3

accepts the existing political structure as a mirror of the natural order. And through a similarly unconscious process (complicated by the tenuous existence of the South's mythic aristocracy in the first place), the social structures associated with enclosed flower gardens produce in Ellen Glasgow's characters a type of sheltered mind. The present book is the story of Miss Glasgow's personal rebellion against the pattern of social and mental life often metaphorically represented through gardens, a deceptively natural and rich metaphor which carries the student of her work deep into qualities of southern life around the turn of the century. The nature of her garden, however, sets her apart from the mainstream of American fiction and marks the pioneering character of her contribution to our national literature.

The Garden of the American imagination has traditionally been "the West, the vacant continent beyond the frontier," an always "new and enchanting region of inexpressible beauty and fertility." This, according to Whitman and the popular imagination, is "the real genuine America." It is the Edenic agricultural paradise of "fecundity, growth, increase, and blissful labor in the earth," the escape of Rousseauistic man from the supposedly urban causes of human depravity. Most important, this Garden of the World is, in Henry Nash Smith's words, "grandly and abstractly, a place where afflicted humanity raises her drooping head"; it is the happy abode where the hero of Jefferson's democratic and agrarian nation, the "independent yeoman," lives his productive existence according to the Rights of Man, the simple manners and rational patterns of Americans. In short, *the* Garden is the cliché dwelling place promised by the American Dream.[1]

There is, however, another, equally old garden of the American imagination. Although both find their prototype in Eden, the two begin with opposite images of man and society, and emphasize conflicting qualities. The first, the American Eden, is at bottom Rousseauistic; it assumes the inherent nobility of man, the probable

[1] Henry Nash Smith, *Virgin Land, the American West as Symbol and Myth* (New York, 1959), 4, 12, 139, 144–48.

corruption of social institutions, and the moral holiness of the natural state.

The other garden draws upon an assortment of philosophic and religious notions, whose most articulate expressions include the writings of Thomas Hobbes as well as the Calvinists. It stresses the fallen condition of man and nature. Man is dependent upon strong civil and moral authorities to protect him from himself and others of his kind. Because men in a state of nature are constantly at one another's throats or pocketbooks, they are willing, in their less bloody moments, to sign away their freedoms to someone (a father, a monarch, a theocrat) or to some institution (a constitution, a tradition, a code of conduct) which exists to protect them—primarily from one another.

It is this artificial state that Shakespeare describes in *Richard II* as "our sea-walled garden, the whole land" characterized by "law and form and due proportion." Thomas Huxley's famous Romanes Lecture of 1893 pictures this second garden as man's transcendence of the Hobbesian state of nature, an escape from the tooth-and-claw struggle for existence. As men advance from animals to civilized creatures, they gradually create an artificial environment, a "garden," to guarantee justice (righteousness) for members of their society. The garden here is human civilization thought of as an accumulated body of laws, traditions, codes, and manners. Whereas the primary values of the American Eden are freedom and natural (even wasteful) fecundity, the emphasis in the other garden falls upon order, harmony, stability, and, perhaps, controlled fruitfulness.

It is this other garden of the American consciousness that appears most often in Ellen Glasgow's novels from *The Voice of the People* through *In This Our Life*. Obviously it is, in her imagination, the embodiment of a specific cultural order in America, the Virginia tradition into which she was born and against which she struggled throughout her life. In her novels, more often than not, microphylla roses, an old-fashioned imported product of careful cultivation, set the tone which dominates the garden of Virginia tradition.

Originally, both gardens were indigenous to Miss Glasgow's Virginia. Captain John Smith's idyllic *Description of New England* (1616), centering on Virginia, bodies the new land forth as a second Eden in terms as appealing as a Europe-weary reader could ask. And no one contributed more to the myth that the American agrarian was the new Adam than Thomas Jefferson of Virginia. But as early as 1832, Virginia and its legislature "abandoned Jefferson's ideal of a republic based on small subsistence farmers," and, relinquishing the ideal of prosperity founded upon freedom, settled for products of forced labor and a political order grounded in fear. The crux of the crisis was slavery; the ideal which triumphed, the southern dream of the plantation.[2]

For the simple myth of the landowning yeoman and his plow, the plantation ideal substituted a more complex if somewhat unfocused image. At its center should have been the sweat-streaked, grumbling slave with a hoe, but this less than romantic figure was generally placed far in the background so that the focus of the southern imagination instead fell, as in John P. Kennedy's sometimes satiric *Swallow Barn*, on "aristocratic masters, brilliant and charming heroines, and devoted slaves." In contrast to the "rapidity of change, crudity, bustle, heterogeneity" of Jacksonian democracy in the emerging West, the plantation was "inimical to change," and presupposed "generations of settled existence" and "the beauty of harmonious social relations in an orderly feudal society."[3]

William Taylor's *Cavalier and Yankee* documents the way the literary legend of the pre-cotton South was created after 1817, at which time the few planters of Tidewater Virginia were already in retreat, by such parvenu writers as William Wirt. Although a town dweller with little plantation experience, Wirt nostalgically romanticized the "high civilization" of colonial Virginia in his grossly mythopoeic *Sketches of the Life and Character of Patrick Henry*. Wirt's popular dream kingdom was elaborated by the novelists John Esten Cooke and William Alexander Caruthers of Virginia, Kennedy of Baltimore, and William Gilmore Simms of South Caro-

2 *Ibid.*, 152–53.
3 *Ibid.*, 172–73.

lina.[4] Preconceptions about the plantation were so irresistible that, to quote Henry Nash Smith once more, "the large and important yeoman class of the Old South almost dropped from sight and has had to be rediscovered by historical research." [5] The real women and blacks of the Old South underwent similar eclipses. (Even historical digging has not been able to re-create a complete image of the Negro of the Old South; he has remained an Invisible Man lurking somewhere beneath the fuzz of Uncle Remus, the obsequiousness of Uncle Tom, and the eunuchism of Nigger Jim.) The myth reigned supreme.

But did the Civil War not destroy the plantation system of the Old South? Did the rose garden of the South still exist in Ellen Glasgow's lifetime? How much the Civil War did to cancel the plantation ideal (or even the plantation itself) is debatable. Histories are not entirely reliable in answering such questions. Since objective "history" implies a consensual selection and interpretation of facts to accord with the world view of some ruling class ("lies agreed upon"), such histories are possible only if a stable ruling class exists either in the period of the events or during that in which a specific history is written. But such was not the case in the years after 1865, and, in matters of central importance to the past and future of the southern system (i.e., the southern Negro and his relationship to the southern white), a ruling-class consensus still does not exist. Therefore, rather than expect objective histories of the Reconstruction and New South periods, we often must be content with modes which allow for imaginative exaggeration in the selection and interpretation of facts. For example, viewed from the northern and western point of view, the period of the seventies, eighties, and nineties provides a satire of individual greed *(The Gilded Age)* passing often as an epic of national development ("Pioneers! O Pioneers!" and "Passage to India").

For the southern white, however, this period is a romantic com-

4 William R. Taylor, *Cavalier and Yankee: The Old South and American National Character* (New York, 1961), 67–94. See also Edmund Wilson's commentary in *Patriotic Gore: Studies in the Literature of the American Civil War* (New York, 1966), 440–42.

5 *Virgin Land,* 153.

edy which casts Thaddeus Stevens as the chief blocking figure and sees Black and Radical Republican governments as the evil society of the present with the antebellum plantation as the golden age in the past. The comedy moves toward the inevitable ceremony of conversion and reunion represented, in the popular imagination, by the wedding of a self-effacing heroine, the belle of the South, and her hero, the Yankee officer (Thomas Nelson Page's *Meh Lady*, etc.)— a reunion effected in reality by the closed-door Compromise of 1877, which put Hayes in the White House, and by the reemergence in national politics, after 1874, of the Democratic Party squarely based upon the sometimes solid South.[6] The new society represented by this reunion was that of white Americanism. The irreconcilable character who had to be sacrificed in the comedy's scapegoat ritual was the black American and, more often than not, the representatives of divine Providence were the Ku Klux Klan (Page's *Red Rock* and Thomas Dixon's *The Clansman*).

Finally there is the largely suppressed black man's view of the era, a tragedy of hope generated then destroyed, of a people rebelling against a social order which claimed the authority of the natural order, of a people finding a champion in Lincoln and the Union Army, then winning the war, but losing the victory during the Confederate-style reconstruction of 1865–66, partially regaining their claims to human equality under the protection of the Radical Reconstruction but falling sometimes into excesses of petty human greed and pride before they were sacrificed after 1871 in the name of national unity and the superiority of white civilization, so that finally even most of the blacks were gulled into believing the white man's view of things: that whites are inherently superior to blacks and that the white man's desire for a social order based on racial separation does, in fact, represent the will of the white-faced God who created the natural order.[7] The black man might still enter the rose garden in 1873, the year when Ellen Glasgow was born; he

[6] Cf. Paul H. Buck, *The Road to Reunion* (Boston, 1937), *passim*; and E. Merton Coulter, *The South During Reconstruction, 1865–1877* (Baton Rouge, 1947), 36off., 377.

[7] John Hope Franklin, *Reconstruction: After the Civil War* (Chicago, 1961).

might bring his hoe with him still, but he must leave his hope, his masculine pride, and his human dignity at the gate.

On one point at least, the three imaginative reconstructions of the period agree: the legend of the Old South survived the war virtually intact, especially in Virginia, which lost the war, won the Reconstruction through evasion, but lost (and seems to be only now recovering from) the Redemption. Historians friendly to the southern view have exaggerated the effects of Reconstruction's Carpetbaggers, Scalawags, and Black Rule upon the southern states. C. Vann Woodward contends, "In no Southern state did Radical rule last so long as a decade." [8] The average period of a state under Radical authority was "less than three and a half years." Virginia seems to have escaped genuine Radical rule entirely;[9] this miracle of evasion was effected by confusion in the Radical ranks and unity among native conservatives including "a combination of Confederate Democrats, conservative Republicans, the old-line Whigs, [and] . . . Negroes," guided by Richmond's capitalistic leaders.[10] The politics of the ruling class in Virginia after the war was still Whiggish although the professional interests of that class had shifted from plantations to commerce and industry.[11] In 1866 Richmond began to replace its "burnt district" with impressive structures, and by 1880 it was "the second-largest manufacturing city in the South [behind new Atlanta] with . . . 598 establishments, almost $7,000,000 capital investment, and almost $21,000,000 annual output, paying over $3,000,000 in annual wages." [12] In the countryside, the "small planting class continued to dominate" as before; there was no meaningful redistribution of land. In some cases, names on the titles of plantations changed, but, through sharecropper and tenant arrangements, the large farms remained under the ultimate control of large landowners.[13] Even those southerners who had only a tenu-

---

[8] C. Vann Woodward, *Origins of the New South, 1877–1913* (Baton Rouge, 1951), 22.

[9] Franklin, *Reconstruction*, 197.

[10] Woodward, *Origins of the New South*, 4.

[11] *Ibid.*, 20.

[12] Coulter, *The South During Reconstruction*, 255.

[13] Woodward, *Origins of the New South*, 178; Franklin, *Reconstruction*, 179.

ous claim, or none at all, to planter status in the antebellum period and only mercantile connections in the present, plowed their capital gains into the dream of the Old South and its Lost Cause by building mansions with white columns, donating for Confederate monuments, and subsidizing former Confederates for public office.[14] They wished their wives and daughters to dwell in rose gardens even if they themselves had personally to "mind the store."

As a dream the rose garden, with its nostalgia for an imaginary golden past, would have even greater power of attraction over the mind than it had as a sometime reality before the war. Paradoxically, the deeper the commitments of industrialists to the New South and the more impoverished the conditions of sharecroppers became, "the louder the protests of loyalty" to the Old Order. By 1895 the legend of the Lost Cause had been "taken into custody by Southern Womanhood" and had become a cult marked by religious ardor and sentimentality. The mythic view of the past was a "soothing salve" to compensate for the region's "prevailing sense of inferiority." [15] It caused a totally subjective, magical world to come into being of such unquestionable beauty and purity that it filled completely the consciousness of all those who believed it, keeping their minds away, as the case might be, from the truths of defeat, poverty, or the meanness of commercial and industrial success. As James Branch Cabell has hinted, it was a willed project of self-deception.[16]

French Impressionist Claude Monet painted what must be the paradigm of the rose garden in this period, "Au jardin." The human forms in the foreground are extraordinarily real while in the background the foliage of the garden itself fades into the dreamlike splotches, strokes, and streaks of nascent Impressionism. Three young ladies, with parasols and billowing long dresses of white, blue, orangish pink, seem frozen, entranced by bouquets of roses: pink, crimson, yellow, white; their faces are washed with a sentimental serenity. A fourth, with bright auburn hair, hurries alone

14 W. J. Cash, *The Mind of the South* (Garden City, 1956), 133–35. For a discussion of the South's dual mind after the war, see James Branch Cabell, *Let Me Lie* (New York, 1947), 143–59.
15 Woodward, *Origins of the New South*, 155–57.
16 Cabell, *Let Me Lie*, 143–59.

from the end of a path into the decomposing shadows, as though startled, then attracted by an intruder (the rose in her hand, a sparrow, a lover?) in the static garden.

Although created several thousand miles from Ellen Glasgow's Richmond, Monet's "Au jardin" represents essential qualities of the rose garden whatever its particular locale. The garden (not the painting) is evasive, ideal, static. We must ascribe every act to the noblest motive—it is the rose, not her lover or any other mundane call, which draws the fourth girl into the shadows. The tone is sentimental, as was so much European and American life in this period of Victoria, Gentility, and the Second Empire. The young French ladies are fortified, sheltered exactly like their Virginia counterparts, within a boundary of mindless complacency—three of the four seem unaware of the "haunting fear and uneasiness" waiting beyond the wall of foliage. Ideally, the southern gentlemen of the period built such walls to guard their ladies from the complementary threats of black men, sexuality, and socioeconomic upheaval (their actual motives remain for Miss Glasgow's own commentary). No doubt nineteenth-century Frenchmen agreed with Thomas Huxley in England and contemporary southern males that the civilization they together defended represented the "summit of human achievement." [17] Social leaders in the South manufactured flimsy genealogies detailing each step of progress toward their present pinnacle of culture, and thereby, like an Old Testament historian, persuaded the North, their lower-class neighbors, and even themselves that their faith was solidly founded in continuous tradition.

This was the garden into which Ellen Glasgow was born in 1873. If it was temporarily in confusion, the cause probably had less to do with Reconstruction than with the state of the national economy, for her father was among the industrial leaders of booming Richmond, and 1873 was a year of crushing national panic. But the garden recovered sufficiently to become a stifling force throughout Ellen Glasgow's early years, in part causing, and serving as the target of, her later intellectual rebellion.

Perhaps the simplest clue to the way the rose garden functioned

[17] Cash, *Mind of the South*, 133–36.

in Miss Glasgow's imagination is to note the pattern that recurs in the table of contents to key novels from all phases of her career. The books of *The Wheel of Life* are titled "Impulse," "Illusion," "Disenchantment," and "Reconciliation"; those of *Virginia*: "The Dream," "The Reality," "The Adjustment"; those of *Life and Gabriella*: "The Age of Faith" and "The Age of Knowledge"; those of *The Sheltered Life*: "The Age of Make-Believe," "The Deep Past," and "The Illusion"; those of *In This Our Life*: "Family Feeling," "Years of Unreason," and "All Things New"; and those of *Beyond Defeat*: "The Shadow," "The Substance," and "The Light in the Sky." The pattern common to each is not simply the sense of conflict essential to all dramatic literature, but a full-blown intellectual dialectic, moving from thesis (usually illusion of one sort or another) through antithesis (reality) to synthesis; the latter is usually pragmatic or ironic—except for *Beyond Defeat* where the reconciliation is clearly meant as a paradigm of the good life. This dialectic mirrors Ellen Glasgow's stormy personal development—biographical, intellectual, and literary. The thesis or illusion in her development is the shielded garden of her young girlhood. The antithesis or reality is the world beyond the garden, the Darwinian world uncovered by the new science of the late nineteenth century, a world which dazzled and attracted as she saw it creating or transforming itself before her eyes. The synthesis was her own imaginative fusion of the illusion and the reality, a synthesis with which she was never satisfied and which she continued to revise until in her final (posthumous) novel she created a model of agrarian freedom much closer to Jefferson's ideal than to the rose garden.

The story of Ellen Glasgow's first twenty years is largely an illusion into which ominous shadows of the real seep from time to time, suggesting dangers beyond the garden. Her first two novels show her experimenting with aspects of Darwinian reality. It is not until her third book, *The Voice of the People,* that she brings the two worlds together in her initial full-sized picture of Virginia. During the first twenty years, Ellen Glasgow's immediate family provided all the evidence needed that the protective garden has its own dark recesses.

A PERPETUAL CONFLICT OF TYPES

The factors which prepared Ellen Glasgow to embrace rebellion as a way of life were part of the general atmosphere dominating her first twenty years. The early sections of her autobiography, *The Woman Within*, show that, conditioned for resistance, she initially adopted the outlook of critical realism itself more as a mode of rebellion against the Victorian traditions of her family and region than as a tool through which one discovers truth. Later she would return to the modern critical attitude which grew out of Darwinism, because its strenuous view of life matched the world of her childhood; a world that, for all its sheltering evasions, seemed a place of unending conflict: between man and woman, between man and society, between man and his past, and often, though not always, between man and nature. Memories of childhood convinced her that the chief alternative to constant struggle must be something like the imaginative sympathy Darwin identified as the root of moral conduct. She thus found in the theories of the great evolutionist a confirmation and illumination of her own intuitions regarding human nature.

The following account of these early years draws of necessity upon the autobiography and is therefore, in part, a summary (seen from a critical distance) of Ellen Glasgow's image of her own life. Of special interest are her views of her relationships with her parents, pets, and servants, with nature, organized religion, words, her peer group, poverty, southern chauvinism, and northern publishers. The sense of unending conflict, of suffering and alienation, is present in the autobiography itself. Where additional sources are accessible (especially heretofore unexamined materials regarding the illnesses of her mother and of Cary, her sister, and the mysterious death of Cary's husband, the major intellectual guide of Miss Glasgow's early years), they support Miss Glasgow's notion that her early life was starkly tragic—even more so than she herself admitted. The new materials reinforce the novelist's suggestion that this tragic sense prepared her to accept and hold to the Malthusian-Darwinian image of man's place in the universe. But the roots of this struggle were present long before she herself was born in 1873.

In Richmond, in 1873, the Francis T. Glasgows embodied a compromise with the then emerging New South which was probably never mentioned by the older members of the family, for any such allusion would have reminded them that their notion of the social structure of the Old South was a myth rooted in an illusion. Within its body the family attempted to reconcile, sometimes none too smoothly, the opposites which historians have identified as the source of the most significant genetic and ideological conflict of the white South. Historians also argue that the large social conflict represented in the Glasgow family goes farther than any other single factor toward explaining the transformation from the rationalism of the region's eighteenth-century statesmen to the emotionalism of its spokesmen during the crucial decades leading to, and away from, the Civil War.[18] This conflict of types, in turn, became the central opposition of temperaments present in Ellen Glasgow's fiction.

Mrs. Glasgow, to be sure, was a descendant of the Tidewater Anglo-Episcopal plantation aristocracy. As the former Anne Jane Gholson, she could, if pressed, show a connection with the famous Randolphs (through Colonel William Randolph of Turkey Island), another with the original Virginian Woodsons (who had crossed the Atlantic in 1619), and even a tie with the cosmopolitan de Graffenrieds (through Christophe de Graffenried, Landgrave of the Carolinas under Queen Anne).[19] But her line backwards to such Virginians of real distinction was a weak one, running chiefly through females, and seems in retrospect only to symbolize the widespread infirmity, even before the war, of that once grand class. For Anne Jane Gholson's closest relatives, and those to whom she was most indebted, were her grandmother's in-laws, the Creed Taylors of "Needham." The Taylors had adopted Anne Jane when her mother[20] died shortly after the child's birth, December 9, 1831. Taylor (1766–

18 See James McBride Dabbs, *Who Speaks for the South?* (New York, 1964).
19 Also with the Yateses, the Bakers, the Pendletons, the Blands, the Booths, the Gholsons, and the Creeds of Virginia; see Ellen Glasgow, "A Dull Note for Genealogists," *The Woman Within* (New York, 1954), 299–300. Hereinafter cited as *Woman*.
20 Martha Anne Jane Taylor, 1805–31.

1836) was chancellor of the Richmond and Lynchburg Superior Court of Law and Chancery, and the founder (in 1821) of a "famous law school" and experimental moot court.[21] But his estate, Needham, fifty miles southwest of Richmond, in Cumberland County, seemed at times to serve as an orphanage for his nieces; for the chancellor, whether from benevolence or family necessity, had similarly adopted the mother of Anne Jane Gholson twenty-one years earlier when Anne Jane's grandmother (and the chancellor's sister-in-law) died. Anne Jane's father, William Yates Gholson—son of a United States congressman and a former student of the chancellor's law school—deposited his daughter, along with her only brother, at Needham when, after his wife's death, he moved, first, to Mississippi to practice law and, after a few years, to Cincinnati, where he eventually became a judge of the Ohio Supreme Court (1860–65). Gholson thus passed responsibility for the education and marriage of his only daughter on to the Taylors.[22] But the chancellor died in 1836, leaving the marriage of Anne Jane Gholson to the care of his "high-strung and nervous" wife.[23] It is understandable, then, that Anne Jane's marriage in 1853 did not take place as securely within the Anglo-Episcopal Tidewater tradition as the chancellor might have desired.

Francis Thomas Glasgow was a hard-shell Scotch-Irish Presbyterian and, more important for the economic well-being of the chancellor's adopted granddaughter, a rising southern industrialist. These are details generally played down by critics who see Ellen Glasgow as the novelist of the aristocratic Anglo-Episcopal Tidewater South and contrast her as such with Thomas Wolfe, who clearly is the spokesman of the middle-class Scotch Piedmont South.[24] Aside from the fact that two of her most important novels,

21 Thomas P. de Graffenried, *History of the de Graffenried Family, from 1191–1925* (New York, 1925), 197, 199. See also Matthew P. Andrews, *Virginia, The Old Dominion* (New York, 1937), 370, 621.

22 De Graffenried, *History*, 200.

23 Sally Woodson Taylor, the model for those ladies in Ellen Glasgow's novels who either read *Mysteries of Udolpho* in bed, like Mrs. Lightfoot in *The Battle-Ground*, or had their portraits done by St. Memin (de Graffenried, *History*, 197–98).

24 C. Hugh Holman, *Three Modes of Modern Southern Fiction: Ellen Glasgow, William Faulkner, Thomas Wolfe* (Athens, Ga., 1966), 9–25.

Barren Ground and *The Vein of Iron*, deal with similarly non–Tidewater Presbyterian Virginians, it is likely that the presence in her own family of representatives of the conflicting Souths contributed to the detached doubleness of vision which enabled Ellen Glasgow to focus critically, in her fiction, on either South.

Francis Glasgow was the grandson of that Arthur Glasgow (1750–1822) who had emigrated, with his mother and his elder brothers, from Ulster in 1766—rather late compared with the Woodsons—and had followed the Pennsylvania Road, then the twists of the James River 120 miles west from Richmond "into the spacious fertile valley of the Shenandoah between the Blue Ridge Mountains and the Alleghanies." [25] There the Glasgows "took possession" of four or five thousand acres which today include two small towns, Buena Vista and Glasgow, just south of Lexington, Virginia. They prospered well enough on their plantation—called Green Forest because Glas Gow means green forest in Gaelic—to replace an earlier log dwelling, immediately after the Revolution, with a brick house (*Woman*, 298, 301). When this house partially burned (about 1830), it was rebuilt in brick and stone by Arthur Glasgow's second son, Robert. Robert married his cousin, Catherine Anderson—the descendant of a second Scotch-Irish family, who had settled in neighboring Botetourt County—and had nine children, the fifth of whom was Francis Thomas Glasgow, born September 13, 1829.[26]

As the fifth child, Francis' inheritance would consist less of property than of those intangibles traditionally passed on by Scotch-Irish families: a framework of "solid and austere virtues," the desire for an education, and, in this case, a group of workable family connections. In 1844 the boy entered Washington College (now Washington and Lee University) in nearby Lexington and "was graduated, with the degree of A.B., in 1847." Then Francis followed the James east to Richmond where he read law until, in 1849, Joseph Reid Anderson, his mother's brother, and president of the Tredegar Iron Works, invited Francis to join the Richmond

---

25 Monique Parent, *Ellen Glasgow, Romancière* (Paris, 1962), 122. All translations from Parent are by J. R. Raper.

26 *Ibid.*, 123.

concern, an association which was to endure for more than sixty-three years.[27]

How this uncompromising industrialist from the Valley met the "infinitely tender and fragile" Anne Jane Gholson, "a flower of the Tidewater," is not recorded, but the linking of industrialists with members of the slavocracy was a familiar pattern of the period.[28] On July 14, 1853, they were married in Richmond, and before the war began in 1861 she had given birth to four children, the first born dead in 1854.[29] Although Francis, we are told, had freed his personal slaves before the war, he gave his full support to the South, becoming, family tradition says, one of "the first to volunteer for service in the Confederate Army." [30]

It is strange that one seemingly little concerned with slavery would be so enthusiastic. But here, as in many facets of his career, Glasgow was simply identifying his interests with those of Tredegar Iron Works and his uncle, Joseph Anderson. Anderson, who has been called the "most conspicuous manufacturer of the slavocracy," became in 1845 the first ironmaker in America to employ trained slave labor. Indeed this effort to cut production costs in order to compete with northern and Welsh manufacturers worked so well that Anderson continuously increased the number of slaves Tredegar owned, and moved steadily, despite his economic ties with the tariff-minded Whigs of the Northeast, toward the proslavery position of southern planters.[31] Faced after secession began with a largely southern market and the threat of complete economic failure, Anderson became a dogmatic secessionist.[32] (It might be added that Anderson had long made a specialty of munitions for the

---

27 De Graffenried, *History*, 200.

28 Parent, *Ellen Glasgow*, 126; *Woman*, 299; Kathleen Bruce, *Virginia Iron Manufacture in the Slave Era* (New York, 1939), 262. They may have met through Mrs. Glasgow's maternal grandfather, Samuel Taylor (1781–1853), a leading Richmond lawyer. For the larger significance of the conflict stressed here between the Anglican and Scotch-Presbyterian Souths, see Dabbs, "Puritans of the South," 79–99. Dabbs believes this conflict was the essential tension of southern life. My emphasis is based completely on the conflict implicit in Ellen Glasgow's autobiography and novels.

29 Parent, *Ellen Glasgow*, 127–28.

30 *Ibid.*, 123.

31 Bruce, *Virginia Iron*, 234–35, 259–63, 267–71, 427.

32 *Ibid.*, 334–35.

United States government.) Francis followed his uncle's lead.

Fortunately for his family, however, Glasgow's employer, now *General* Anderson, "refused to permit his enlistment because he could be of greater service" to Virginia and the Confederacy at the Tredegar Iron Works,[33] which was to be, after Anderson volunteered its services, the chief supplier of munitions of war for Lee's army of northern Virginia, and the company that overhauled and outfitted the Confederate ram, the *Merrimac*, with iron plates and guns.[34] The Glasgow family thus spent the war years in the Valley of Virginia, "the only available supply of ore" and "a territory frequently overrun by Federal troops," where Glasgow was Tredegar's agent for five blast furnaces in Botetourt and Rockbridge counties. His responsibilities included the transportation of iron to the Manassas Railroad and the James River—sometimes a distance of twenty miles—for shipment to Richmond, and the management of a labor force which included convicts and slaves hired from plantation owners. When word of the Emancipation Proclamation secretly reached the slaves, they rebelled against the Tredegar management. Glasgow, it is recorded, punished the Negro leaders to prevent further disaffection.[35] During these violent years, Anne Jane Glasgow gave birth to a third daughter, Cary Gholson. When, for six months immediately after the war, the Tredegar Works was taken over by Union troops, Francis Glasgow carried his family back to the war-devastated family plantation, Green Forest, which he worked to rehabilitate and where his second son and eventual heir, Arthur Graham Glasgow, was born less than two months after Lee had surrendered at Appomattox sixty miles away.[36]

The fire of war and the threat of a common enemy had so fused

33 "The removal of the Confederate capital to Richmond was largely dictated by the necessity of holding the Tredegar Works, and the same necessity largely governed Confederate military strategy throughout the war." Anderson himself served as a brigade commander at the battles of Mechanicsville and Chickahominy in June, 1862; wounded, he returned to Richmond in July, 1862, to take charge of Tredegar, running the vital firm with extraordinary efficiency. *The Dictionary of American Biography*, I (New York, 1928), 268–69. Hereinafter cited as *Dictionary*.

34 Andrews, *Virginia*, 436; Bruce, *Virginia Iron*, 352–58; de Graffenried, *History*, 200.

35 Bruce, *Virginia Iron*, 371–93, 399.

36 De Graffenried, *History*, 200–201.

the two classes from which Anne Jane Gholson and Francis Glasgow came that the distinctions which once had counted—national ancestry, church, region, occupation—were largely forgotten, even by the families involved, and, in retrospect at least, the Valley and the Tidewater, the Scotch-Irish Presbyterians and the Anglo-Episcopalians, the industrialists and the planters, of the Old South seemed one. But there were deeper differences of class conditioning which, even if forgotten, would still matter profoundly—at least to members of the generation which spanned the abyss between the Old and the compromised Souths. A childhood spent in the ease of Needham had not prepared Anne Gholson for the years during which she would face the hardest tasks of housekeeping in the war-ruined Valley; nor had it fortified her constitution sufficiently to nourish the eleven children she bore her hardier Scotch-Irish mate. Her husband was able eventually to return to Richmond to become a managing director of the partially burned Tredegar Works, valued in December 1865 at $725,000, more than in 1861 (Anderson lost his cause but little else). But their ninth child, born April 22, 1873, at the corner of First and Cary Streets, Richmond, would suffer the effects of Mrs. Glasgow's physical and emotional exhaustion. The Glasgows named their fifth daughter Ellen Anderson Gholson Glasgow (*Woman*, 5–6).[37]

VICTIMS

Ellen Glasgow's autobiography stresses her view of her parents as temperamental opposites. The images she associated with each suggest that while Mrs. Glasgow was perhaps the prototype of those characters in her daughter's fiction who combine highly developed moral sympathies with an infirm personal will, Francis Glasgow foreshadowed the heroes of strong will but ruthless indifference to the well-being of others. In fairness to Francis Glasgow, it should be pointed out that his daughter's portrait of him has been contradicted by his heir, Arthur Graham Glasgow, and his grandson, Car-

[37] *Ibid*, 201. Parent, *Ellen Glasgow*, 122–23, 128; see especially 129–30 for the difficulties involved in fixing the novelist's birthdate and year.

rington C. Tutwiler, Jr., who contend that Miss Glasgow's image of their progenitor is a myth, an effort to portray him as a "sort of Virginia ogre: a Richmond Father Brontë; a Confederate Bronson Alcott, neither responsible nor sympathetic." [38] As the case may be, the historical Francis Glasgow is not finally at issue here—only the Francis Glasgow who existed in his daughter's mind and influenced her image of man. If *The Woman Within* is correct, Ellen Glasgow associated her three earliest recollections, all cruel ones, with her father.

Her first memory seems to embody the hostility of the physical universe. She was born so small and frail that for her first three weeks she was carried on a pillow rather than in the arms. She was initially "stabbed into consciousness" by the sun, beyond a window-pane, which impressed her opening mind as a "bloated mask of evil": "a face without a body" staring in at her, "a vacant face, round, pallid, grotesque, malevolent" (*Woman*, 3–5). Through an unfortunate process, the child came to view her father, like the sun, as an oppressor, and her mother, like the will-less infant, as an eternal victim in this hostile universe—a bizarre application of the sun-earth, male-female archetypal relationships.

A second recollection involved the dawning of the sympathetic imaginaton in her own nervous system, the birth of her feelings of compassion and benevolence, afterwards repulsed by her father's hardness and frugality. She recalled that her first image of a victim of merciless power was a large black dog that had come running toward her perambulator, fleeing in terror from stones thrown by a shouting pack of men and boys. Instantly, the child sensed a "strange transference of identity, the power to suffer for something outside" herself—the root of the Darwinian moral sense: "I run out into the street. My mammy . . . swoops down and gathers me up into her arms. But I have seen what it means to be hunted. I run on with

[38] Carrington C. Tutwiler, Jr., "Excerpts from Ellen Glasgow—The Writer as Reader," *The de Graffenried Family Scrap Book*, ed. Thomas P. de Graffenried (Charlottesville, 1958), 216–21. Miss Glasgow's view of her father fits a pattern common among American women of the nineteenth century, the "sisterhood of suffering," "a tradition handed down from mother to daughter, of masculine brutality." Christopher Lasch, "Emancipated Women," *The New York Review of Books*, IX (July 13, 1967), 28.

the black dog. . . . I am beaten with clubs and caught in a net." She would forever suffer with abused, inarticulate victims, and hate those who abused power (*Woman*, 8–10). Years afterwards, this incident would blend with the cruelty she sensed in her father when he refused to allow her to bring back to Richmond a small pointer she had become attached to during a summer on the family's farm. She turned against her father: "I never forgave Father, who did not like dogs." Pat went instead to an indifferent overseer whom she disliked: "For years I agonized over Pat's fate" (*Woman*, 27–28, 51–52). How much she agonized is suggested by the fact that, from Eugenia Battle in *The Voice of the People* to Asa Timberlake and Kate Oliver in *Beyond Defeat*, a character's treatment of dogs and other animals is perhaps the surest hint of his capacity for imaginative sympathy, and of Ellen Glasgow's personal feeling about him. Pat was himself eventually resurrected as one of two canine companions of Kate Oliver and Asa Timberlake in the apocalyptic vision of Miss Glasgow's final novel.[39]

Her third early memory represented the seemingly universal failure of one man (or one group of men) to understand the pain or needs of others. She recalled Uncle Henry, an old Negro, whom she had seen struggle as he was "brought out from his cellar and put into the wagon from the almshouse." He was, she later realized, penniless and would have starved in his cellar, but he did not "want to go to the poorhouse." He was "still young enough to dread that." He cried, he resisted. A group of little boys began to jump up and down. At first Ellen imitated the boys, but suddenly she stopped and burst into tears: "A flood of misery pours over me. I am lost and hopeless. Nothing that I can do will stop them from taking the old man away." Her father demonstrated a want of understanding and generosity that linked him, in the girl's mind, with the unfeeling power that oppressed Uncle Henry. When, in "the hungry eighties," Ellen wanted a doll with real hair, her father told her she could not have it "because we had 'lost everything in the war.' "[40]

[39] For an interesting though ironic clue to the source of the second dog's name, Percy, see "Alienists and Agent" in Chap. 4, below.

[40] Ellen Glasgow, *A Certain Measure* (New York, 1939), 12. Hereinafter cited as *Measure*.

The Tredegar Works had, it is true, been in the hands of a receiver from 1876 to 1878, but a managing officer in a firm which intended in 1884 to exhibit its "freight cars, spikes and other products" at the World's Industrial Exposition in New Orleans[41] would probably have bought a doll for his young daughter—if he had had the sympathy and imagination to see the world through eyes other than his own. The same wall that kept the boys from understanding the old man's plight kept the father from understanding his daughter (and, as it turns out, his wife). In her first two years, the girl intuited that if that wall stood, nothing she could do would "make the world different" (Woman, 10–11).

LIGHTS LIKE FLOWERS

But these were only premonitions of the lonely exile to come later, for during the first seven years the shadows were lightened, if not vanquished, by contrasting images of sympathy, sacrifice, and beauty that seemed to cluster about her mother. The child's earliest impression of joy, at two or three, came when an old lamplighter passing down Cary Street raised his stick to the tall lamps on the corners, and one after another, the lights bloomed out, shining, "like a row of pale daffodils" (Woman, 7–8). Because her mother seemed another pale flower, Ellen gravitated instinctively towards her already failing gaiety and brightness, even after a tragic shape dimmed the woman's light: when Ellen was three her oldest brother died, bringing on the exhausted mother an anguishing, long nervous illness.[42] Ellen was especially drawn to her mother because, unlike her husband, Mrs. Glasgow displayed a feeling for animals and a generosity towards former servants in need (Woman, 13–14).

Too weak to care for her daughter properly, Mrs. Glasgow extended her love through the agency of Lizzie Jones, a woman with "unusual intelligence, a high temper, and a sprightly sense of humor." Much later Ellen Glasgow was to look back, in a typical

41 Dictionary, I, 268–69; J. Malcolm Bridges, "Industry and Trade," Richmond, Capital of Virginia: Approaches to its History (Richmond, 1938), 75.
42 The death of Joseph Reid Glasgow (1860–76), who was named for his uncle, left Arthur Graham Glasgow as Francis Glasgow's primary heir.

southern fashion, on the years spent with Mammy Lizzie, 1876–79, as the most carefree of her life. Lizzie Jones offered the best treatment possible for a child who, as a consequence of poor prenatal nourishment and serious, early attacks of diphtheria and scarlet fever, was so pale and nervous that doctors thought it unlikely she "should ever live to grow up" (*Woman*, 12, 24, 87–88). Lizzie took the girl for excursions about the heart of Richmond: Capitol Square, St. Paul's Church, the Governor's mansion, and the City Alms House, which had been an important military hospital. Sometimes they haunted "strangely romantic" cemeteries where Confederate heroes nursed their glory, or disturbed the shadows of old houses with dwindling gardens along Cary Street where the past lived out its sheltered life (*Woman*, 18–22). And after 1878 when her father bought a farm north of Richmond called Jerdone Castle, Ellen and Lizzie Jones ranged about the wide fields of corn and tobacco, through the broomsedge and scrub pine, and on into the virgin woods. Summers were given to natural things—earth, sky, hills, fields, trees, grass, flowers—for which the girl developed a love that throughout life was to be, in a profound naturalistic manner, second only to her "sense of an enduring kinship with birds and animals, and all inarticulate creatures" (*Woman*, 26–27).

To the outings, the frail child responded first with "an inborn love of adventure and a vital curiosity" and then, slowly, with an infant imagination. In the evenings, states the autobiography, she and Lizzie spun out a continuous adventure of even greater excitement: "Out of the dim mists of infancy a hero named Little Willie had wandered into the strange country of [Ellen's] mind, or, it may be, at the start, into Mammy's." Little Willie joined the circus, became lost in the woods, or was pursued by bears—even lived with the Swiss Family Robinson (*Woman*, 20, 23–24).

The girl's mind was thus creating fictions long before she could write them down. Because doctors had warned her mother against teaching a child who seemed too sickly to live, Ellen and the alphabet were left to themselves. Her father's elder sister, Aunt Rebecca, related plots of *The Waverly Novels* so perfectly, we are told, that Ellen eventually could no longer tolerate the barrier which kept

her from a limitless stream of new adventures, and charged into
Old Mortality, taking it apart letter by letter, "spelling out the
words." She would learn her letters; then she would teach Lizzie
hers (*Woman*, 24–25).

EXILE

But in the spring of 1880, just after Ellen's seventh birthday, Lizzie Jones left the Glasgows. The sight of her departing carriage,
Miss Glasgow later wrote, tore the child's world apart. The excursions and evening stories were over. "Little Willie had vanished.
He never came back." At seven, the precocious girl sensed that already the most ordered and complete time of her life was finished;
Lizzie's departure "was the beginning of that sense of loss, of exile
in solitude, which I was to bear with me to the end" (*Woman*,
29–30).

Alienated by temperament from her father, separated by sickness
from her mother, and now divided from Lizzie, Ellen Glasgow, in
the year 1880–81, searched for a new center of meaning and order;
religion, words, and social groups outside the family offered themselves, but each proved unequal to her immediate emotional needs.
According to *The Woman Within*, a few weeks after Lizzie's departure, the child found herself overwhelmed by a religious conversion at a revival conducted by visiting evangelist, Dwight L.
Moody. When the preacher singled out "the little girl in blue on
the front bench" to lead the assembly in the Gospel hymn, "Rescue
the Perishing," her Aunt Rebecca, with whom Ellen attended,
helped the child, full of shame and horror, perform her religious
duty. But when Moody left Richmond, it meant the permanent end
of Ellen's evangelistic fervor; "organized" religion was too much a
community affair for an ego more secure in the company of dogs,
trees, and open land. In later years her religious sense would mature
toward the older mystic and philosophic traditions of the East, positions more easily synthesized with Darwinism than was Moody's
(*Woman*, 34–35).

In the same year, the girl's insecurity inspired her first literary effort. According to the autobiography, "one summer day, lying on the blue grass at Jerdone Castle," she suddenly caught herself chanting aloud the desire to drift with the clouds. Realizing her chant was poetry and she had made it, she rushed into the house and wrote out a hymn: five 4-stress lines, rhyming aa, bb, c. Based on her own frustrating captivity in "this land of mist and snow," the verses express the wish to leave "behind me the world's sad choices" and to listen, "at the foot of my Father's throne," for "angels' voices" alone. Exhilarated by this ability to sublimate her loneliness, she relished "that strange exile to which all writers who are born and not made are condemned." But this joy lasted only a few days, until she overheard one of her sisters reading the "precious verses aloud" amid bursts of "kindly ridicule and amusement" from her guests. The young poetess plunged into despair, and the emotional energy which had fed her creativity escaped underground where it flowed on in a strong steady course until sixteen years later, after she had published her first novel anonymously, Ellen Glasgow allowed her name to be printed on the title page of *Phases of an Inferior Planet* (*Woman*, 36–37).

If her creative energy had found its buried channel, it was still necessary to maintain day-to-day relations with her mother, her brother Frank, her sister Rebe, and two friends, Carrie Coleman and Elizabeth Patterson.[43] Safe with her coterie, she enjoyed the realistic war dramas recounted by Miss Virginia Rawlings, a family companion and governess who had shared the "war terrors and anxiety, and the worse horrors of Reconstruction" with the Glasgows, and then "stayed on permanently, as one of the family" (*Woman*, 38).

When, however, in October, 1880 or 1881, Ellen was finally sent to school for her first term (probably to that run by John Henry Powell and George F. Merril on Cary Street), it was without the company of Rebe or Elizabeth. This first attempt, she later contended in the autobiography, lasted less than one day. During the

---

[43] Francis Thomas Glasgow (1870–1909), who committed suicide, and Rebe Gordon Glasgow (1877–1967) were at this time the brother and sister closest to Ellen in age and interests; see Richmond *Times Dispatch*, April 8, 1909, p. 10.

morning, she feared that she might be forced to spend ten years in a torture chamber crowded with pupils and hard benches. During the first recess, she watched, in nervous despair, as another girl ate the biscuits, chicken, muffin, and apple she was herself too sick with fear to want. After the recess, she felt one of her nervous headaches beginning, broke out in a cold sweat, and feared she would throw up. She overheard an older girl whispering behind her back, "Look at the white rabbit!" She "dashed out of the door, into the paved yard, through the gate, down the empty street to [her] sure refuge with Mother." Like the dog that had run towards her perambulator, she felt she was being pursued by the hostile class. As a good sheltering southern mother, Mrs. Glasgow "understood": Ellen would not have to go back to school (*Woman*, 41–50).[44]

After this experience, Ellen underwent schooling of a less public sort in a seminary, at 307 West Franklin Street, run by Miss Etta Munford. Even though this second episode lasted "less than a year," she profited sufficiently to write, years later, a novel based, in part, on Miss Munford, one of four sisters of the "great" Munford family. After the male Munfords were killed in the Civil War, the sisters lived on in impoverishment, forced into teaching as the only way to earn their livelihood. This situation Ellen Glasgow would describe in *Virginia*.[45]

Systematic education thus failed Ellen in one of its most important implicit functions: it did not provide the bashful, sick girl with access to a community larger than the closest circle of family and friends—she was, she later confessed, even frightened by her grown sisters (*Woman*, 58). Schooling itself became a private endeavor carried on, for the most part, either in the family's "good old library" where every evening her father read aloud, or in the solitary room where she read under the guidance of her sister Cary,[46] or in the lonely open spaces of Jerdone Castle under the tutelage of

44 Parent, *Ellen Glasgow*, 316.

45 De Graffenried, *Scrap Book*, 217. See Ellen Glasgow to Signe Toksvig (December 4, 1944), *Letters of Ellen Glasgow*, ed. Blair Rouse (New York, 1958), 364–65. Hereinafter cited as *Letters*.

46 Ten years Ellen's senior—and the "most brilliant mind I have ever known" (*Woman*, 57). For the tragic future of this brilliant mind, see note 17 to Chap. 7, below.

the wind and the trees, which she worshipped with the orthodox animism of childhood (*Woman*, 42, 51, 57). It was clearly not an education to increase the girl's mathematical powers or her knowledge of geography nor, more unfortunately, to inspire in her a sense of solidarity with mankind (*Woman*, 58–60).

But this process of learning drove her nearer an answer of sorts to a prayer she had, she tells us, uttered every night since she was seven: "O God, let me write books! Please, God, let me write books!" (*Woman*, 36). For the curriculum she had stumbled upon provided a more intensive experience of nature and of lower-class people—poor whites and former slaves living near Jerdone Castle—than she would have received in ten years spent in classrooms. It also furnished an equally important and extensive familiarity with the world of words. Before she tried school at eight, she had read, or had had read to her, the fairy tales of Andersen and the Brothers Grimm, Scott's *Waverly Novels*, and Shakespeare's tragedies (but not the comedies—her father never "commited a pleasure").[47] She felt she knew Dickens well, and could recite a varied collection of English poetry, although Dryden seems to have been her earliest favorite (*Woman*, 45, 47, 53).

Two of Ellen's new centers of experience, the lower classes and literature, were imaginatively fused with the child's sense of exile when, at seven or eight, she first thought to preserve a story on paper. "Only a Daisy" is a 250-word treatment of the Cinderella fantasy:[48] a lonely daisy sprung up in a field of roses feels strangely discontented until one day the young Earl from the nearby castle receives the daisy, rather than the roses, as a remembrance from his beloved whom he is about to leave. The Earl presses the daisy to his lips and then hurries away into darkness leaving the "little daisy ... content at last to be 'only a daisy.' " Miss Glasgow, looking back on the story years later, saw in it the theme of many novels that came after: "the outsider, the man struggling up from an unprivileged status into a circle of inherited privilege; the lonely newcomer, the

47 De Graffenried, *Scrap Book*, 217.
48 "Only a Daisy" was first published in Parent, *Ellen Glasgow*, 133. It is also available in Richard K. Meeker's "Introduction" to *The Collected Stories of Ellen Glasgow* (Baton Rouge, 1963), 9–10.

person who does not belong entering a settled society and fighting for a place in it." [49] Miss Glasgow's interpretation indicates she considered the youthful fantasy the prototype of her later novels of manners, a form traditionally recognized by the sympathy the author commands for a hero who finds himself excluded from a shallow "society devoted to snobbery and slander."[50]

An alternate interpretation is that the fantasy fulfills Ellen's desire to be taken from her present exile in a world of hostility where she (the daisy) feels inferior, into an imagined world where her parents (the Earl and his beloved) would express affection both for their daughter and for each other. The fantasy also reveals the ambivalence of Ellen's feeling for her father; she wishes both that he would love her and that he would die (go away into darkness). Whatever the story's value as a precursor of Ellen Glasgow's novels, it is clearly the daydream of a young girl who desires love from her parents—especially her father.

The story expresses less hostility toward the mother—perhaps it even reveals some confidence in her love—for the mother, disguised as the young girl, "turned and went," not into darkness, but "into the house." This aspect of the daydream was, unfortunately, no key to the immediate future, for in the next few years the crisis of Mrs. Glasgow's health destroyed whatever security Ellen had received from her mother's love and drove the already lonely child further into exile. In about 1884, a "severe shock, in a critical period," caused Mrs. Glasgow's frayed nerves to give way, changing her abruptly "from a source of radiant happiness into a chronic invalid, whose nervous equilibrium was permanently damaged." Night after night at Jerdone Castle, Ellen and Rebe would lie listening through an open door to a voice from their parents' adjoining room where Mrs. Glasgow "walked the floor in anguish, to and fro, back and forth, driven by a thought or a vision, from which she tried in vain to escape" (*Woman*, 61–62).

Miss Glasgow's autobiography does not identify the specific

[49] Quoted from Robert Van Gelder, "An Interview with Miss Ellen Glasgow: A Major American Novelist Discusses Her Life and Work," *New York Times Book Review*, October 18, 1942, pp. 2, 32.
[50] Northrop Frye, *Anatomy of Criticism* (New York, 1966), 48.

cause of her mother's breakdown. Monique Parent, in interviewing neighbors of the Glasgows, learned that a Richmond rumor "attributed the illness . . . to the shock [Mrs. Glasgow] felt on discovering the illicit relations of her husband with various Negresses." [51] This rumor seems less improbable if one takes into account the social context, especially the inconsistencies of southern racial attitudes. Sociologists point out that while the southern caste system emasculates the black male, both psychologically and physically (in the communal ritual known as the lynching), it has a special place for the sexuality of the black female. While the public version of this duplicity asserts that only lower-class white males cross the color line for sexual pleasures, the fact is that the highest-class white men also have black mistresses. After all, more than 80 percent of American "Negroes" have some white blood, and, over the centuries, the planter class has had a great deal more contact with blacks than has the upland group of poor whites—two facts which taken together undercut the public version of this relationship.[52] The chief problem is to square the rumor with the devout Presbyterianism of Mr. Glasgow, but the inconsistency here is probably only an apparent one, for in this darkest corner of the southern psyche, religion and church morality are still the tool of racism's ambiguous need. The rumor gains added support from the presence of the once widespread relationship between the southern gentleman and the Negro woman as a recurring theme in Ellen Glasgow's more important novels, including *Virginia* (1913), *Barren Ground* (1925), and *The Sheltered Life* (1932).[53] In each case, she handles the miscegenation with an authority, an absence of melodrama, and an emphasis on emotional consequences which suggest she may have been writing from childhood memories, or half-memories. This is especially so in *Virginia* where aspects of Cyrus Treadwell's character were apparently modeled after her father. This painful experience should

51 Parent, *Ellen Glasgow*, 137n.

52 John Dollard, *Caste and Class in a Southern Town* (Garden City, 1957), 138–39, 156. See also Wilson on Mary Chesnut in *Patriotic Gore*, 289–98.

53 *Virginia*, the first to exhibit important use of this relationship, was also the first written after Miss Glasgow left her father's house for New York, where she lived until his death in 1916—*Virginia* (New York, 1913), 172–75. See also *Barren Ground* (New York, 1925), 7 *et passim*; and *The Sheltered Life* (Garden City, 1932), 52 *et passim*.

be taken into account in any effort to judge her own stormy relationship with her father. The latter conflict must, in turn, if Freud is right, partially explain those dimensions of Ellen Glasgow's later personality—the confessed absence of a maternal instinct, the forcefulness of her rebellion, her vacillations about marriage—which may seem excessively masculine, for, according to the Oedipus / Electra theory, a warm affection for the father (with latent sexual overtones) is essential to the development of femininity.

A second contributing cause of Mrs. Glasgow's own illness may have been her change of life, the "critical period" mentioned in the autobiography. She was fifty-three in 1884; she had borne her husband a child every two or three years from 1854 to 1877. Her excitability, depression, and insomnia suggest the involutional melancholia which sometimes accompanies the female climacteric. But whatever the cause or causes, no adequate cure was employed. Mrs. Glasgow refused even a mild sleeping potion. Helpless physicians could only advise that she "divert her mind by cheerful thoughts, or . . . try a change of scene" (*Woman*, 62).

The effects of the illness on Ellen's world were excruciating. On the nights when her mother walked in the neighboring room, she would cover her ears with the sheet and pillow to shut out the sounds and to bury her painful sympathy. She came to recognize the "atmosphere of despair," of hopelessness—the "air of melancholy" which had washed over the family—as an accepted way of life. In sympathy for her mother she brought an impassioned judgment against the family, the physician, the universe—against God: that a nature, such as her mother's, "composed of pure goodness" should be so smothered and that two young children should be companions to such melancholy, were signs that the universe lacked all reason and all justice (*Woman*, 62–63). This precocious insight—which she affirmed throughout her life and which paved the way for her acceptance of evolutionary theory—into man's absurd position in the universe opened a gulf between Ellen and her few friends. For this reason, Lizzie Patterson and Carrie Coleman, her childhood companions, seemed to drift away just as the only brother with whom she was close, Frank, was sent by Mrs. Glasgow to a military school.[54] It was not, however, until Mr. Glasgow—having already moved his family, in 1887, from Cary Street into a "big gray house" at One West Main Street—sold Jerdone Castle that the ultimate blow fell on the temporary order Ellen had created for herself; Mrs. Glasgow unfortunately had "conceived a horror" of the only place where Ellen had found health and the place where the girl had begun to write (*Woman*, 63–68, 73).[55]

Eventually Mrs. Glasgow took Rebe for a visit of several months with her only brother, a doctor in Holly Springs, Mississippi. Her departure did little to bring joy or affection to Ellen, for it forced the girl more directly into conflict with Mr. Glasgow, toward whom all her natural love was already expressed as hate. According to her autobiography, Mr. Glasgow thought the absence of his wife offered an opportunity to rid the family of Toy, a dog he considered "sick and old and troublesome." When Ellen learned her father had had the family pet put into a bag and "had given him to two men who worked at the Tredegar," she went straight to him, convulsed with a rage shot through with memories of all the hurt, hunted animals and people she had ever seen. In frustration, she hurled a china vase against the wall—then hurried to compose a letter to her mother. Her mother never answered, however, because, unknown to Ellen, an older sister had retrieved the letter from the postmaster to spare Mrs. Glasgow additional shock (*Woman*, 69–71).

This unexplained silence pushed Ellen still farther into loneliness and deeper into hatred of the family. Their "sanctimonious piety that let people hurt helpless creatures" became the special object of her disgust. She struck at her father where he was most immediately vulnerable: she would never again honor his command that she attend the "divine services" of the Presbyterian Church (*Woman*, 71–72).

But complete rebellion brought Ellen its special compensation: complete freedom. Deprived after 1887 of parents, of sister, even of her roots at Jerdone Castle, Ellen was also free of the intellectual

[54] The older brother, Arthur, had left home in 1881, before his mother's shock. In 1885 Arthur graduated from Stevens Institute of Technology in Hoboken, New Jersey (de Graffenried, *Scrap Book*, 203).
[55] Parent, *Ellen Glasgow*, 139.

and emotional commitments of her family and region; her solitary mind discovered itself free to fly wildly through everything in the family library: "I was overwhelmed by a consuming desire to find out things for myself, to know the true from the false, the real from the make-believe. I was devoured by this hunger to know, to discover some meaning, some underlying reason for the mystery and pain of the world" (*Woman*, 72–73). Total exile—the unconquerable anguish—had thus forced upon Ellen the greatest consolation of her life: the will to search for answers.

BELLE OR REBEL

In the early winter months of 1890, sixteen-year-old Ellen Glasgow made her debut into society at the highly respected Saint Cecilia Ball in Charleston, where she was spending part of the winter. Ellen found herself "eager for gaiety." For once she did not have to dissimulate a light disposition. As she recalls in *The Woman Within*, she let herself be carried away by the flattery of the Charleston gentlemen, perhaps without realizing that, in light of the selection process a young lady passed through before the Saint Cecilia Society honored her with an invitation, the cavaliers were committed to making her feel brilliant.[56] Ellen could not help but contrast the Charleston success with her failure two years before at Frank's school, the Virginia Military Institute, in Lexington, where she had been neglected, a wallflower. But in Charleston she was the youngest girl present and one of the belles of a "brilliant and unforgettable evening": "I was graceful on my feet, a natural dancer. I wore a frock of white organdie, with innumerable flounces, which whirled around me in the waltz. There was a red rose in my elaborately curled hair" (*Woman*, 77–78).

But the real beginning Miss Glasgow made that winter in Charleston took place outside the dance society's gay Hibernian Hall, for it was also a young Charlestonian who first presented her to new critical theories of economics and science. Until 1890 her in-

[56] Mrs. St. Julien Ravenel, *Charleston: The Place and the People* (New York, 1927 [1906]), 424–29.

tellectual adventures had been confined to the romantic and idealistic literature housed in the library maintained by her father—a
man moved most easily, she recalled, by novels which turned upon
the return of a "prodigal daughter" (*Woman*, 86). There Ellen, in
1886, had gone through Dickens again—this time on her own. The
next year she read *Les Misérables* and, shortly afterwards, Moore,
Defoe, and George Eliot, as well as Eugene Sue's *Mysteries of Paris*
and Stevenson's *Dr. Jekyll and Mr. Hyde*. She also broadened her
childhood love for the southern poets, Poe and Lanier, to include
Byron, Keats, Shelley, Browning, Arnold—and Wordsworth, who
was to become her lifetime favorite.[57] In 1890, however, she came
under the influence of a youthful and independent intellect in step
with the critical realism that characterized the final decades of the
nineteenth century.

Twenty-two-year-old George Walter McCormack, of Charleston
and the University of Virginia School of Law, later to be Ellen's
brother-in-law, guided her during the next four years, sometimes
rather haphazardly, through the major works of John Stuart Mill,
Henry George, Charles Darwin, and Ernst Haeckel, plus an assortment of other scientists, economists, and cultural theorists that included Lecky, Gibbon, Romanes, Draper, Buckle, Weismann, Clifford, Bagehot, Spencer, and Huxley.

Himself an unsuccessful Reform (Populist) candidate for the
Congress of 1892, McCormack took her first to the economists.
Mill's sympathy with the struggle for women's rights and his respect
for the capacity of human reason to aid mankind's progress probably reinforced Ellen's own opinions, but the idea which must have
seemed most illuminating to the disaffected daughter of an iron
works manager was the thesis of Mill's *Principles of Political Economy*, that there is an important distinction to be made between the
natural laws of production and the man-made rules of distribution.
If the rules of distribution are not absolute laws of the natural
order, as Smith, Malthus, and Ricardo had assumed, then society
bears an ethical and moral responsibility for the manner in which
the wealth it produces is distributed: "Society could tax, subsidize;

[57] De Graffenried, *Scrap Book*, 217, 219.

it could even expropriate and redistribute." But Mill's socialism was mild, perhaps too mild for a young lady looking for a cause, for Mill defended the profit motive—at least until the "better minds" could gradually "educate" the "others" to respond to less "coarse stimuli" than profit.[58] Thus when, following up a suggestion from Walter McCormack, Ellen "found, on the dusty shelf of a second-hand bookstore, a copy of *Progress and Poverty*," she, like many eager readers of Henry George, thought she had found, in the single tax on land, *the* answer (*Woman*, 78–79).

Accordingly, when in June 1890 she was invited to the second of her successful social outings, this time to Commencement at the University of Virginia, she was, we are told, sufficiently confident of her background in Mill and George to stand examination by the university's Professor of Political Economy and of the Science of Society, George Frederick Holmes. An admirer, a correspondent, and the chief American opponent of the great Positivist Auguste Comte during the early 1850's, Holmes, in the seclusion of his study, administered an examination based on that given his students.[59] Ellen "passed with distinction" (*Woman*, 78–79).

Triumphant, she rushed back to Richmond as though licensed to try out her new ideas and her rebellious, if contradictory, ambitions. That year she gave her first party but refused the "usual 'coming-out-party' and the 'formal presentation to Richmond society' " because she was already well into a youthful novel she was calling *Sharp Realities* (*Woman*, 79–80). Furthermore, something she had learned during the weeks of Commencement had given her the

[58] Robert L. Heilbroner, *The Worldly Philosophers* (New York, 1961), 106–11. For influence on Miss Glasgow's thought, see also the article by Christine Terhune Herrick, "The Author of *The Descendant*," *The Critic*, XXX (June 5, 1897), 383, and the column, "Chronicle and Comment," *Bookman* (New York), V (July, 1897), 369.

[59] The acquaintance with Holmes came perhaps through McCormack who had attended the University from 1885 to 1887—"Necrology," *Alumni Bulletin of the University of Virginia*, I (July, 1894), 35. Hereinafter cited as *Bulletin*. Holmes approved of Comte's interest in empirical methods but vehemently opposed Positivism's writing off the supernatural as an unprofitable realm of inquiry. On Holmes see: Harry Clemons, *Notes on the Professors for Whom the University of Virginia Halls and Residence Houses Are Named* (Charlottesville, 1961), 57–61; Richmond L. Hawkins, *Auguste Comte and the United States, 1816–1853* (Cambridge, 1936); and "The Letter Book of George Frederick Holmes," *Bulletin*, V (November, 1898), 74–77.

seed of a second project: when one of the older women chaperoning the party observed the careless way Ellen threw herself into "several light romances" that "bloomed and dropped," the older lady became suspicious that Ellen was dangerously ignorant of the facts of life; she "delicately but painfully enlightened" the seventeen-year-old girl. To this reproof Ellen responded by conceiving a novel, later to be named *The Descendant*, about an illegitimate boy who becomes a social reformer (*Woman*, 78).

In planning such a novel, however, she had allowed her imagination to run far beyond her experience; therefore in 1890 she joined the Richmond City Mission, "the youngest 'visitor' in its membership." Sympathetic by temperament with the underdog and filled from her reading with intellectual preconceptions about poverty and the need for reform, she had now to learn what her economists meant when they spoke of social evils. Ripe for revolution herself, she wanted to know why other people did not "rebel when they had nothing to lose," and "what it was that kept the poor in their place." Her idea of revolution, however, was rebellion against inhumanity rather than an overthrow of social institutions; when she had difficulty seeing the poor in their horrifying squalor as *human* rather than as inanimate matter, she began to doubt the value of revolution. The following year she changed the focus of her interest from those people resigned to pauperdom at the City Mission to the more independent poor at a private charity hospital, called The Sheltering Arms, because she thought she might find more human fortitude among the "poor who were 'too proud to beg.' " She made one or two visits a week to the hospital and came to feel she was "very close to their personal lives"; for a few months she called herself a Fabian Socialist but soon concluded that Fabian gradualism was "flabby with compromise." She now realized that her visits to The Sheltering Arms were a naïve "effort to learn something of life from the outside," and grew disenchanted with her "foolish dreams" of the revolution—a skepticism that hereafter dominated her social philosophy: "I could see, in the sky, no promise of better things, not the faintest glimmering signs of an approaching millennium. . . . History proved . . . that the blood of revolutions had never washed a people's soul clean of cruelty and greed and intolerance" (*Woman*, 80–82).

FUEL FOR THE FIRES

Thus in 1891 the disgruntled young reformer was forced back once more upon the occupation which was gradually emerging as her "very private and personal destiny": literature. For several years Ellen's older sister, Cary, had tried to discourage her writing, for Cary, having "tried and failed as a girl," wished to spare Ellen "a renewal of that old disappointment" (*Woman*, 82–83). But Ellen only read into her sister's discouragement an encouragement to do better, and, by August, 1891,[60] the latter was aiding Ellen's search for a critic to read a four-hundred-page novel, *Sharp Realities*, which Ellen considered an indignant departure from the sentimental tradition of American literature (*Woman*, 97). In *The Writer* magazine of Boston, Ellen had discovered, we are told, a corporation called "The Writer's Literary Bureau" which, "for the sum of fifty dollars," offered young authors the opportunity to have a "distinguished" literary critic read their manuscripts, advise them, and "assist them in selecting the right publisher." This advertisement in mind, the sisters decided Ellen should go to New York with a group of girls whose parents felt their daughters should be exposed to the world of music, especially the opera. She would stay in a boarding house maintained by a southern lady for "girls of good families." To convince Mr. Glasgow that the trip was practical, Ellen agreed to see an ear specialist about "some slight trouble" she had begun to notice when she was fifteen; although the Richmond doctors had assured her it was nothing serious, she was still anxious. Finally, when Cary, who became Mrs. George Walter McCormack in 1892,[61] promised secretly to give her sister fifty dollars from Mr.

60 Here I have assumed that a letter to Mrs. Francis Smith dated August 29 [no year] (see *Letters*, 23), was in regard to *Sharp Realities* rather than *The Descendant*, because if Holmes helped Ellen with *The Descendant*, the letter to Mrs. Smith would most likely have been unnecessary (*Woman*, 106).

61 McCormack and Cary Glasgow were married March 24, 1892; see Richmond *Dispatch*, March 25, 1892, p. 1. In the same year, McCormack ran for the House of

Glasgow's wedding present, there were no barriers left; Ellen sent the manuscript of *Sharp Realities* to the unknown literary adviser (*Woman*, 95–96).

The Woman Within gives an interesting account of the two weeks Ellen Glasgow spent in New York during the winter or early spring of 1892. It tells of her stay in the boarding house, her evenings at the opera, her walks along Fifth Avenue, her visit to a bohemian restaurant, The Black Cat—all incidents which would turn up in the New York settings of her first two published novels. The autobiography also mentions the aurist, who simply reassured her that there was no danger of her becoming deaf and that she "had better go home and forget about it."

The most humorous account is the encounter with her literary adviser, who turned out to be a grizzled masher more intent on seeing her figure in the altogether than on commenting about her plotting and characterization. This image of January drooling pathetically over May seems to have stayed with her, and to have become in 1926 the controlling idea of her great comic novel, *The Romantic Comedians*. At the time, however, she saw little comedy in the incident. She managed to struggle free, she tells us, without granting the kiss he demanded, but "his mouth, beneath his gray mustache, was red and juicy, and it gave me forever afterwards a loathing of red and juicy lips." Perhaps, in fear, Miss Glasgow unconsciously connected the intruding head with the oldest image in her memory, a red face, "round, pallid, grotesque, malevolent," staring down on her. There is in this anecdote, it seems, a possible key to the dearth of descriptions in her novels of the sexual aspects of love (*Woman*, 95–99).

Moreover, the episode shattered the young woman's preconceptions of professional men of literature—especially of those whose public pronouncements expressed such delicate respect for the innocence of young lady readers like herself; she was "bruised, . . .

Representatives on the Reform ticket, but was defeated; see Richmond *Dispatch*, June 19, 1894, p. 1. In 1892 Ben Tillman's "Reformers" had adopted (word for word) the Farmers' Alliance's "Ocala Platform" by which the Populists swore; see Woodward, "Southern Populism," *Origins of the New South*, especially 235–36, 241, 261.

disgusted, . . . trembling with anger." Although the manuscript, if not Cary's fifty dollars, was recovered before the young novelist returned to the more restrained circles of Richmond, its recovery was to no avail: in Richmond in disgust she tossed the unwrapped manuscript, she tells us, into "an open fire" and resolved never to write again (*Woman*, 97).

But Ellen's resolution was too impetuous to reckon adequately with several forces already working inside her. First, she was obsessed with rebellion: against contemporary literature, against inhumanity, against her father. Every Christmas since she had learned to read, one of her maiden aunts had given her a romance of the Civil War written by a southern novelist of the Thomas Nelson Page-John Esten Cooke school. The "standardized pattern" of these novels allowed "a gallant Northern invader (though never of the rank and file)" to "rescue the person and protect the virtue of a spirited yet clinging Southern belle and beauty," thus symbolizing the longed-for reunion of the nation. And every Christmas Ellen's "slowly kindling fire of revolt" against this evasive and idealized conception of the war and the South grew hotter. Breaking with the sentimental elegiac tone of southern literature would not be enough, for when she looked at the larger literary horizon she found it dominated by figures of a similarly sentimental tradition, the genteel Victorians. To revolt against the southern tradition, which only reflected the demands of northern publishers, was to revolt, she felt, against the entire contemporary movement; this seemed a proper challenge to the rebellious young woman (*Measure*, 11, 48–49, 54).

Second, the idea of the bastard who grows into a reforming newspaperman—an idea whose seeds had been sown during her social visit to the University of Virginia—seemed to draw together the separate strands of Ellen's rebellion. The theme of illegitimacy would allow her to express personal grievances against her father and southern society. Moreover, a bastard would need to struggle against the inhumanities of society, and by having him become a reform-minded journalist, she could embody her image of one type of the modern American radical—derived possibly from the early career of Henry George (*Woman*, 79–80).

Thus in the summer of 1892, only months after the resolve to quit writing forever, Ellen Glasgow could no longer resist the story of a poor-white bastard of an unknown father who, at nineteen, leaves the unfriendly Virginia village of his birth. If her protagonist and purpose were irresistible, the setting and method were less certain. Since "thrusting a revolutionary mood into the conservative pattern of Virginia culture" would violate all the probabilities (*Measure*, 55), she decided to have her social outcast escape to less familiar surroundings, New York, the only big city in which she "had stayed as long as two weeks—or even two days" (*Woman*, 98). Her radical would walk Fifth Avenue, he would eat in a small bohemian restaurant called the Chat Noir, he would fall in love with a young painter from a boarding house like that in which Ellen had stayed.

The lack of an adequate literary method proved considerably more difficult. She spent months discovering for herself "the simplest rules which an experienced craftsman might have shown [her] in a few days or weeks." Her only critic was within. Her only help was "the native instinct that warned . . . unfailingly, 'This is not right! That word will not do!' " But this instinct was negative; she did not know the exact way she had to follow to make her work better. For want of instruction from some "friendly critic," there was much wasted time and disappointment that might have been avoided "by knowing not only what one wanted to do, but the whys and wherefores of doing it" (*Measure*, 51–53, and *Woman*, 94).

Chapter II

Darwin in the Garden, 1893–1895

DEATH TO DEATH

Ellen Glasgow's Richmond acquaintances included no friendly critics who had mastered the art of fiction. The next three years would bring a marked reduction in her friends of any sort, for now her only instructors were to be time, books, and death. While the quality of this instruction would be above question, the effects would be, not aesthetic growth, but increased skepticism, deeper critical detachment from the rose garden, and greater knowledge of the Darwinian arena beyond.

Miss Glasgow's struggle to give form to her feelings of rebellion continued into 1893 and on through the summer. In September, when Mrs. Glasgow felt cheerful enough for a vacation, she took Rebe with her to a resort in the Virginia mountains. Mrs. Glasgow responded well to the change, but shortly after her return home, she "became ill with typhoid fever." In a week, on October 27, she died.[1] The impact upon her three youngest children was crushing; Rebe, Ellen, Frank felt their world rock suddenly, then fall to pieces. Frank, who had been the most unselfishly devoted to his mother, "retreated into . . . invulnerable reserve," and never again in his life—which ended with suicide in 1909—did Ellen hear him mention his mother's name. For the three, she had been "the supreme figure" in their universe. Only Mr. Glasgow seemed to have

1 See Richmond *Dispatch*, October 28, 1893, p. 1.

no need for comfort; he gathered his remaining family about him, we are told, and, "with an inscrutable face, . . . read aloud his favorite belligerent passages from the Old Testament." [2]

Miss Glasgow's reaction was shock and puzzlement. For a second time, her frustration was so great that it could only break through in a gesture of self-destruction: again she allegedly burned the manuscript of her novel—two years' work this time. The pattern is characteristic. Her health failed; she suffered a recurrence of her childhood headaches. The doctors advised, not golf, cold baths, or long walks, but withdrawal, a permanent rest cure. For the winter months she was confined to her room, and in the year of her mother's death, she "did not leave the old gray house" at One West Main: "All my impulse and ambition seemed to be buried with Mother." She began to sense that her capacity to endure—her fortitude, her "vein of iron," she would later call it—was not, by itself, enough to support life. Could one, she wondered, maintain the will to live, to struggle against an unjust order of things, "hostile and even malign"—if life ultimately lacked meaning, purpose, and, therefore, justification (*Woman*, 89–90)?

That winter she began her search again—not in economics this time but in science—seeking out of despair a *raison d'être*. She borrowed the few scientific works at the state library, and in the spring, in the small garden back of the house, she read "all day, stopping only for a cup of tea or a plate of soup." Walter McCormack came again to her aid; he and Cary, living now in Charleston, sent "a subscription to the Mercantile Library in New York." Other relatives warned that reading made attractive young ladies too "strong-minded," so Ellen took the regular parcels of new books to her room, and when Rebe fell asleep at night, she "would slip from the adjoining bed, and steal down the dark stairs" to the library. There, she tells us, she would light an oil lamp and read on, "breathlessly, searching always for something [she] never found" (*Woman*, 89–91).

Although this search failed to justify her struggle simply to remain alive, it did provide a workable explanation for the existence of struggle itself. When Walter McCormack recommended Dar-

2 *Woman*, 83–85.

win, she turned from German scientists to the great Victorian; she studied *The Origin of Species* until she "could have passed . . . an examination on every page" (*Woman*, 88). She read Darwin chiefly because her father feared and hated him; despite knowledge of the details, she as yet comprehended little of "the Darwinian hypothesis." But this was only the first of many times she was to look to Darwinism for something like the consolation of philosophy. The eventual impact would be the total reorientation of her world view. For, in psychological terms, by rejecting her father's ideology and turning to Darwinism, she was, inadvertently, remaking both the reality principle and superego of her own psyche. Years later, in an essay she wrote for Clifton Fadiman's 1939 volume of contemporary creeds, *I Believe*, she described the effect of this early discovery of *The Origin of Species*:

> This single book . . . led me back, through biology, to the older philosophic theory of evolution. The *Darwinian hypothesis* did not especially concern me, nor was I greatly interested in the scientific question of its survival. . . . What did interest me, supremely, was the *broader synthesis of implications and inferences*. On this foundation of probability, if not of certainty, I have found—or so it seems to me—a permanent resting place; and in the many years that have come and gone, I have seen no reason, by and large, to reject this cornerstone of my creed.[3]

What Darwin proposed implied the total annihilation of southern ideology, replacing its emphasis upon hierarchical order, stability, uniformity, and protection of the innocent, with an emphasis on change, diversity, and struggle.[4]

In the shadowy past of the southern mind, all concepts of race, caste, and class (the familiar expression "bottom rail" is an example) go back eventually to the rationalizations of the great chain of static being; they are therefore related to the "Linnean dogma" of fixed species. Darwin began, on the other hand, with an awareness

---

3 *I Believe*, ed. Clifton Fadiman (New York, 1939), 101–102 (italics added).
4 William Berryman Scott, *The Theory of Evolution* (New York, 1917), 18–19; Robert Scoon, "The Rise and Impact of Evolutionary Ideas," *Evolutionary Thought in America*, ed. Stow Persons (New Haven, 1950), 6–8.

of a variability among plants and animals so immense that they defied classifications as fixed species. Although fixity accorded better with his religious and scientific presuppositions, he could not avoid the induction that species are mutable. His chance reading of Malthus in 1838 added a second axiom to Darwin's thought, the stress upon struggle. Malthus stated that because populations always increase geometrically while the amount of productive land can increase only arithmetically, many more individuals are constantly being born than their environment can possibly sustain. A struggle must necessarily ensue between individuals of the same species for means of subsistence. When Darwin related the "struggle for existence" to the evidence of variability, it seemed logical to him that "under these circumstances favorable variations would tend to be preserved and unfavorable ones to be destroyed." If such advantageous characteristics were, as seemed evident, transmitted and accumulated over the generations through the process of biological heredity, "the result . . . would be the formation of new species." [5] Thus Darwin's special hypothesis posited natural selection as the process which explained the origin of new species. He, unfortunately, could not explain the mysterious origin of new varieties, but, unlike his predecessors, he built his argument in such manner that his major thesis, the central importance of natural selection, does not stand or fall on the mechanism through which varieties occur and are inherited. For scientists, including John Stuart Mill, the British keeper of the principles of induction, Darwin's thorough exposition established the very high probability of the theory of organic evolution. It remained for his followers to fill out the skeleton he had constructed.

For Francis T. Glasgow, however, it must have seemed that Darwin was intent upon turning the garden of civilization into a jungle. The naturalist, in truth, was simply describing a neutral wilderness with the potential for both gardens and jungles. But to Ellen Glasgow's rigid Presbyterian father, the implications of Darwin's hypothesis of origins was anathema, for the cultural impact of

[5] Scott, *The Theory of Evolution*, 19; Richard Hofstadter, *Social Darwinism in American Thought* (Boston, 1955), 39.

Darwin's contribution went far beyond its purely scientific meaning. His argument, if correct, implied the need for a radical look at widely accepted theories of reality, human nature, and morality. It seemed, almost inadvertently, to shatter the cornerstone of two essential structures of Western civilization: the mythos of the Jews and the ontology of the Greeks. The threat to the former was the more obvious, though Hebraic religion and Greek philosophy are so fused in Christian idealism that defenders of orthodoxy often did not distinguish from which side they were being threatened. Mr. Glasgow's Presbyterianism, with its Old Testament righteousness and its feudal or medieval view of creation as a frozen hierarchy (see *Paradise Lost*, V, 469–501; VII, 191–550, for a later, popular statement) was especially vulnerable, as his liberated and taunting daughter knew.

Darwin's *Origin* was the new *Genesis*. The world, it became evident, is much older than the Bible implies with its hypothetical Creation in 4004 B.C. An anthropomorphic God, walking about Eden, creating species of plants and animals, became a superfluous hypothesis. The chain of being or *Scala Naturae*—familiar alike to aristocrats, poets, deists, theologians, and naturalists of the eighteenth century with "its order . . . generally conceived as the immutable product of divine creation"—crumbled before Darwin's transmutation of species.[6] With the toppling of the tree of knowledge, the myth of the first garden and the religious sanctions for Judaic-Christian morality also fell, as Kant had long before feared. Theoretically, the demise of William Jennings Bryan following the 1925 Scopes trial in Dayton, Tennessee, where the conflict between biblical and scientific authority had been dramatized for the nation, was the symbolic death agony of the Judaic mythos as fundamentalists construe it.

Underlying the chain of being and thereby seeming to support both Presbyterianism and southern social theory was the multifaceted tradition of Platonic realism commonly called idealism. The

[6] H. W. Magoun, "Evolutionary Concepts of Brain Function Following Darwin and Spencer," in Sol Tax (ed.), *Evolution after Darwin, Vol. II: The Evolution of Man* (Chicago, 1960), 187.

ladder of nature implies a frame of reference, called "typological thinking" by scientists, which has its roots in the "earliest efforts of primitive man to classify the bewildering diversity of nature into categories." According to anthropologist Ernst Mayr, this process has its formal philosophical codification in the *eidos* (kind, sort, species) of Plato, which assumes: "a limited number of fixed, unchangeable 'ideas' underlying the observed variability, with the *eidos* (idea) being the only thing that is fixed and real while the observed variability has no more reality than the shadows of an object on a cave wall . . . . The discontinuities between these natural 'ideas' (types) . . . account for the frequency of gaps in nature." The idealistic philosophy of Plato dominated much philosophy of the seventeenth, eighteenth, and early nineteenth centuries and furnished the foundations for Linnaeus' scheme classifying plants and animals according to species which seemed fixed. This apparent permanence, combined with the hierarchies of the chain of being and the normal self-flattering tendencies of the human mind, provided ample support for the static racial and class divisions of Virginia society; the American caste system has traditionally been pinned to such biological differences as color, features, and hair form rather than cultural ones.[7] In opposition to typological thinking, "Darwin introduced into the scientific literature" a new process, "population thinking," according to which the type (*eidos*) is an abstraction, an average. "Only the variation is real. . . . No two ways of looking at nature could be more different." [8] This new view of types and variations (or hybrids) reduces to absurdity such southern and racist dogmas as the idea of a "pure" Anglo-Saxon, Norman, African, aristocrat, or a hereditary poor white.

Darwinism also ran counter to the high-mindedness of the genteel South, counter to its evasive idealism intent on attributing human actions to "specifically human qualities like spirituality or the categorical imperative." *The Descent of Man* (1871) left no doubt

---

[7] Dollard, *Caste and Class in a Southern Town*, 63.

[8] Ernst Mayr, *Evolution and Anthropology: A Centennial Appraisal* (Washington, 1959), 2; quoted by W. H. Gantt, "Pavlov and Darwin," in Tax (ed.), *Evolution after Darwin*, II, 225.

of "the evolutionary bridging between body and soul." [9] Formerly considered a little lower than the angels and higher than the beasts, man became, in the Darwinian arena, simply the human animal. Humanistic, as well as Judaic-Christian, values were placed in question. As an animal, man must acknowledge violent struggle and sexuality as part of his condition. Where Darwin was accepted, a vast ethical vacuum came into existence that the individual had to fill with whatever authority he might accept without deceiving himself. Mr. Glasgow stood stubbornly with the tradition; the authorities his daughter considered—though perhaps never without reservations—were those who appealed to the theory of evolution as the basis of ethical thought.

Finally, Darwinism undermined the most compelling quality of the southern social dream or any ideal: its absoluteness, its transcendence of all temporal vicissitudes, its condition of pure static being. According to the distinguished neurophysiologist, Ralph W. Gerard, Darwin "crystallized the problem of cumulative change," the need for an intellectual comprehension of "becoming" to replace the Greek philosophy of "being"—a distinction existentialists express at present in their slogan, "Existence (becoming) precedes essence (being)." Biologists subsequent to Darwin have come to stress the importance of the very capacity to change; they have discovered that "selection operates to enhance not only particular adaptive mutations but also mutability in general." The ability to change in itself marks an important progression for organisms in the evolutionary scale. Expressed in social terms, the importance of becoming means that "stereotyped behavior and fixed views do not favor cultural development; the new idea, a sort of social mutant, . . . is needed." [10]

For Ellen Glasgow—born into the most tradition-ridden society of America—the disadvantages arising from the stereotyped behavior expected of the white woman and from the South's fixed views

9 Alfred L. Kroeber, "Evolution, History, and Culture," in Tax (ed.), *Evolution after Darwin*, II, 1.

10 Ralph W. Gerard, "Becoming: The Residue of Change," in Tax (ed.), *Evolution after Darwin*, II, 255–63.

of class, were commonplace. She responded intuitively to the "all-embracing philosophy of organic evolution," and agreed, on instinct, with the ancient theory that struggle and change are the conditions of existence. She would not be moved by the inquisitional machinations of her father: at first, she tells us, he simply tried "rebuke, then moral suasion, and, after that, since milder methods had proved futile," he stormed about Ellen in his righteous rage. Thus her first exposure to Darwin took place within a context of conflict more emotional than intellectual. Darwin supplied some of the weapons she needed to equalize her otherwise one-sided war against an enemy supported by the complacence of an entire society. But conflict did not generate fanaticism on her part. She retained emotional reservations concerning Darwin's "special scientific theory of natural selection"; she was not as confident as some that the fittest survive—perhaps the strongest but not always the best.[11] Experience was teaching otherwise (*Woman*, 91–93).

The summer following Mrs. Glasgow's death produced whatever additional proof Ellen needed that there was little reason to be optimistic about the results of the eternal struggle. June brought Cary and Walter McCormack "up from Charleston for a brief visit." Walter, according to Miss Glasgow's autobiography, was on his way to New York—"ostensibly upon a legal matter"—and Cary would stay in Richmond. He looked ill; "his face . . . was drawn and pallid. He was suffering from a severe spinal malady which gave him attacks of acute pain." In contrast to the strong-willed Mr. Glasgow, McCormack, it seemed, was not equal "to the simple drudgery of securing the bare necessities of living." Hinting something of the matriarchal dominance in southern life since the Civil War, Ellen later attributed his failure to the privations that "so many Southern men of his generation" had endured. "He had never been robust in health"; his struggle for an education in the "wasted country" had left him, at twenty-six, exhausted. Yet Ellen's attitude was one of deep respect: McCormack was the first man she had known "with an intellect of the highest order"; he had managed to overthrow the

---

11 Hofstadter, *Social Darwinism*, 38–39, 50.

"last of [her] inherited prejudices": a scorn for men. If nature, in truth, chose the "best" to survive, McCormack, she felt, should have prospered (*Woman*, 88, 99).

The afternoon before McCormack left, Ellen and he went walking. He listened as she confessed her own miseries; her grief and illness were becoming so unbearable that she would welcome any escape. McCormack replied that, for himself, sheer curiosity to see "what folly the world would 'commit next' " kept him clinging to life.

But afterwards from New York, Cary and Ellen heard nothing. As the days passed, they grew anxious. The next word to reach them reported McCormack's death. *The Woman Within* omits any account of the death, an apparent suicide, from a bullet through his left breast. The details described by the New York papers were bizarre. About two o'clock, on a hot Sunday afternoon, June 18, 1894, a "rather slender" but "very good-looking" young man, well-dressed in a "black diagonal coat and waistcoat and light striped trousers," walked into a lower westside hotel, Smith and McNell's, at 199 Washington Street, and registered in a "tremulous hand" as S. J. Otey, Atlanta, Georgia. He took a room for two days and ordered supper in his room. Later at 9:40 p.m., a porter, hearing "the report of a revolver in the room," summoned the night clerk. The stranger, "clad only in his underclothing," was "lying back on the bed dead," a "heavy 38-calibre revolver" beside him. His suit was "neatly hung up on the hooks"; his valise "contained only a complete change of underwear." Twenty-one cents were found in the room. His other effects included: "a half emptied bottle of medicine" filled "from a prescription on Saturday" at a Broadway drug store; a guide book, entitled *A Week in New York*, and "a novel entitled *A Ruling Passion*[12] inscribed on the fly leaf: 'S. J. Otey, corner Washington and Fourteenth Streets, Augusta, Ga.' "

Dispatches were sent to southern papers, including the addi-

---

12 Possible novels with this title may be narrowed to *The Ruling Passion, A Comic Story of the Sixteenth Century* by Philip Francis Sidney (Hull, 1821), in which the passion is pride of royal Scottish ancestry, or *Ruling Passion* by "Rainey Hawthorne," or Charlotte Eliza Lawson Riddell (London, 1845), in which the passion is love of property.

tional facts that the underclothing was marked "G. W. McC." and that pieces of legal documents found on the floor of his room indicated that "the man was interested in some suit before the Courts in Charleston, S.C., which has been sent to a referee." One such dispatch reached McCormack's Charleston law partner, who telegraphed New York Assistant District Attorney Gordon Battle, a friend of Walter when they were at the University of Virginia. But before Battle saw the body, it was identified by a "pretty and stylishly dressed" young woman who "called at the hotel and asked to see" it. She claimed the man was "Jasper I. Beall, who had asked her to marry him, and she had refused." She contended that Beall "at one time had gone under the name of A. J. Otey. He was a Southerner, and for many years lived in Atlanta Ga., but came North about three years ago and located in Perth Amboy, N.J. where he became the editor of a newspaper." Later, after Battle identified McCormack and notified the families, he and the hotel manager called on the young woman and "convinced her" that the dead man was not Beall, but McCormack.[13]

How much Ellen and Cary were told of the unusual events following McCormack's death is uncertain, for while the Richmond and Charleston newspapers alluded to the mistake in identity, they did not mention the young woman who first claimed the body. Instead, in genteel fashion, they were quick to insist that McCormack's family life was happy and that he was prospering in his profession. A Charleston editorialist conjectured that "his death was undoubtedly due to mental depression caused by bad health, resulting from too close application to business matters." There was some confusion in the papers whether McCormack had been in New York to make business arrangements "that would result in his removing his residence" there, or "to receive treatment from a specialist" for the "morbidness and depression of spirits" which had

[13] See "Came to the City to Die," New York *Herald*, June 18, 1894, p. 3, and "Not Her Rejected Lover," New York *Herald*, June 19, 1894, p. 3. Cf. "Suicide Was G. W. McCormack," New York *Times*, June 19, 1894. No Oteys are listed in the Augusta city directory for 1889 or in the Charleston directories available. Beall, however, is a Charleston name, though I have not located a Jasper Beall. A Walter M. Otey appears in the 1929 Atlanta city directory.

followed his frequent attacks of dyspepsia during the past year.[14] If
Ellen had access to the New York papers, the events they described
probably served to harden the judgment she had already reached
regarding the human male; even at their most sensitive and intelligent, as in Walter McCormack, men are, it must have seemed, very
likely scoundrels, victims of their own drives. Fictional parallels to
McCormack's fate appear in the murders of Jonathan Gay (*The
Miller of Old Church*) and George Birdsong (*The Sheltered Life*)
and in the suicide of Peter Kingsmill (*In This Our Life*)—all three
faithless lovers.

It is evident that the grief which had lowered above Ellen Glasgow since her mother's death seven months before, now pressed
down heavily. She entered with total empathy into Cary's anguish:
because Walter "had been fond" of her and because they "had
understood" one another, she believed herself the "only person who
could feel and know why he had chosen the one way of escape."
Walter's escape, by increasing Ellen's despair, compounded her personal need to find deliverance. According to *The Woman Within*,
the first year of mourning for Walter passed with little relief. Cary,
who still believed "in personal immortality," felt that since she had
"always read and studied with Walter," she would be "more com-
panionable . . . when they met in eternity" if she continued to read
widely. With this "pathetic hope," she led Ellen, in 1895, back to
the study of literature, economics, biology, and ethnology. They returned as well to English novels, running through them, especially
Fielding and Hardy, in massive lots. When Ellen thought "she
knew thoroughly the major English novelists, she . . . engaged a
tutor in French, and in a short time was reading de Maupassant,
Flaubert, and Balzac in the original." [15] In this context she also reread *The Origin of Species* and Spencer's *Synthetic Philosophy*,

---

14 See Charleston *News and Courier* for: "Who is Suicide?" June 18, 1894, p. 1;
"The McCormack Tragedy," "Editorial, George W. McCormack," and "A Sad Mystery," June 19, 1894, pp. 1, 4, 8, and "To Be Buried at Richmond," June 20, 1894,
p. 8. See Richmond *Dispatch* for "Sad Case of Suicide," June 19, 1894, p. 1; "Mr.
McCormack's Funeral," June 20, 1894, p. 7, and "Funeral of Mr. McCormack," June
21, 1894.
15 de Graffenried, *Scrap Book*, 219.

replacing her earlier intuitive appreciation with a more profound, conscious understanding (*Woman*, 101–102).

THE ARMIES OF DARWIN

But this time she did not stop with Darwin and Spencer; by 1897 we know her studies included William Graham Sumner, Walter Bagehot, Thomas Huxley, and August Weismann. We do not know the order in which she read them and can only infer from her writings and their general reputations what aspects of their thought most held her attention, but some inferences are necessary for several reasons.

First, this group of thinkers and their followers laid the foundations upon which creative writers in the late nineteenth century built the traditions of a new novel (Flaubert), a new drama (Ibsen), and eventually a new poetry (Robinson and later the Imagists). Darwinism, through its positivistic assumptions, aided the rebellion against romantic idealism (a revolt caused in part by the rise of modern industrialism and, in America, the disenchantment of the civil war) and consequently accelerated the growth of the realistic novel. In brief, the realistic movement, in which Ellen Glasgow would become the primary southern figure, emphasized: the manners and passions of socially mobile, commonplace characters embedded in a fully realized and concrete setting and governed by social, economic, and natural determinants; objective, impersonal reportorial styles emphasizing "lifelikeness," especially when combined with close attention to dialects and the natural rhythms of speech and thought; and an ironic, dramatic method which keeps the otherwise intrusive narrator from destroying the reality his characters' world has for the reader.

In addition, the Darwinian explorers of the human condition were creating the chief body of knowledge about the human animal on which novelists of Ellen Glasgow's generation could draw. The factor which more than any other separates the reader of the mid-twentieth century from the fiction of the turn of the century, and draws him instead to that of the twenties, was the advent of

Freudianism (including Jung and Adler) as a force in literary circles. Freud created the image of man and society which attracts one automatically to *Winesburg, Ohio, The Sun Also Rises, Look Homeward, Angel, The Sound and the Fury, Tender Is the Night.* But Freud was not translated into English until 1910,[16] so that it is unlikely any important American novelist, other than Henry James perhaps, profited directly from psychoanalytic theory before that date. Until recently, readers have generally looked down on American writers of the turn of the century (even Twain, James, and Dreiser), assuming their knowledge of human nature to be naïve. It can, however, be shown that prototypes of such key concepts of Freud as the id, the superego, and the psychoanalytic breakthrough were present decades earlier in the Darwinian and neo-Darwinian notions of the instincts, the power of cultural inheritance, and the change of individual behavior caused by a change of environmental determinants. Indeed, in some areas it would seem that Darwinian theory created a less reductive image of man than the emphases of Freud.

In *The Descent of Man* Darwin argued against reductivism in favor of two emergent human faculties: Mind and the Moral Sense. Here he simply exhibited the data he had collected which seemed to indicate that attributes distinguishing men from the next highest animals are differences of degree rather than kind and are therefore capable of being developed from those of the next highest species; in this manner, "man is descended from some less highly organised form." [17] The gravest challenge to this thesis was the undeniably high standard of man's moral sense, the apparent cornerstone of human societies. To account for the cooperation characterizing the moral sense, Darwin redefined the "struggle for existence"—not as a competition between individuals of the same or similar species—but as a struggle between "communities" of the same or similar species. In this way, natural selection tends to choose

---

16 Frederick J. Hoffman, *Freudianism and the Literary Mind* (Baton Rouge, 1967), 48–51.

17 Charles Darwin, *The Origin of Species and The Descent of Man* (New York: The Modern Library, n.d.), 909, 911–12.

individuals belonging to communities protected by moral qualities, or, in the case of animals lower than man, by the social instincts,
including "family" ties.[18] It was precisely in the social instincts—
which allow animals to "take pleasure in one another's company,
warn one another of danger, defend and aid one another in many
ways"—that Darwin found the trait capable of development into
man's moral sense. The foremost social instincts include "sympathy" upon which rest "the appreciation and the bestowal of praise
or blame"; this sensitivity figures importantly in most social interactions involving mutual aid. But the "moral sense" as it operates
in man could emerge only after the development of the mind allowed primitive man to reflect on his past actions and motives and,
through this self-awareness, to approve of some and disapprove of
others. "Ultimately man does not accept the praise or blame of his
fellows" as his guide, "but his habitual convictions, controlled by
reason [i.e., his 'conscience'], afford him the safest rule." By implication, civilization consists, in part, of the conversion of such
private habitual convictions into public customs and institutions.
The advancement of human morality (and, consequently, of civilization) depends upon gradually rendering the sympathies more
tender and slowly extending the sense of community, beyond the
family, the clan, the nation, the race, and mankind, to include "that
disinterested love for all living creatures [which is] the most noble
attribute of man," a biocentric ethic of which some great naturalists, including Darwin, are seemingly capable.[19] Darwin's model of
human nature, then, involves an essential tension between two life-
protecting instincts: the instinct which preserves the individual in
the struggle for existence, self-interest or egoism; and the instinct
which tempers that struggle and lies at the foundations of human
society, the social instinct or altruism, the key to the moral sense.
This, more than any other, is the model upon which Ellen Glasgow
built her own image of human nature.

Miss Glasgow thus opposed the reductive tendency among many
of Darwin's followers, although she took care to read and reread

18 *Ibid.*, 443.
19 *Ibid.*, 494, 911–14.

them. Their most powerful spokesman was Herbert Spencer, who had already used biological concepts as arguments relevant to human societies before Darwin published *The Origin of Species*. His *Social Statics* (1850) was an attempt to strengthen laissez-faire economics "with the imperatives of biology." In so doing he failed to recognize the essential Darwinian tension between self-interest and the social instinct. Instead, he accepted the Utilitarian "ultimate standard of value—the greatest happiness of the greatest number"— and set up "as an ethical standard the right of every man to do as he pleases, subject only to the condition that he does not infringe upon the equal rights of others." The state has no function but police duty: man can only adapt to the conditions of life, not attempt to make them more agreeable; human perfection is inevitable. Spencer transformed Calvinistic Election into social theory; arguing for a process called social selection, he "opposed all state aid to the poor" on the ground that "they were unfit . . . and should be eliminated." It is the nature of progress for only the fit to survive. Following the publication of Darwin's theory of organic evolution, Spencer in 1864 launched a vast deductive argument for cosmic evolution, *The Synthetic Philosophy*, in which he combined the most recent theories of the conservation of energy from Helmholtz, Ostwald, Haeckel, and others, with a wildly expanded version of Darwin.[20] In this scheme of things, he sought to reduce man to a limited stock of matter and energy.[21] Inevitably Spencer's great synthesis of all knowledge failed, but not before it had been used, under the guise of William Graham Sumner's Social Darwinism, to rationalize the rapacity of James J. Hill, John D. Rockefeller, Andrew Carnegie, and similar profiteers of American business, North and South, and had spawned the naturalistic fiction of Frank Norris, Theodore Dreiser, Jack London, and Hamlin Garland.[22] Then his theories passed forever into the popular lore clustered about all the myths of American individualism, from whence they periodi-

20 Hofstadter, *Social Darwinism*, 32, 36, 40–41.
21 Robert Mackintosh, *From Comte to Benjamin Kidd: The Appeal to Biology or Evolution for Human Guidance* (New York, 1899), 80–82.
22 Hofstadter, *Social Darwinism*, 34, 35, 41–43, 45.

cally reappear as a tired argument against social reforms under government sponsorship.

In the 1860's, Thomas Huxley, otherwise Darwin's most articulate and successful advocate, stood in agreement with Spencer that Nature unimproved was the surest arbiter of ethical conduct, that Nature working in the here and now left no sinner without sorrow and allowed no righteous man to be punished. But as the century matured, Huxley found himself unable to clear his own mind of the Hobbesian or Calvinistic categories and tendencies he had acquired early in life; by the time he conceived the Romanes Lecture of 1893, on "Evolution and Ethics," he dissented vigorously from his master's confidence that natural selection and ethical conduct are reconcilable. He violently widened the gap between biology and civilization that Darwin had sought to close in his discussion of the moral sense. According to Huxley, men become ethical only as they set themselves against the principles embodied in the evolutionary process of the animal world. The state of nature, he believed, is dominated by Hobbesian internecine warfare, not by an instinct capable of being developed into man's morality. He came to see evolution entirely in terms of the cruel Darwinian struggle in its plain and literal sense, and was too humane to believe that the example of animal conduct justifies such behavior among business men and politicians. As a society advances it gradually eliminates the struggle for existence among its members; it creates an artificial environment, a "garden," to guarantee justice (righteousness) for its members. In an advanced society only the poor and the criminal are actually engaged in a struggle for life, and they, Huxley believed, are such a small part of the whole that they have little selective effect. The major reason Huxley disagreed with Darwin was that he construed the moral ideal to be abstract "justice" rather than an existential response, "sympathy." Animal sociability explains the rise of sympathy but not the development of the sense of justice. He found nature utterly lacking in justice; after the struggle, the "fittest" survive but not necessarily the "best or noblest." He recognized the tautology of Spencer's slogan, which might be more accurately phrased, "Those that survive survive." Ugliness and evil have survived as well as goodness and beauty. Huxley's view was not the popular one in an era habituated to the survival-of-the-fittest argument as justification for the crimes of empire. Even Leslie Stephen and Walter Bagehot agreed that "among human societies it is probably fair to assume that in the majority of cases the most moral are the strongest." Ellen Glasgow, however, stood with Huxley against the success ethic, which, in effect, teaches, "If it works it's wonderful—simply because it works!" [23] She did not, on the other hand, think evolution and ethics irreconcilable, for she, unlike Huxley, was able to find in the lower animals instincts which, when combined with language, the product of man's mind, are capable of development into human moral systems. Most importantly, she discovered early in her career that Huxley's "garden" itself has a pernicious effect, the distortion of essential human drives. Huxley's "garden" would become in her novels the symbol for "the sheltered life."

Indeed, Ellen Glasgow's second exposure to Darwinism provided ammunition for future attacks upon the sheltered life and marked her total emancipation from her father's world view. The students of Darwin, such as Weismann, Ritchie and Bagehot, who spoke not only of biological but of cultural evolution ran completely counter to the southern faith in hereditary determinism, unchanging human nature, and the holiness of tradition; for Weismann and the others implied that cultural evolution via language (i.e., changes in the conceptual environment) is of far greater importance to human progress than blood or biology.[24] It was against the South's dependence upon simple heredity, unchanging human nature, and tradition that Miss Glasgow would eventually direct her most effective assaults.

[23] Thomas H. Huxley, *Evolution and Ethics, and Other Essays* (New York, 1896), 7, 13, 57, 80–86. See also Mackintosh, *From Comte to Kidd*, 148–52; Hofstadter, *Social Darwinism*, 95–96; Gertrude Himmelfarb, *Darwin and the Darwinian Revolution* (Gloucester, Mass., 1967), 402–408. Cf. Ellen Glasgow's poem, "England's Greatness," in *The Freeman and Other Poems* (New York, 1902); cf. also her reaction to the suicide of George Walter McCormack, *Woman*, 100.

[24] August Weismann, *Essays upon Heredity and Kindred Biological Problems*, II (Oxford, 1892), iii, 36, 47, 51n., 65–69. Also Mackintosh, *From Comte to Kidd*, 125–131.

THE BEST DEFENSE

Such would be the future benefit of Ellen Glasgow's 1895 immersion in the furious main currents of Darwinian thought. But her own awareness of these far-reaching effects would require time, for nothing less was at stake than a change of selves, a transformation of superegos, the first of several conversions of consciousness in Ellen Glasgow's stormy mental life. Sartre has said that because he never knew his father he has always been free: "Had my father lived, he would have lain on me at full length and would have crushed me. . . . I readily subscribe to the verdict of an eminent psychoanalyst: I have no Superego." [25] Ellen Glasgow was not so fortunate; she had to fight day by day, for her freedom. She did not always succeed. If it seems paradoxical that her freedom depended on the authority of so long a list of Darwinists, one must be reminded of the awful pressure southern provincialism exerts to force the conformity of all southerners to its monolithic world view: to resist she needed every support she could reach. In part because she rebelled, many spokesmen for a free South have since existed.

The immediate benefit of all her reading, however, was only temporary intellectual excitement, a few hours at a time away from the melancholy memory of George Walter McCormack's death. It was pointless. Books eased Cary's torture occasionally, but Ellen more and more sensed the real question rising in her own mind: is there not a limit to one's ability to endure when there is only struggle? After her mother's death the same question had made her writing seem futile; now it appeared the only defense with which she might temporize: if she was "to survive in the struggle," she had to "go back to [her] work" (*Woman*, 101–102).

The image of the rootless, reforming newspaperman that had obsessed her before her mother's death still lived in her memory. Luckily, two years before, when she burned the manuscript of his story, she had, in her grief, "overlooked" the first six chapters (*Woman*, 94). Now, to save herself, she went to work in earnest. She still lacked an explanation for the nature of things that would jus-

---

[25] Jean-Paul Sartre, *The Words* (New York, 1964), 18–19.

tify an individual's struggling against the inhumane powers of society and nature. In the fight of her young reformer, however, she was certain she could at least present a less sentimental and less genteel record of the oppressive forces she knew from experience governed an individual's freedom than was available in any popular American novel.[26] Fired once more with rebellion, she told only Rebe and Cary what she was about; she wrote in secret, either shut up in her room or during the night hours. To preserve her ruse, we are told, she periodically joined "the family at their pleasures and diversions." [27]

Before 1895 was ended, she had completed the first draft of *The Descendant*. When she read it aloud to Cary and Rebe, Cary was enthusiastic, and, to occupy her own mind, offered to supervise the revisions. She knew no more about technique than Ellen, but possessed "a rare instinct . . . for the elemental sources of character." With the revisions completed, the rebellious girl presented the offspring of her mind's hatred to her father, an accomplished fact: "Father, I have written a book." Mr. Glasgow, the anecdote goes, was dumbfounded; to the staunch Calvinist, *The Descendant*, taking its texts as it does from Schopenhauer, Ibsen, Mill, Haeckel, and Darwin, was a deliberate act of cruelty that matched any of his own.[28] But revenge was no longer Ellen's interest; her mind was on a different struggle: "If only I can have one book published, . . . I think I should die of happiness." And this time there could be no looking in magazines for a "distinguished literary critic" (*Woman*, 103).

---

[26] There is no certain evidence that she, at this time, knew these precursors of American naturalism: E. W. Howe's *The Story of a Country Town* (1883), Hamlin Garland's *Main-Traveled Roads* (1891), Stephen Crane's *Maggie* (1893), or Harold Frederic's *The Damnation of Theron Ware* (1896). The novels of Frank Norris, Theodore Dreiser, and Jack London, of course, followed the publication of *The Descendant* (1897).

[27] Isaac F. Marcosson, "The Personal Ellen Glasgow," *Bookman* (New York), XXIX (August, 1909), 619–21.

[28] *Ibid.*, 619.

Chapter III

No Remedy For Time, 1895–1896

The Descendant

PUBLISHERS AND LESSER GODS

For a young woman in revolt with no fear of the gods and dubious respect for social conventions, Ellen Glasgow shook with surprising awe before the sovereigns of the book world.[1] Publishers, according to her autobiography, were akin to all the strange races—agnostics, conjurors, magicians, dipsomaniacs, and advocates of free love— that she had, she declared, known only in books. She and Cary sensed such creatures were not to be approached without some more experienced guide, but both were, at the same time, wary of advisers who advertised. After several wasted months, Cary recalled that their old acquaintance at the University of Virginia, George Frederick Holmes, had once mentioned his own friendship with the president of the University Publishing Company, a southern-owned New York firm that published textbooks which were "Unsectional, Unpartisan, and Unpolitical . . . Prepared by the most Eminent Southern Scholars and entirely acceptable to Southern teachers and Parents"—including readers, spellers, and histories by Holmes himself.[2] Holmes was asked for a letter of introduction.

Before the professor could respond, however, a second way opened through a new and exciting friend, Louise Collier Will-

[1] The ultimate statement on southern writers and northern publishers is, of course, Thomas Wolfe's long and almost Oedipal conflict with Maxwell Perkins novelized in *You Can't Go Home Again*. Cf. *Woman*, 106.

[2] Coulter, *The South During Reconstruction*, 329–30.

cox.[3] Not only was Mrs. Willcox (1865–1929) a writer herself, but her brother Price Collier dwelt among the lords of the book world; he was "the final critic" at the New York Macmillan's. Mrs. Willcox supplied the required letter introducing Miss Glasgow to her brother, and *The Descendant* was shipped off to him. Two weeks later, Miss Glasgow followed (*Woman*, 105–106).

Thus in the winter of 1895–96, Ellen Glasgow made her second stay in "the brownstone boarding-house in the upper Forties" which specialized in proper southern ladies—this time without the former entourage of culture-seeking acquaintances. Immediately she sent the letter of introduction to Collier, who, in prompt reply, invited her to lunch at Delmonico's. The outing was an exposure of a new sort for the self-educated young lady from Virginia. Schooled at Harvard and in Geneva and Leipzig before serving as European editor of the *Forum*, Collier (1860–1913) was cosmopolitan in background and outlook.[4] He served wine to his youthful dinner companion (whose father held temperance views), complimented her on her youth, and, without having looked at the novel, patronized her with a short lecture to the effect that she ought "to stop writing, and go back to the South and have some babies," because the measure of a woman's greatness was the quality of her babies, not that of her books. Although Miss Glasgow did not stay in the restaurant long enough to dispute this advice, she held, she felt, the unanswerable refutation: she wanted to write books, and had never "felt the faintest wish to have babies." She sensed that the maternal instinct had been left out of her by nature. She had no doubt given the matter a great deal of thought, for all her authorities stressed the central function of that instinct in the development of the moral sense. Instead of the maternal instinct, she had been given a strong sense of compassion which told her it would be "an irretrievable

---

3 Mrs. Willcox was eventually an editor with *Harper's Weekly, Harper's Bazar, North American Review*, and a reader for Macmillan and E. P. Dutton. *Who Was Who in America, 1897–1942* (Chicago, 1942), 1349.

4 His books included: *England and the English from an American Point of View* (1909), and *America and the Americans from a French Point of View* (1896). For essential details on Collier see *National Cyclopaedia of American Biography*, XV (New York, 1916), 232.

wrong to bring another being" into a world where she herself had suffered so many abuses.

The luncheon with Collier was followed by a month or six weeks during which he arrived at his decision *not* to have Macmillan's publish *The Descendant* (*Woman*, 106–109). Meanwhile, Miss Glasgow attended the annual meeting (January 9) of the "benevolent old gentlemen" of the Carnegie-supported Authors' Club, where she learned nothing about craft—only "that the enjoyment of the second best was not confined to the South." [5] Then, with *The Descendant* again in hand, she set out to see whether her second, and less promising, letter of introduction could be as useless as the first. Her autobiography recounts, instead, the sympathetic reception she received from the small University Publishing Company. The novel was given to a Mr. Patton, who was supposed to have trade book publishers among his acquaintances.[6] Then there followed another anxious afternoon and night during which she tried to imagine what passages Patton would like best as he went on (*Woman*, 111).

Perhaps she wondered too whether he would perceive and approve of the ways she had used the teachings of her scientists to question tenets of the southern tradition. There was also the opposite danger that Patton might see the mark of her reading all too quickly, for her style was heavy with its influence. The opening paragraphs, for example, did not quite achieve the proper effect. She wished to show that her protagonist, even as a child, was afloat—open to the most powerful forces of the cosmos—and that there was something so belligerent, even sinister, about those forces that, unless the boy found a way to adapt or resist, he would perish. She began with little Mike sitting upon the roadside and "a stiff wind . . . rising westward, blowing over stretches of meadow-land that

[5] Cf. "The Authors' Club to Get a Tea Set," New York *Times*, February 25, 1896, p. 2, and *Woman*, 109–110.

[6] Regrettably, I have been unable to identify the Mr. Patton Miss Glasgow saw (*Woman*, 110–11). The University Publishing Company failed to survive the rash of bankruptcies of 1912. See *American Booktrade Directory* (New York, 1928), 34. It is possible that Miss Glasgow met Walter H. Page, later her friend and publisher, during this trip to New York and that he saw *The Descendant* in manuscript; see *Letters*, 40.

had long since run to waste." [7] A good start, but other phrases, "death-bed of the Sun," "bloody . . . carnage," "skeletons of human arms," were no doubt excessive. Style, she knew already, was her great handicap. She had "read so widely in the writings of science"— especially in corrupt translations from German—that her literary ear had grown weak. The eventual solution would be "total immersion in the centuries of sound English prose" until her natural ear for rhythm and her instinct for style had been restored.[8] She did not yet fear that growing deafness might erode her verbal power. For the present, her hope was that Patton would be patient enough to look beyond the style to her sympathetic but critical study of Michael Akershem, and judge her worthy to meet a publisher.

The Woman Within describes the enthusiasm with which Patton responded to *The Descendant*. If Miss Glasgow was amused because he was more aware of the romantic interest than of her critical realism, she nonetheless felt relieved to know that she was on her way (*Woman*, 112). Although it would take Patton well into the summer of 1896 to find an interested publisher, Harper's, and take Harper's until March 1897 to bring the book out, she began to look to the near future with a slightly lessened sense of conflict.

OF BLOOD AND TIME

There is a danger with any moderately successful ironic novel that the reader may confuse the protagonist's point of view with the novelist's. This is especially so with *The Descendant*, for Michael Akershem, the protagonist, is a strong-willed, courageous individual whose impassioned, total revolt against society has an immediate appeal. But a line must be drawn between his rebellion and that of his creator; for while *The Descendant* attacks many conventions— primarily the mistaken notion of heredity upon which southern class distinctions are based—it does not, like its protagonist, assault social values per se.

---

7 Ellen Glasgow, *The Descendant* (New York, 1897), 3. Hereinafter cited as *Descendant* or simply by page.
8 *Woman*, 110–12, and *Measure*, 58.

Akershem is a bastard born to a "poor-white" mother, a situation on which southern ideology provides two conflicting judgments. Southerners of Scotch-Irish ancestry and Presbyterian creed, as well as others with similar Calvinistic backgrounds (Methodists and Baptists in rural areas where fundamentalistic sects tend to merge) would see in both Akershem's socioeconomic position and his illegitimacy, the judgment of Providence; to them Akershem is predetermined for damnation. Indeed, this is the unstated assumption of all those living near the northern Virginia village of his birth. On the other hand, more democratic and optimistic southerners would share Jefferson's faith in Locke's doctrine that the mind is a *tabula rasa*; that consequently the economic and legal conditions of birth no way limit Akershem's future; that, if he is a man of "worth and genius . . . completely prepared by education," he might, in Jefferson's words, go on in time to defeat "the competition of wealth and birth." Not only is the latter Akershem's image of himself, but it is probably the social convention held by most Americans who read *The Descendant*; therefore Akershem would strike the reading audience as a sympathetic character. The strict aristocratic position, which sees class like everything else through a veil of god-created hierarchy, is unimportant in this book.

Ellen Glasgow, however, establishes in *The Descendant* a third and less simple position from which to evaluate not only Akershem's situation but that of his judges as well. From the author's Darwinian point of view, while the results of Akershem's heredity are at best ambiguous, there can be no question that his early *conceptual environment* permanently damages him; the Calvinistic doctrine of predetermined damnation controls such powerful social forces that it, in effect, becomes a self-fulfilling prophecy. The Darwinian ambience subsumes both the Calvinistic and the democratic world views and thus dominates the novel. Indeed, Miss Glasgow's thorough exposure to nineteenth-century science—especially to Darwin, "this benign and powerful inspiration" (*Measure*, 58)—is visible in all major aspects, from diction, imagery, and point of view to the complete determinism of the conflict which gives the book its life and provides the critique of southern ideology.

The story line is simple. Michael Akershem, at age seven, realizes that the circumstances of his birth somehow set him apart from his playmates at Plaguesville, a rural community in northern Virginia. As he grows older he learns that as the bastard of a wandering stranger he is an outcast. At nineteen, estrangement drives him from Plaguesville to seek whatever comforts the anonymity of New York may offer. After a depressing struggle to find work in the city brings him to the edge of suicide, he wanders into the offices of *The Iconoclast*, a free-thinking newspaper.

Seven years later, Akershem is widely known as the hated and feared genius who edits *The Iconoclast*. At this high point in his career, he meets Rachel Gavin, a "jolly little Bohemian" from his apartment building: an audacious new woman with a reputation as a talented young artist. A rapidly developing relationship transforms each. Rachel accepts his revolutionary distaste for marriage, and gradually her passion for him entirely displaces her interest in art. In Mike, the old social hatred is slowly domesticated by Rachel's ego-satisfying affection; the representatives of social respectability, whom he had originally scourged, seem less despicable.

But Rachel, the disciple of his former revolutionary moral opinions, begins to strike him as frivolous, careless and unkempt. Michael wishes to disown his entire rebellious past. After a crisis with Rachel, he clashes with a writer on his staff, and, losing his head in rage, kills the younger man. Afterwards he is too earnest to lie in his own defense, despite the pleading of friends.

Eight years later, Akershem, discharged from prison for medical reasons, drifts, without really willing it, back to the block where *The Iconoclast* is published, and then to the old apartment building. Rachel, now successful as a painter but apathetic about living, chances to see him. Shortly afterward Akershem, fed and warmed by her, burns with new determination, but the simple effort to rise from his seat, brings a violent cough from his chest, followed by blood. The past, it appears, is irremediable.

The emotional appeal of such events is elemental, but it is less certain that early readers noticed that Miss Glasgow apparently conceived *The Descendant* as a "diploma novel"—to show potential publishers that she had some mastery of her craft and was thoroughly familiar with the intellectual issues of the day.

Of Miss Glasgow's two achievements—in craft and intellectual content—the latter was by far the more obvious. The conversations, for example, are generously peppered with references to "distinct species," to tracing the origin of life, to "verifying Darwinism by producing the bones of our ancestors," and other topics of interest to scientists of the 1890's. In a period when many popular jokes were variations on the "sexual selection" theme,[9] it was believable to find a character using the sort of "Darwinese" that John Driscoll—the author's spokesman at crucial moments—casually spouts.[10]

Besides Driscoll's diction, the elements most likely to catch the eye are the titles given the four books of the novel ("Variation from Type," "The Individual," "Domestication," and "Reversion") and the epigraphs. On the title page, Miss Glasgow uses a quotation from Ernst Haeckel: "Man is not above Nature, but in Nature"—simply a paraphrase of Darwin's thesis in *The Descent of Man*, that the distinctions between man and the lower animals are not differences of kind but degree. The epigraph to Book I reiterates this basic assumption of the novel: "Omne vivum ex ovo" [11]—not from the sky "trailing clouds of glory." Of the other epigraphs from intellectuals fashionable in the nineties, that from Schopenhauer before Book II emphasizes the relativity of human truth, and that from Ibsen (*Ghosts*, Act II) before the final book points out that the reversion which forms the novel's conclusion is as much cultural as biological; it is Mrs. Alving's condemnation of marriage and past conventions, which begins: "It is not only what we have inherited from our fathers and mothers that walks in us. It is all sorts of [ghosts,] dead ideals and lifeless old beliefs"—an uncompromising attack upon all tradition, whether Scandinavian or southern. Such

[9] They had been for two decades. See Hofstadter, *Social Darwinism*, 24.

[10] See particularly Driscoll's analysis of Akershem's tragedy, *Descendant*, 245–46; also 54, 190–91, 202.

[11] An hypothesis of William Harvey in *Exercitationes de Generatione Animalium* (1651).

added glitter would attract any publisher who prided himself on being boldly modern.[12] If he desired more of the new science, it was there, but disguised or at least assimilated, more or less successfully, into the traditional elements of fiction.

Where Miss Glasgow fails to assimilate her preoccupation with science into the drama of the novel, her ideas seriously distract the reader. Besides awkward diction already mentioned, an unfortunate result of this concern is her handling of point of view. Although she doggedly maintained token resistance to point-of-view purists throughout her career, there are faults in the first novel too serious to attribute to rebelliousness. The narrator is omniscient, and in no way restrained regarding the minds he may poke about in.[13] Because the Jamesian method had not been codified in 1896, this license cannot be considered a serious fault—even when the leap from one consciousness to another is made without apparent forethought. Besides, there are several passages of mental analysis sufficiently dramatized to be called "described internal monologues" (183, 246) and at least one skillful transition from present time to past effected through an association of images (183).[14] Where her untutored handling of point of view fails most is in passages which are discursive rather than narrative; in these digressions, the narrator dismisses characters from the stage in order that the reader might attend to the didactic essay introduced in the midst of the

12 The final quotation traces back as far as Schiller the tradition of pessimism in which she was writing: "Human Life is naught but error." Regarding Schopenhauer, Miss Glasgow took special pains to answer the accusation that the book was "imbued" with the attitudes of the high priest of pessimism; in 1897, she was quoted as saying that she had read only "one or two casual essays" by Schopenhauer and that she never "concerned herself with speculative thought at all" because she felt surer of "tested science and verified history"; see Clarence Wellford, "The Author of *The Descendant*," *Harper's Bazar*, XXX (June 5, 1897), 458, 464. She would later change her mind about Schopenhauer (*Woman*, 91, 172–73).

13 An interesting sidelight on the narrator is that one of his comments clearly establishes him as someone a generation older than Miss Glasgow: "A new form of vice is in vogue, not the skillfully draped creature that we of the fifties remember so fondly" (84). It would probably be a mistake to construe this as the author's instinctive effort to achieve dramatic distance rather than as her calculated attempt to have her anonymous novel taken seriously by creating an impression both mature and masculine.

14 For a less skillfull flashback, see 63–66; here there is no transitional association of images—the narrator simply "carries" the reader back.

story (see, for example, the pronouncement on sexual and egotistical forces determining Akershem's conduct, 173). As she later realized, pseudo-scientific discursiveness seriously flaws a novel—no matter how reductively naturalistic the work's assumptions. Olympian passages have no place in a novel repeatedly asserting the relativity of truth (18, 40, 45, 53–54, 105, 166–69, 186); their presence shows that Miss Glasgow's exposure to the new science was a mixed blessing.[15]

Her feeling for character and instinct for conflict were much surer. In these two areas, the influence of the new science adds to, rather than detracts from, the power of the writing. For when Darwin's work had been synthesized by Spencer with the latest findings of physicists, especially Helmholtz and Haeckel, there became available a great mine of biological, mechanical, and electrical imagery supporting a forceful concept of human nature which writers of Miss Glasgow's generation would use to reveal character and describe the tensions of the human condition.

For the most part, she has assimilated the Darwinian and naturalistic imagery well enough for it not to call attention to itself. It is when the reader begins noting the recurrence of certain kinds of images, that he suspects her source. For example, masses of men and women are often "moving atoms" (50, 268), a metaphor that reduces society beyond the social organism of emergent evolution to Spencer's social molecule. Individuals are often described in astronomical metaphors—"meteor-like" in destruction (Akershem), aberrant bodies (emancipated Rachel), and recoiling bodies (Akershem reverting, 257)—all inorganic and unthinking. This strict determinism sets the basic pessimistic tone of the novel.

Electrical, magnetic, and biological imagery allows the narrator to describe sexual attraction as a sensuous force and seemingly remain, at the same time, within Victorian (if not southern) proprieties. Akershem approaches Rachel for the first time, "his brilliant glance fixing her like magnetism." In a passage which sounds like *Women in Love* (1920),[16] he notices: "the quick play of thought

15 For a longer digression on the evolution of manners and morals, see 83–85.
16 D. H. Lawrence, *Women in Love* (New York, 1960), 57 f.

across her sensitive features. He wanted to make her angry and see the flash come out in her eyes. There was a delicious danger in playing with the fire in her glance. He desired and feared to meet its level brilliance" (47). There are echoes of Darwin's theory of sexual selection—especially his chapters on birds and mammals—in the images used to show the animal nature of Akershem's sexual impulse; Rachel attracts him with her "soft, Southern accent," the soft fur piece about her neck, the curve and quiver of her lips, and the dark coil of her hair that slips from its place to fall "in a heavy wave upon her shoulders" (56, 100, 101, 107).

Electrical and magnetic imagery[17] provides metaphors for Akershem's immense personal power. He is charismatic; he exudes "some dominant, magnetic force . . . so powerful . . . that it seemed to compel rather than allure. . . . To Rachel there was a glorious suggestion of mastery that quickened her to combat. A nature as independent as her own must subdue before a weaker one could gain the power to attract. It was the power that she worshipped, and power there was and to spare in Michael Akershem" (99). Audiences at his speeches are equally helpless: "by a chemical affinity he attracts as satellites a host of feebler intellects" (121).

The influence of Darwin explains repeated attention given the shape of Akershem's forehead. At nineteen, still judged by Virginian views of heredity, he displays "more than a farmer's breadth of brow" (17, 24). Later, even in the anonymous city, his "prominent" brow broadcasts to strangers that he has "genius" (39). Miss Glasgow uses the shape of the brow consistently throughout her early novels as an external indication of native intellectual capacity.[18]

17 To the modern reader, this use of metaphors from physics is likely to seem extremely dated and artificial—until he recalls the important position such metaphors, derived from Helmholtz' statement of the "conservation of energy," occupy in more sophisticated theories of psychology. For a brief discussion of Freud's debt to Helmholtz, see Calvin S. Hall, *A Primer of Freudian Psychology* (New York, 1955), 12–13. For a critical evaluation of the role of energy and mechanistic imagery in the Freudian schema of the mind, see H. Stuart Hughes, *Consciousness and Society: The Reorientation of European Social Thought, 1890–1930* (New York, 1958), 134–35.

18 In Miss Glasgow's first six novels, the following major characters have large or jutting brows: Michael Akershem *(The Descendant)*, Anthony Algarcife *(Phases of an Inferior Planet)*, Nicholas Burr *(The Voice of the People)*, and Arnold Kemper and Laura Wilde *(The Wheel of Life)*; each of these individuals varies from the average in some intellectual accomplishment: reforming journalist, scientist and preacher, law-

Although her original copy of Darwin has been lost, other books in her library contain penciled cross-references to Darwin's discussion of the comparative developments of skull size and mental powers in *The Descent of Man* (although Darwin cautions that the relationship is more safely applied to distinctions between man's skull and that of the lower primates than to variations in human skulls).[19]

More correct from the Darwinian standpoint is the particular form Mike's genius assumes. It is neither a logical precision nor a delicate intuition, but a matter of energy and doggedness, never the mark of the Virginia aristocracy:[20] "Self-taught he was and self-made he would be. The genius of endurance was fitting him to struggle, and in the struggle to survive" (19). Darwin, in this the good Victorian, had strongly underscored the importance of perseverance:

> When two men are put into competition, or a man with a woman, both possessed of every mental quality in equal perfection, save that one has higher energy, perseverance, and courage, the latter will generally become more eminent in every pursuit, and will gain the ascendancy. He may be said to possess genius—for genius has been declared by a great authority [Mill's *The Subjection of Women* (1869)] to be patience; and patience, in this sense, means unflinching, undaunted perseverance.[21]

---

yer and politician, writer and poetess, respectively. Miss Glasgow's attention to chins or jaws is also significant: the will-less and somewhat ascetic minister of *The Descendant* is chinless; Christopher Blake, the revenge-seeking young giant of *The Deliverance*, and Arnold Kemper and Perry Bridewell, the virile pleasure-seekers of *The Wheel of Life*, have prominent, brutal jaws.

19 Darwin's hypothesis regarding the shape of the human skull also explains the recession of the human chin relative to that of other mammals. Darwin theorized that the reduction of man's jaws from those of his forefathers resulted directly from the loss of canine teeth, which loss accompanied man's assumption of an erect position. Moreover, because man assumed his erect position in order to have his hands free, and because the use of the hands for purposes other than locomotion was both the cause and the effect of increases in the size of the human brain, the reduction of the jaws (or chin) correlates with the increase of man's mental abilities. *The Origin of Species and The Descent of Man*, 431–37. There are no markings in the copy of *The Descent of Man* which survives in Miss Glasgow's library; she had first read him in an earlier copy; see Carrington C. Tutwiler, Jr., *Ellen Glasgow's Library* (Charlottesville, 1967), 16.

20 Cf. Taylor, *Cavalier and Yankee*, 69, 84–94.

21 *The Origin of the Species and The Descent of Man*, 874. Darwin concedes that

Akershem earns his success literally "by the sweat of his brow, with a brain which . . . ached like a madman's and yet toiled on" (49).

Why then does Akershem perish, if he is potentially the natural aristocrat in Jefferson's sense, a man endowed by nature with so many enviable qualities: good features, great energy, earnestness, determination, even brilliance? To answer this question, we must move to the place of the Darwinian view of man and culture in the conflict which animates the novel, a struggle embodying Miss Glasgow's first published use of Darwinism as the antithesis to southern ideology. Here resides the most profound influence of the new science, not only on *The Descendant*, but on the whole body of her fiction.

First, however, it is necessary to admit that while Ellen Glasgow is always more interested in character than issues, her first novel is not completely successful at keeping the two in proper relationship. It seems at times a multiple "problems novel" with the focus shifting from one issue to another. A generational conflict seems central at the start when Akershem blasts the villainy of his father and the stupidity of his mother (22), but this is transformed into a larger, class conflict as Akershem levels his attack upon the system, especially the smugness of bourgeois morality. Once Akershem deserts the class of his origin (178), and the narrator begins to satirize reformers (44, 47, 125, 130, 162), and Driscoll, the author's spokesman, gives up reform (45, 53, 202), the class issue is lost. In addition, there is a good deal of Ibsenesque attention given to marriage and sexual emancipation. In New York, Michael moves among women of the bohemian quarter who have elected (often from an ignorance which passes as innocence, it seems) to rid themselves of sheltering social conventions, women who share his own antipathy for the institution of marriage. But the author's defense of emancipation is blunted when liberated Rachel becomes the pathetic victim of Akershem's attempt to live out his theories condemning marriage, and the issue is totally undercut by the antics of a minor

---

this view of genius is not adequate in itself, for the "higher powers of the imagination and reason" are essential also.

character, Mrs. Laroque, a hypocritical misogamist (78, 273–74). Each conflict is intended to dramatize and thereby reveal Akershem's character, but each seems to receive disproportionate attention, blurring the novel's essential conflict within Michael Akershem between his genius and his embryonic moral sense (104).

There can be no question of Akershem's intelligence or his intellectual drive (18, 41) or that his smashing attacks on conventions are soundly based. To document his critique of marriage as an outworn institution to be discarded like an old garment (75), he need only have alluded to Carlyle, to Mill, or—to be on safer grounds—to Darwin,[22] Bagehot, and Weismann. To his admirers, Akershem is the inspired harbinger, like John the Baptist, of a new moral order (47).

The course of the action raises questions, however, regarding both Akershem's qualifications for suggesting alternatives to outmoded conventions and his motives for attacking them. For while he is bright enough to perceive that all social customs, in time, lose their original usefulness, he is without the instinct essential to an individual who in choosing to live free of past conventions unknowingly creates the conventions of the future. As Driscoll tells him, "Call it what you will, your fight against conventions is nothing more or less than a fight against morality" (142). To refute Driscoll, Akershem might again have appealed to Darwin, this time to the argument that true morality is based, not on static moral fiats, but on instinct and intelligence. Akershem might have contended that in overthrowing existing conventions he wished to clear the way for a less rigid morality which would permit the best possibilities of all individuals to find expression. But reared in Virginia, Akershem appeals characteristically to an unspecified abstraction he calls "principle." And, as Driscoll points out, "The only use some people make of their principles is to sacrifice other people to them"; Akershem's *principle*, Driscoll implies, is a euphemism for *selfishness* (142). The fact is that Akershem, as his conduct demonstrates, lacks the basic elements of the moral sense: the developed social instinct, sympathetic imagination, and self-awareness. From this deficiency

22 *Ibid.*, 891 ff.

arises the tragic instability of his personality: a brilliant mind at
the mercy of a powerful will because no moral sense provides the
needed balance (68). The man who appears to be John the Baptist
ends with the sign of Cain throbbing in his brow (13, 240). For
this, the Virginia environment of his childhood is at least partly to
blame.

The manifestations of his imbalance are less ambiguous, however, than the causes, for his violence furnishes the major incidents
of the book. These include: his burning, overflowing childhood
imagination which damns the whole world to hell because he has
been rejected (13–14); his savage and successful scourging of an abstraction he calls "the system" (31); his egotistical casting aside of
his remorseless "Magdalen," Rachel Gavin, so that he can follow
after Anna Allard, a Madonna-like paragon of respectability (146,
156, 187, 188, 265); and, in the total triumph of social irresponsibility, the murder of Kyle (242). Such behavior indicates not only that
he is not the representative of a better moral order, but that lacking
a social sense, he is not equipped to join the human community.

The first character to suspect the dangerous deficiency in Akershem is Driscoll. In Driscoll, Miss Glasgow has chosen a strange combination of traits for a spokesman;[23] he embodies aspects of her
own world view omitted in Akershem. He too is a student of Darwin, but whereas Akershem is interested in the social application
of Darwinism, Driscoll thinks most about the purely scientific aspects: for example, to satisfy himself about some newly discovered
Pleistocene bones, he takes off to Java (190–91). But warring with
Driscoll's modernity is a Puritan conscience which he (like Miss
Glasgow) inherited, he believes, from a grandfather. Whereas Akershem is a libertarian, Driscoll becomes increasingly authoritarian;
the Puritan conscience both incapacitates him for the radical work
of The Iconoclast (153–55) and enables him to foresee dangers in
Akershem's defense of total freedom. In advice that echoes any number of authoritarian documents from John Winthrop's Calvinistic

[23] Driscoll is the only character to appear in both of Ellen Glasgow's first two
novels; cf. Ellen Glasgow, Phases of an Inferior Planet (New York, 1898), 64f, 206f.
Hereinafter cited as Phases or simply by page.

"Little Speech on Liberty" to the pessimistic position of Thomas Hobbes on human nature, he futilely warns Akershem against the unthinking destruction of fixed moral law: "Men aren't so good that they should be allowed full liberty to do evil; it would be pretty sure to end in their doing it. Give it up. If not for your sake, for— Rachel Gavin. . . . Marry her if she will marry you" (142). This advice and other episodes suggest also that, unlike Akershem, Driscoll sympathetically shares the pain of Rachel's compromised social position (156); his moral sense goes deeper than Puritan moral law. This imaginative sympathy, instinctive sensitivity to the pain or pleasure of others, is the basic element of the moral sense without which Michael cannot qualify for the community to which he suddenly aspires. The latter's genius is not enough; it has worked too earnestly to destroy conventions. Nor is the will to be respectable sufficient.

Although Driscoll's suspicions are well founded, he does not act firmly until too late, and then in the wrong way. He becomes the catalyst of Akershem's reversion, for when he learns that Michael has discarded Rachel, he shows his disapprobation in words which abuse the most egocentric sense: "This . . . is a fitting climax to your conduct of late. Would a man who had *acquired an instinct of honor* owe to one woman the debt that you owed, and turn from her to follow like a spaniel at the heels of another? . . . I had thought you an honest fanatic, . . . but now I know you are a damned scoundrel" (240, italics added). Minutes afterwards, when Kyle, Akershem's foil and victim, makes a similar charge, the reversion is complete (242). In shooting Kyle, Akershem has symbolically completed society's work of domestication, for he has killed the mirror image of his former self, the malicious genius who edited *The Iconoclast*. But the act of murder is itself the total release of the primitive.

Akershem resembles the traditional hero less than he does the antihero, and the critical reader might regard him simply as a literary "heel," were it not that he lacks control over his fate. At no point prior to his act of violence does the narrator allow him to examine his own imbalance with detachment. Warned of his selfishness, he violently refuses to listen (142). Told of the heinous influence his theories have on others, he decides, with equal impulsiveness and minimal insight, to become respectable (178–80). Thus Akershem never has the opportunity to choose to live as an enemy of society; he has been created such by internal or external determinants. The reader, therefore, is encouraged by the narrator to take a sympathetic view of his instability.

Ultimately it is probably not possible to identify the exact source of Akershem's social irresponsibility. Reviewers accused *The Descendant* of perpetuating the outdated Lamarckian notion that acquired characteristics are inherited.[24] Lamarck's 1806 argument that species are not fixed by the faultless working of heredity, but have only a limited life, had been an important influence on early Darwinian positions. Lamarck suggested that: "As the circumstances of habitat, of exposure, of climate, of nourishment, of manner of life, are changed, the characteristics of stature, form, proportion of parts, colour, consistency, duration, agility and industry in animals are proportionally changed." [25] The implication of the critics' charge was that Akershem's parents had acquired abnormal sexual and antisocial instincts and had passed their aberrations on to their son, even though he never knew them. Yet there is a scene in the novel in which Akershem discovers Anna Allard reading August Weismann's *Heredity* and becomes irritated that her assessment of the book is a noncommittal "interesting." The reason for his strong reaction is probably lost for the contemporary reader, but Weismann of Freiburg (1831–1914) was the first Darwinian evolutionist to contend that not acquired characteristics, but only those new structures which first arise in the reproductive material, called "germ-plasma," are hereditary. Presumably Weismann's position would free Akershem from the worry that "blood tells" everything—that his own destiny is prefigured by the behavior of a single generation of ancestors.

One may accept Weismann's thesis, however, and still argue on Darwin's authority that heredity is the major source of Akershem's instability. It is obvious from his father's treatment of his mother—

24 See Wellford, "The Author of *The Descendant*," 458.
25 Quoted in Scott, *The Theory of Evolution*, 7–8.

a wandering stranger, he lay with her, then traveled on—that the father was deficient in the moral sense. And variations in the moral faculties, according to Darwin, are transmitted from parent to off-spring.[26] Darwin did not specify whether the variations were genetic or acquired. But moral transmission in one fashion or another was the inevitable conclusion from the observations on which he established the thesis of *The Descent of Man*: that all attributes of man developed from those of the next highest species. To support this thesis he had somehow to account for the relatively high standard of man's moral sense, the cornerstone of human societies. As we earlier saw, it was in the social instincts that Darwin found the trait capable of developing into man's moral sense, and his observations indicated that the foremost social instincts, including "instinctive love and sympathy," are inheritable. Of the two equally important life-protecting instincts which Darwin's concept of human nature said exist in an essential tension, Akershem, like his father, seems to possess self-interest in excess but has the social instinct only in embryonic form. From Darwin's point of view, it is extremely dangerous that a man of Akershem's savagely antisocial outlook should have gained any power at all as the re-creator of society. To the great naturalist, civilization consists primarily of public customs and institutions created out of private convictions based on the moral sense. On the one hand, the advancement of human morality and, consequently, of civilization depends upon gradually rendering the sympathies more tender.[27] However, Akershem's egotistically righteous rebellion is totally without sympathy, even for people closest to him. For Akershem's conduct, the simple explanation, which comes quickly to the mind of anyone nurtured on either Calvinism, southern class thinking, or Spencerian evolution, is "bad blood."

The narrator, however, hints that environment or circumstances, not heredity, perverted Akershem's extraordinary energies: "Had his life been otherwise, the strength might have been welded to gentleness, the courage to humanity. But otherwise it had not been.

26 *The Origin of the Species and The Descent of Man*, 496.
27 *Ibid.*, 480–81, 494.

Circumstances are mighty and man is weak" (50). Akershem himself feels that he has been "a victim to adverse circumstances. . . . He
believed that the hope for future generations lay in sweeping such
possible injustice aside" (81). He attacks conventions, supposing
them to be the source of such injustice.[28] The nature of circumstances shaping him is much more complex, however, than he realizes. For Darwin, while stressing the great importance of heredity
in producing the moral sense, has also assigned a function to nurture: "The feeling of pleasure from society is probably an extension
of the parental or filial affections, since the social instinct seems to
be developed by the young remaining for a long time with their
parents." [29] It is precisely this essential relationship with parents
which is missing in Akershem's early years. That he possesses some
innate embryonic social instinct is pathetically evident when, in the
absence of other companions, he seeks the company of the pigs he
must feed (15). Presumably he might have enjoyed the company of
people as much—if gossip regarding his birth had not caused the
community to judge him damned, and then, by word and deed, to
remind him constantly of their verdict.

Here Ellen Glasgow delivers her earliest published indictment
of the southern class system, as reinforced by religion, for its op-
pression of a large group of individuals. The existence of the class
into which Akershem was born, the lower-class white group lacking
capital, talent, and ancestry, has been "one of the continuous features of southern social organization," [30] an embarrassing feature.
From William Byrd's Lubberlanders, through Faulkner's Snopes
family and Caldwell's grotesques, to Flannery O'Connor's fallen
band of "freaks and lunatics," the image southern writers have
created of those on the lower rungs of southern society is almost

---

[28] That the narrator does not share his view completely is obvious from one per-
plexing sentence: "But conventions are created and stamped with the Divine signa-
ture, not for the one, but for the many" (238). This statement supports the present
interpretation of *The Descendant*, but it does not accord with Miss Glasgow's view in
her next novel that conventions stifle the instinctively moral man. Nor does it accord
with the otherwise dominant materialism of this period of her life, unless the evolutionary process be considered "Divine" because it is ultimate.

[29] *The Origin of the Species and The Descent of Man*, 478.

[30] Dollard, *Caste and Class*, 75.

uniform in its comic superciliousness. If Miss Glasgow's handling of Akershem is detached, it is the irony of drama and critical analysis rather than condescension. Her mode here remains low mimesis, realism.

In theory, the poor whites should have disappeared when the Civil War destroyed the plantation system and ushered in economic democracy. An independent yeomanry should have risen from the ruins of the aristocracy.[31] Instead, the war brought no meaningful redistribution of lands: "large landowners continued to own and control many acres which some observers . . . mistakenly recorded as the property of the small farmers who lived on them";[32] the poor whites had simply disguised themselves as sharecroppers or tenant farmers.

The continuing presence of this group after the war puzzled northern visitors who could not readily reconcile such poverty "with the national faith in opportunity and boundless progress." Had the poor simply been picturesque "highlanders" or Elizabethan enclaves, they would have been acceptable. Had they not boasted embarrassingly English, Scotch, and Irish names, they might have been dismissed, in an age of jingoism and self-styled superior races, as "backward natives" like those "the leading imperial powers of Western Europe were . . . seeking to 'develop.' " Instead, here was a substantial group of Anglo-Saxons who obviously were unable to improve their situation and seemed to have no ambition or love of adventure in them—an embarrassment to all Anglo-Saxon vanity. Northerners came to view the poor whites as the "most numerous element in the Southern population" and used this inference as the "standard means for rationalizing the poverty" of the South.[33]

Ellen Glasgow's portrait of Akershem strips both the northern and southern veils from the myth of the poor white. First, he is aflame with ambition and the love of adventure (9). Second, he possesses a brilliance which he probably inherited from his poor-white

31 Woodward, *Origins of the New South*, 175–76.
32 Franklin, *Reconstruction*, 179.
33 Woodward, *Origins of the New South*, 109–10.

but bulging-browed mother (7). Third, he, not economic democracy, is the likely product of the North's intervention in southern life between 1861 and 1877. The warlike description of a sunset which opens the book with images of a "death-bed . . . bloody after the carnage" suggests an allusion to the initial stage of that intervention, while Akershem's unexplained but exotic non-Anglo-Saxon name (he is sometimes called Shem, the root of the word Semite) implies his father might have been a carpetbagger of the second phase. Thus Miss Glasgow transforms the romantic symbol of national reunion, the marriage of the southern belle and the Yankee officer,[34] into a more realistic one, the furtive copulation of a woman of the fields and a Yankee peddler.

But Miss Glasgow's indictment of southern responsibility for Akershem's destiny is even more caustic than her implication of northern blame. By gestures omitted and committed, the small Virginia community of Plaguesville not only fails to domesticate young Akershem but creates in him an irrational sense of conflict. Blame falls on social attitudes based primarily on an all-pervasive southern Calvinism. The opening paragraph provides a clue to the attitude of conflict which permeates the religious thought of the community; tree branches in the fire of the setting sun are compared to "skeletons of human arms . . . withered in the wrath of God" (3). In this world view, all man's essential relationships—with the transcendental, with nature, and society—are based on mutual antagonism. The majority of those in the community are lower middle class with a strong concept of inherent depravity. Even the middle-class children use this religious dogma to humiliate Akershem; in his presence they gleefully harp on that section of the Catechism concerning damnation (5–6). The family of Farmer Watkins in which Akershem lives does no better. Watkins imagines himself to be a one-time gentleman farmer reduced (probably by the Civil War) to small-farm status: his "father never put his hand to the plough" (11). The limit of Watkins' goodness is simply the lack of any active vice. Though more humane than his wife, he lacks the active virtue to protect Akershem from the vicious tongue

34 Buck, *The Road to Reunion*, 215–16.

and cruel will of a woman whose mind is totally governed by Calvinist ideology. For Mrs. Watkins, Akershem is depraved from birth because he is the "offspring of harlots and whatnot" (11). She believes the adversities of her own family are the judgment of God for their harboring the boy, and falls back on this religious theory to justify the economic exploitation of Akershem; he is expected to do the dirty work, "tote the slops," while she goes to prayer meeting (12). Akershem flees from this hostile family group to lonely rage.

The minister who received Akershem the night of his birth seems to embody a more humane and democratic position. When Mike's peers call him damned, the minister reassures the boy, "No, . . . you have nothing to do with that, so help me God" (6). Advised by the schoolmaster of the boy's brilliance, the minister undertakes his education (18). What seems a Jeffersonian concern for young genius is, in fact, largely hypocritical. For warring against the minister's "germ of human kindness," or moral sense, is his stern religious code of righteousness; like those he should guide, he sees "in the child only an embodied remnant of Jehovah's wrath" (7). The boy's genius confounds his own belief in the doctrine of Election; it is a stumbling-block to his faith in "divine purposes" (19–20). Torn between a compassionate conscience and this socioreligious ideology, the minister succumbs finally to the latter; he cannot accept the way Michael and his own pretty Emily look at one another ("But would you want your daughter to marry one?"). He decides to shelter his daughter from harlot's spawn by expediting Akershem's escape to the North (23–24). This rejection represents the final failure of southern society to domesticate the young genius. Social rejection, which continues to oppress Akershem in New York, forcing him to greater and greater extremes of antisocial behavior, becomes the means by which Calvinism fulfills its own prophecy that the young outcast is predetermined for damnation.

Nothing that time afterwards brings to Akershem can overcome the damage of his hostile early environment. He has not had the experiences that *instill in the individual* that "watchman of society, charged to restrain the anti-social tendencies of the natural man within the limits required by social welfare"—a faculty which Thomas Huxley, and later Freud, called conscience. Huxley's description of the genesis of this faculty, like Darwin's, is the reverse image of Akershem's childhood: "We judge the acts of others by our own sympathies, and we judge our own acts by the sympathies of others, every day and all day long, *from childhood upwards*, until associations, as indissoluble as those of language, are formed between certain acts and the feelings of approbation or disapprobation. . . . We come to think in the acquired dialect of morals. An artificial personality, [conscience], is built up beside the natural personality." [35] In place of positive sympathies, Akershem received from the community only withering righteousness, which nips the social instinct in the bud. Consequently no sense of responsibility for others, no moral sense can develop.

Instead, he learns to rage, rage against his persecutors: the system, all of society. It is the one way he has been taught to relate himself to the human community, which he neither understands nor trusts. By the time he meets Rachel, who gives the affection he once lacked, it is too late to develop the regard for others which restrains impulsive, ego-satisfying extensions of will in normal personalities. For Akershem, others do not really exist—at least, not with the same palpable reality he discovers in himself.[36]

Still, when all factors are considered, the source of Akershem's deficiency as a social being cannot be unambiguously settled. The incipient chorus figures assume "bad blood." The omniscient narrator hints unclearly about circumstances, a view shared by the protagonist himself, who is hardly disinterested. This ambiguity remained a problem for Miss Glasgow to explore in her later novels,

[35] Quoted in William H. Marnell, *Man-Made Morals, Four Philosophies that Shaped America* (New York, 1968), 229 (italics added).

[36] *The Descendant* was not the only book of the middle nineties to attack the arrogance of modern intellectuals. In 1895, while Miss Glasgow was writing her book, Max Nordau's *Degeneration* was translated from German into English. Nordau viciously tears into the French Parnassians and Decadents Ibsen and Nietzsche as egomaniacs. His concluding statement on Nietzsche gives the tone of the book: "It still ever remains a disgrace to the German intellectual life of the present age, that in Germany a pronounced maniac should have been regarded as a philosopher, and have founded a school"—*Degeneration* (New York, 1898), 472. Nordau's description of egomania (241–66) fits Akershem.

although her leaning toward environmental determinism is already implicit in the situation dramatized in these opening chapters. There can be no question, however, that Akershem's lack of a developed moral sense explains his reversion in crisis, the release of the savage instinct to kill which is restrained in normal men.

It is through Driscoll that Miss Glasgow presents her final analysis of Akershem's atavism. When he hears of the murder, Driscoll understands that Michael's aberration was not willed, but "the result of conflicting circumstances," of "disregarded but controlling laws." Then Driscoll specifies to himself, in words which smack of Huxley, the opposing forces which crucified Akershem from the inside outward: "He saw in him not the man revolting against the system, but the abnormal development revolting against the normal. He beheld in him an expression of the old savage type, beaten out by civilization, and yet recurring here and there[37] in the history of the race, to wage the old war against society" (246). Driscoll blames himself for not having understood such primitive intensity of energy unrestrained by social instincts and concomitant moral conventions. He sees that his attempt to shame Michael depended upon conventions which did not govern Mike. The tragedy might have been averted, Driscoll realizes, had he "ventured one appeal to that better nature which was overthrown and vanquished"—presumably, Michael's undeveloped germ of sympathy, his sincere unwillingness to hurt Rachel, had he been able to perceive the effects of his infidelity (246).

Thus, several important aspects of *The Descendant* suggest the influence of Miss Glasgow's early and thorough immersion in the science of the second half of the nineteenth century—especially in Darwinian biology with its ethical, sociological, and psychological implications. These include both the distracting and the forceful elements of the novel. On the negative side can be placed the un-

---

[37] Cf. Darwin on "reversion": "With mankind some of the worst dispositions, which occasionally without any assignable cause make their appearances in families, may perhaps be reversions to a savage state, from which we are not removed by very many generations" (*The Origin of the Species and The Descent of Man*, 504). Miss Glasgow chooses to suggest, rather than assign causes. For example, Driscoll's analysis plays down, though it does not rule out, the early environmental factors.

certainty of the diction, the nondramatic quality of the point of view, and the predictability of the imagery. Far more important, however, is the positive debt to Darwin of the dramatic conflict that arises from the disparity between Akershem's mental achievement and his moral capacity. His instability and his ultimate reversion reflect the Darwinian view of human nature. Similarly, the ambiguity surrounding the true determinant of Akershem's imbalance mirrors the controversy of the 1890's between the Neo-Lamarckians and the followers of Weismann regarding the transmission of acquired characteristics. Here Miss Glasgow puts her intellectual accomplishments to literary use for the first time, to launch a forceful assualt upon a familiar cornerstone of southern class ideology, its simplistic notion of the relation between blood and experience, especially in the life of a man born white, poor, and southern.

In the social and literary contexts of both the South and the North in 1897, Miss Glasgow's subject and treatment, her materialism and her pessimism, seemed rebellious. As an expression of the first decade of American literary naturalism, *The Descendant* probably stands in skill and power somewhere below Crane's *Maggie: A Girl of the Streets*, Norris's *McTeague* and *The Octopus*, and Dreiser's *Sister Carrie*. Compared with such books, however, Miss Glasgow's novel is radically social, for it underscores the existence of instincts which make it possible for men to relate, however hypocritically, to one another in a mode other than aggression and belligerency. *The Descendant* therefore illustrates one aspect of what the author much later called the major theme of her work: "The conflict of human beings and human nature, of civilization with biology." Furthermore, although not a total artistic success, *The Descendant* remains an often moving, and critical study—in some depth—of one type of the reformer.

THE GARDEN OF THE EMPIRE

In the spring of 1896 Ellen Glasgow decided that, with Mr. Patton making the rounds of the publishers for her and with her second novel more than half finished, she was in a position to accept an invitation to spend the summer in England. The letters, still unpublished, sent home to Cary during this first visit abroad deserve the closest possible attention, for they afford a seemingly candid glimpse of her inner tensions and continuing sense of conflict. Not only are they the only body of direct and contemporaneous information available regarding Miss Glasgow's life before she became a published novelist (everything else we know has been filtered through publicists, newspapers, or memories), but they are probably the least dissimulated group of letters surviving from her pen. They clearly confirm her dedication to Darwinian thought and her questioning of the Victorian mentality, whether domestic or foreign.

The splendid invitation came from her brother Arthur, now in his early thirties and still unmarried. Eleven years earlier, after graduating from the Stevens Institute of Technology in Hoboken, New Jersey, he had begun a career in gas engineering which, after taking him to private and public utility companies in Maine and Missouri, culminated in his 1891 appointment as general manager and chief engineer of the Standard Gas and Light Company of the City of New York. A year later Arthur joined another graduate of Stevens Institute, Alexander Crombie Humphreys, fourteen years Arthur's senior, to form Humphreys and Glasgow of London, designers and constructors of water-gas plants in all parts of the world, and builders of the first successful water-gas plant in England. In 1894, the company, under Humphreys' direction, organized the New York firm of Humphreys and Glasgow.[38] Arthur, however, remained in London and took very comfortable lodgings in Victoria Street near St. James Park. Now he wished to have one of his unmarried sisters come measure his success and was willing not only to pay the hundred-and-twenty-or-so dollars of her round trip fare but to provide her with the right clothes. Cary, Rebe, Frank, and her father urged Ellen to accept.[39]

[38] For information on Arthur Graham Glasgow and A. C. Humphreys, see de Graffenried, *Scrap Book*, 203–204; *Progressive Age* (1907) XXV, 127, 567; *Who Was Who in America* (Chicago, 1963), III, 328; and *Dictionary*, IX, 370–71.

[39] *Woman*, 117–18, and letter, April 28, 1896, from Ellen Glasgow to Cary McCormack in Ellen Glasgow Collection, Alderman Library, University of Virginia. Subse-

Consequently, on Saturday morning, April 18, Miss Glasgow boarded the Cunard liner *Etruria* in New York. The last she had heard from Patton was that the Century Company was enthusiastic enough about her manuscript to have her rewrite the first chapters. Having complied, she was ready to sail for Liverpool.

Her early letters from abroad reveal her characteristic independence, but they are notable also for an unusual freedom from anxiety and a grand zest for new experiences. They suggest that Miss Glasgow was making an unprecedented effort to break with the oppressive sense of struggle and futility which had darkened her view of the world.

Her spirit was high; the voyage was entirely enjoyable. People on board were attentive, and the captain expressed a desire to be introduced to her and to have her come up to the chart room. More importantly, the Humphreys, whom Arthur had asked to care for his sister during the voyage, proved extremely pleasant. Although Scottish in his earnestness about work and his tendency to view problems in blacks and whites, Mr. Humphreys always seemed unselfish, as a matter of course.[40]

Arthur met the travelers in London and guided them to Queen Anne's Mansion at St. James Park where his sister found her own "delightful room with bath adjoining, at a short distance" from the Humphreys.

Her first morning in London, Miss Glasgow, Arthur, and two of his friends went to walk in Hyde Park; there she was struck by the "swarms and swarms of women promenading after church just as they are described in English novels." In the afternoon, she went by herself on a visit of personal urgency—to Westminster, but she felt she saw very little, for there was no one to talk to her.

Monday, her second day in London, she awoke already anxious that her trip might be wasted unless she showed herself to the parts of London she considered most important. Guide book in hand,

---

quent references to the Ellen Glasgow, Mary Johnston, and James Branch Cabell collections of this library will be cited as Alderman.

40 Ellen Glasgow to Cary McCormack, April 28, 1896, in Ellen Glasgow Collection, Alderman, and *Dictionary*, IX, 370–71.

she found herself charging about London as audacious Rachel Gavin had run about New York. But unlike Rachel and more like the heroine of the novel she had in progress, Miss Glasgow found total independence less than satisfying. Walking slowly homeward through the crowded city, she discovered herself wishing she had "some congenial person along": "If only Frank had come we should have had such a good time." Moreover, without a guide, there was the possibility that she might miss the Tower and the Zoological Gardens.

Then Arthur introduced her to the family of his friend and colleague, Corbet Woodall. The Woodalls, sensing her need for a guide to England, invited her to see a few important buildings with them and then to visit them on the coast of Scotland during the summer. Their second invitation raised for Miss Glasgow the uncertainty of her plans for the remainder of the summer. The Humphreys intended to stay in London for only two weeks. After they left, she and Arthur would probably have to live in a hotel. She did not much relish staying with Arthur, for aside from the fact that his office duties meant he had almost no time to escort her about, she had little patience with some of his pretenses. She had already expressed this uneasiness in a letter to Cary: "I hope I shan't disappoint him for he wants me to be stylish." Furthermore, the "poor fellow," as she sometimes thought of him, had "so much sentiment about his relatives" that he planned to have someone look up the family record for the enlightenment of the Glasgows in Richmond. Conseqently she was pleased when Arthur not only permitted her to accept the Woodalls' invitation to Scotland, but agreed to buy her some of the bright suits and lawn dresses she had noticed English women were wearing.[41]

After seven or eight weeks of London, Miss Glasgow's initial awe and enthusiasm gave way to a pose of critical detachment regarding British culture and of weary indifference to the expectations of her London judges. Although she might rush out in a hansom to spend the afternoon in the Royal Academy, she still confessed that she

[41] The above account of the first two days in England is based on Ellen Glasgow to Cary McCormack, April 28, 1896, in Glasgow Collection, Alderman.

hardly enjoyed the special summer exhibition of modern British artists: the modern British school "is so watery." Similarly, during the gala procession for the marriage of Princess Maud of Wales to Prince Charles of Denmark, she could not help thinking that the red, white, and silver banners lining all the streets were not so pretty as decorations for the annual Confederate reunion in Richmond. The Queen seemed "very red," the Prince of Wales very ordinary.[42]

After almost two months of sight-seeing, one of the aspects of England which still elicited a measure of enthusiasm was the Woodall family, for their invitation to visit Scotland in early August still stood. During the third week of July, Miss Glasgow dined at her ideal of an English home, Walden, the Woodalls' place in Chislehurst. Corbet Woodall, governor of the Gas Light and Coke Company, was, she noted, quite wealthy.[43] At dinner, after mixing an amount of hock and champagne, she became considerably vivacious. She tried to talk a great deal because it was apparent that the Woodalls thought such conduct interestingly American. But Arthur watched so closely that she was not relaxed; she wondered what he might do if she really acted stupid.

The next afternoon sitting on the Woodalls' lawn, Miss Glasgow had the very strong sense that Mr. Woodall had made a special point that she be at Walden when he was there. Now he insisted that she not return to America with the Humphreys, but continue with his family in Scotland and at their town house. She contrasted herself favorably with Mr. Woodall's daughters, "nice, simple, awkward English girls," without the emancipation and dominancy that the American "girl" of the nineties claimed. To these simple creatures, Ellen knew she was "a wild strange vision."

But she also knew, if she trusted the mirror or her recent photographs, that she was neither simple nor awkward. Pictures of her at twenty-three revealed a young lady, soft, dark, and secret. The frailty and sickness of childhood had given way to a pleasing full-

42 Ellen Glasgow to Cary McCormack, July 23, 1896, Alderman.
43 Twice president of the Institute of Gas Engineers, Corbet Woodall was knighted in 1913. He was born in 1841 and died May 17, 1916. *Who Was Who, 1916–1928* (London, 1929), 1145.

ness reflected in the soft brown of her eyes, the chestnut billows of hair wrapped Gibson-fashion about her head, and the gentle clear curve of her neck and shoulders. The mixture of patrician and Scottish bloods had produced a curve of nose a little prominent for her softly rounded face. Only the tightness of her thin lips suggested the old fear of opening herself to others.[44]

Adding to her difficulty was her morbid fear that the deafness, which doctors had discounted four years before, might be growing. The "terror of not hearing strange voices" produced a melancholy which, according to her autobiography, she felt "was tracking her down, like a wolf waiting to spring." "The sound of the word 'deafness' or even the sight of it in a newspaper" sent chills of horror through her nervous system (*Woman*, 118–19). Perhaps too, the still unacknowledged deafness produced a sort of social blind spot which sometimes caused her—because she could not, with entire sensitivity to slight intonation, judge the responses of strangers—to act unnecessarily lively and even to misinterpret the attention of men like Mr. Woodall.

Whatever the reason, Miss Glasgow, at twenty-three, obviously took pleasure in the imaginary flirtation she had with much older married men (Woodall was fifty-five and had been married over thirty years). There is evidence too that in some cases her interest was reciprocated. Besides Woodall, there was a young Englishman she had met on the *Etruria*; but, she lamented, when the latter invited her to take tea, to go into several shops and then to Hyde Park, his wife came along. Even unselfish Mr. Humphreys assumed a place in her fantasies. Perhaps fantasy provided an alternative to dwelling on deafness. Perhaps too, she had been so nurtured on domestic conflict—both in her family life and in the novels she read—that she considered intrigue essential to an affair.

Besides the Woodalls, there were aspects of England which held deep personal significance for Miss Glasgow because they related di-

[44] Description of Ellen Glasgow based on two photographs: "Ellen Glasgow in her twenties," opposite 68 in *Woman*, and photograph with Wellford, 464; remainder of above visit to Woodalls based on Ellen Glasgow to Cary McCormack, July 23, 1896, Alderman.

rectly to her scientific and literary commitments. She seems to have been forced, not always to her displeasure, to pay token homage to popular elements of English culture—theaters, the music halls, dress shops, royal processions, country houses, cricket matches—before she could shake free to visit, in a proper manner, the Paleontological display at the Natural History Museum, the Zoological Gardens, or Darwin's grave in Westminster.[45] Then, on July 24, she stood for half an hour on one piece of English soil she seems to have hallowed, that by "the grave of Darwin, lying beside Herschel, with Newton a few feet away and Sir Charles Lyell near his head." She found it difficult to comprehend intellectually and emotionally the full significance of the words, "Charles Robert Darwin, Died November 12, 1882." She was irritated by the blasphemy of unknowing tourists: "Hundreds of irreverent feet cross [the grave] every day. Hundreds of high pitched voices chatter about the ears of all those mighty dead, when there should be only silence and thought." [46]

In her own moment of silent thought, Miss Glasgow felt she penetrated deep into the essential British contribution to the history of man: not its vulgar, doomed empire of military power but its intellectual tradition. This insight gradually assumed the form of a twenty-line poem, "England's Greatness," one of several she enclosed that summer in letters to Cary.[47]

The distinction she thus arrived at between the England of the empire and the England of the intellect, to some extent, guided her conduct during the remainder of her European tour. It reinforced

[45] This tour was conducted by Mr. Woodall's eldest brother, William Woodall (1832–1901), who, as a Liberal member of Parliament from Hanley, had led the women's suffrage party in the 1880's and served from 1892–95 as Gladstone's Financial Secretary of War. *Who Was Who, 1897–1916* (London, 1953), 778, and *Dictionary of National Biography*, 2nd Supp. (London, 1912), III, 702–703.

[46] Ellen Glasgow to Cary McCormack, undated letter in Alderman which may safely be dated, from its reference to the Bank Holiday two days later, as Saturday, August 1, 1896.

[47] This may be the poem enclosed in the September 9 letter to Cary, but need not be since Miss Glasgow also wrote other poems at about the same time (see "The Master Hand" and "To a Strange God," for examples). These poems were first published in *The Freeman and Other Poems*. "To a Strange God" also attacks the cultural complacency of imperial England.

her growing repugnance to evenings with her brother's business friends, who seemed to represent—or, at least, to make a great display of—the fruits of the empire. Rather than another boring dinner or visit, she felt she "had rather take a plunge from London Bridge." Even the Humphreys, who had remained at Queen Anne's long beyond their scheduled two weeks (perhaps for Miss Glasgow's benefit) and who at the first of August were at last moving out to their Norwood home, had become oppressive: "I always feel much freer when I am not with the Humphreys. . . . Mrs. H— is exceedingly sweet and kind. But I have nothing in common with them."

This coolness was in part the recrudescence of her old social antipathy caused by a childhood of illness and loneliness, and aggravated now by her morbid sensitivity over the deafness she feared was increasing daily. For she had concluded once more that she, in general, did not care for people anyway: I "much prefer being by myself as I feel more at home in the midst of a crowded thoroughfare than in any house I have entered. . . . The Chimpanzees in the Zoo are the most interesting persons I have met. They don't have to be entertained." Even her brother could not match the chimpanzees as social companions: "Arthur is very kind and seems well disposed, but I am always nervous about amusing him, and I can't do it. I don't know how." [48]

She continued to react differently, though, whenever she had an opportunity to participate in the England of the intellect. It was perhaps shortly after her visit to Westminster that she first took tea with Mrs. W. K. (Lucy Lane) Clifford and began the long friendship with the lady whose home in St. John's Wood once was—and remained, though to a lesser extent—a gathering place for the literary and scientific giants of England, including Leslie Stephen, Huxley, Tyndall, and Henry James. [49] It was here that Miss Glasgow,

[48] Ellen Glasgow to Cary McCormack, undated letter [August 1, 1896], Alderman.

[49] Mrs. Clifford, who had been aided financially by George Eliot after her husband, a mathematician and philosopher, died in 1879, had in 1885 published an anonymous problem novel, *Mrs. Keith's Crime*, the success of which may have contributed to Miss Glasgow's willingness to have *The Descendant* published anonymously. Mrs. Clifford lived until April, 1929. Stanley S. Kunitz and Howard Haycroft, *Twentieth Century Authors* (New York, 1942), 288–89.

according to her autobiography, met "an attractive elderly man" who said to her, "I suppose, like all other Americans, you have been to Westminster Abbey, to lay a rose on Chaucer's tomb?" When she replied that she "had taken a rose to Westminster Abbey, but it was for the grave of Charles Darwin," the stranger appeared "interested, and before leaving, he came back to talk" with her once again. After he had gone, she asked Mrs. Clifford who he was; the latter answered, "Why, that's the eldest son of Charles Darwin." For once in her life, Miss Glasgow would have welcomed the opportunity to apologize for her ignorance (*Woman*, 120).

Oxford was another place where Miss Glasgow could explore the England she valued. Since the first Monday in August was a holiday, Arthur invited his sister to spend that weekend on a small trip. She chose Oxford over Stratford-on-Avon, the other possibility Arthur suggested, a choice consistent with her seemingly lifelong indifference to Shakespeare. She carried on the trip up the Thames several novels Arthur had given her by Hardy. Hardy's most recent, *Jude the Obscure* (1895), replaced Baedeker as a guide to the cloisters and quadrangles of Oxford—or "Christminster," as Jude had known it. She found its medievalism seductive but superfluous: there was nothing in all of it which held an interest for the "scientific spirit of inquiry"; it was the past that students of Christ Church and St. John's absorbed—"neither the present nor the future." [50]

After a restful drive in the green English country (during which Arthur was evolving a plan to buy Creed Taylor's plantation, Needham, and call it his family home), they returned on Tuesday to London for a week at the Metropole before she traveled with the Woodalls up to Scotland. The trip to Scotland, however, fell short of her summer-long expectations. Her ancestry and her childhood adoration of Sir Walter Scott had prepared her to enjoy the trip by train to Glasgow and then by river steamer west to Bute, as a journey to her home in the past. The ride through the Highlands and the four weeks with the Woodalls on the Kyles, or northern coast, of the island of Bute, jutting down into the Firth of Clyde, af-

[50] Ellen Glasgow to Cary McCormack, undated letter [August 1, 1896] and August 2, 1896, Alderman.

forded unforgettable beauty. It would have been Miss Glasgow's "first happy summer since early childhood" if, throughout the excursion, she had not remained nervously ill trying, in mistaken pride, to pretend away the "secret wolf of deafness" which hunted her, even in her dreams.[51]

The second week in September she found herself back in London, with Arthur, and uncertain whether she was enjoying herself or not, her world-weariness had set in so strongly. Or, rather, she asserted it was the surfeit of experience that wearied her. Perhaps this pose too was, like the nervous illness, a way to hide from herself the fear which proved enervating. At any rate, she found herself alone much of the time, unhappy, and depressed. When she remained in the hotel, she grew so despondent it was unbearable. During the days, she escaped into the streets, or haunted the National Gallery, where she "enjoyed the pictures more everytime," especially serenely exotic and visionary paintings by Turner and Claude.[52] Or, again, she would linger over those works which represented domineering women and weaker males, like Sebastian del Piombo's "Holy Family," with its contented Joseph at the Madonna's feet.

In the evenings she sat late in the Metropole reading room—after all other female guests had gone to bed and "the lights in the reception room" were out—to write letters. She longed to hear from Richmond but confessed that she had "nothing else to write of" except the paintings and to assure Cary she would be glad to accompany her to Japan soon (a trip never taken), for she had heard that "Japan is a dream from which [one] dreads to awaken." She could not resist unburdening herself:

> Nothing makes life very bearable; one may travel from the North Sea to Jericho, and one cannot alter one jot or tittle of one's nature or destiny. I believe that happiness lies not [so much] in getting what you want, as in learning to want what you get, 'for he is a wise

[51] Ellen Glasgow to Cary McCormack, July 23, August 2, 1896, and undated letter [August 1, 1896], Alderman, and *Woman*, 120.

[52] Cf. Ellen Glasgow to Cary McCormack, September 9, 1896, Alderman. The paintings are undoubtedly Turner's *Dido Building Carthage* and Claude Lorrain's *Embarkation of the Queen of Sheba*.

man and hath understanding of things divine who hath nobly agreed with necessity.' I have now an abundance of the comforts of life—but a dinner in ten courses is wearying to a lack of appetite, and the more I have the more I want.

Beneath the professed resignation there was the old sense of struggle plus newer unresolved anxieties, not only about her health, but also regarding Mr. Patton and *The Descendant*. To Cary she added: "Suppose you write Mr. Patton and ask for news of my book. Of course, it will be another disappointment, but this suspense is so wearing." When, a few days earlier, she had stood before Andrea del Sarto's *Self-Portrait*, the eternal hills of his art seemed to stand triumphant against the forces of decay. Now she feared that her own chance of ascending similar hills through fiction was very poor, and in this despair she as yet found no freedom.[53]

The change in Ellen Glasgow between the time she boarded the *Etruria* and her stay at the Metropole had been immense. The energy and openness which had driven her into a great realm of new experiences had dissipated. She no longer rode the omnibus up one street and down the other, curious for the London sights. Now London was "the clanging town" whose streets she walked to escape despair. What energy she now experienced was centripetal: her mind had turned homeward, her interests had constricted inward.

Then the chance arose to go over to Paris with some friends of Arthur. Her response to Paris was less than glowing: "I saw nothing more interesting or improving than dressmaking establishments. Once, it is true, I escaped [perhaps from the Humphreys again?] into the Louvre, and I have a vague recollection that I was shown the tomb of Napoleon." Such indifference to Paris suggests that her attempt to pretend away deafness was each day less and less successful (*Woman*, 120–21).

As she soon discovered, however, another project in indirection—

53 Cf. Ellen Glasgow to Cary McCormack, September 9, 1896, Alderman, and "The Master Hand," *Freeman*, 39. See also the title poem "The Freeman," which concludes, "I know / The freedom of despair." The reference to Japan suggests that this may have been when she read Lafcadio Hearn. See Herrick, "The Author of *The Descendant*," 383, 390.

turning her back on publishers—was slowly moving towards a less grim issue. In Paris, into her almost cosmic indifference, there arrived an unexpected answer to the suggestion in her letter to Cary: a cable from home stating "that Harper had eagerly accepted *The Descendant,* and [was] enthusiastic about it." There were no details. Later she "learned that Mr. Patton had taken the manuscript to Harper instead of back to the Century Company," and had submitted it with no name on the title page. In a period when eight out of ten popular successes in America were by European authors and even "established American authors were having a difficult time," anonymity was perhaps the best policy for a young American novelist—especially a woman. No one, she learned, at Harper's had suspected that *The Descendant* was "the work of a girl who had spent only two weeks in New York."

Even without details the blue slip had transformed Miss Glasgow. According to her later account, she went out from the little Hotel Louis Le Grand into the streets. She later thought of this moment as one of the few when she had experienced the sensation of joy. Paris, with "its gray September skies, its damp roving winds, its yellowing leaves underfoot in the parks," meant nothing: "All I felt . . . was . . . happiness." [54]

In late September she sailed for New York. During the loneliness of the voyage, the wolf sprang. When she reached New York, she was in constant pain, "in the clutch of . . . wolfish terror." Deafness had suddenly forced her to depend so completely upon others that one of the officers of the liner had to see her "safely behind the bleak door" of her boarding house. Never again would "the terror of deafness . . . release its grasp" on her mind (*Woman,* 122). The summer of 1896, given to evading the morose sense of conflict that had dominated her childhood, ended in new despair.

---

[54] Cf. *Woman,* 121; the very helpful unpublished dissertation (Duke, 1957) by William W. Kelly, "Struggle for Recognition: A Study of the Literary Reputation of Ellen Glasgow," 6–7; and Alice Payne Hackett, *Fifty Years of Best Sellers, 1895–1945* (New York, 1945), 11.

Chapter IV

The Limits of Rebellion, 1896–1898

Phases of an Inferior Planet

TESTING THE FAMILY TIE

In her now open fear of deafness, Ellen Glasgow spent only one day in New York following the return from Europe. Early that morning she paid the necessary visit to Harper's, to arrange for the publication of *The Descendant*. *The Woman Within* records that she found their representative (probably Colonel James Thorne Harper) delightful, enthusiastic, charming, helpful, and "astonished to find that I was, not Harold Frederic, but a Southern girl." He had confused the "crude innocence" of her book "with the depressing theological flavor of *The Damnation of Theron Ware*." Then the same afternoon she was bound for Richmond, where she hoped her sisters would help her adjust to not hearing. Hereafter she would find it increasingly difficult to meet others, even to receive callers in her drawing room, unless either Cary or Rebe was there as a mediator.[1]

Cary, however, the autobiography neglects to add, had personal health problems to face. She had spent the latter part of the summer at the White Sulphur Springs in West Virginia, to which Mr. Glasgow habitually took the family when he felt a serious need for a change. Here Cary treated her seemingly arthritic hand—a malady which, during the remaining years of her life, compounded the gradual but serious deterioration of spirit and nerves initiated by

1 *Woman*, 122–23.

Walter McCormack's death.[2] Until Cary's death in 1911, the dependence of Ellen upon Cary would be at best a matter of the ill aiding the ill.

Mr. Glasgow's own stay at "the White" had been cut short by national political developments. In July the Democrats, among whom Glasgow had always included himself, meeting at Chicago, had nominated a candidate whose policies Glasgow found repugnant. Although first and last a businessman of retiring disposition who "cared little for public life," Glasgow felt that William Jennings Bryan's bimetallic platform threatened iron interests as much as it threatened gold. Glasgow had done what he could for "the people"—he had served on the board of the state penitentiary—but in the choice between the Populists and business, his sympathies were with the economic Elect. To make matters worse, Virginia Democrats were following the less aristocratic southern states—especially North Carolina—in solid support of the Commoner.[3] Glasgow decided he might forgive the party one mistake, but he did not have, he felt, to sacrifice his own interests or those of the nation: he called himself a "Gold Democrat" and took charge of the "Richmond Committee Opposing Free Silver."[4] In November, Glasgow lost his fight in Virginia, for the state went with the South and West for Bryan. But Glasgow's war against bimetallism was, of course, won—at least for the present election—by like-minded voters in the industrial and commercial Northeast: McKinley narrowly defeated Bryan, and Tredegar was spared.

It is likely that Glasgow's political stand did a good deal to aggravate the estrangement already existing between him and his rebellious daughter. Just five months after the election, *The Descendant*

2 Cf. *Woman*, 102, and Ellen Glasgow to Cary McCormack, September 9, 1896, in the Glasgow Collection with the following letters in the Mary Johnston Collection: Coralie Johnston to Mary Johnston, June 7, 1900; Cary McCormack to Mary Johnston, July 27, 1905, and Sunday [1904]; Lucy Coleman to Mary Johnston, Monday [1906], Alderman. In the latter, Miss Coleman writes, "Cary . . . has been rather unwell, even for her." See also note 17, Chap. 7 below.

3 Wayne C. Williams, *William Jennings Bryan* (New York, 1936), 130. See 129-95 for details of the 1896 convention and campaign.

4 "Francis Glasgow Ends Long Career," Richmond *Times-Dispatch*, January 30, 1916, p. 1. Also *Woman*, 302.

would make its appearance. Michael Akershem, although created before Bryan emerged at the Chicago convention, had traits that might cause readers to associate him with the Great Commoner. Both proposed radical reforms, and both were charismatic speakers; in "gold" circles Bryan was criticized as the candidate who captured the rabble at Chicago with a single speech. Moreover, both seemed to speak for what Bryan's party called "the people." To be sure, Miss Glasgow handled Akershem's tendencies toward demagoguery with great critical detachment, but on the level of noncritical emotion at which most people, like Mr. Patton, read *The Descendant*, there was a large amount of sympathy for the son of the poor farm woman. The novel clearly indicated that the author, if faced with a simple choice between the good of the people and the good of business, would stand—though as a woman she might not be able to vote—with the people. Although Mr. Glasgow would have preferred, in any other situation, to remain a private man, he had made his position on Bryan public. When in March, 1897, his daughter made her own views even more widely known,[5] Mr. Glasgow was humiliated. As a Calvinist he was given to absolute distinctions between a right cause and a wrong. Either he or his daughter was clearly in the wrong. For a while, at least, we are told, he was sufficiently uncertain who had erred to remain absent from his pew in the Second Presbyterian Church.[6]

A less forbidding effect of her father's open participation in the campaign of 1896 may have been an increase in Miss Glasgow's interest in the political process as a significant means by which society is changed. Her first protagonist, Akershem, took no part in politics; his efforts to reform were limited to journalistic and oratorical attempts to mold public opinion. In the new novel, which Miss Glasgow was halfway into when she visited England, the protagonist is likewise concerned with easing the fears of the New York poor. Anthony Algarcife, a very successful clergyman, gets more satisfac-

[5] It is difficult to say how many people in Richmond—beyond Rebe, Cary, and perhaps a few other members of the household—knew Miss Glasgow was the author before the Richmond *Dispatch* reprinted an article from the June 5 *Critic* disclosing the authorship. See "By a Richmond Girl," Richmond *Dispatch*, June 12, 1897, p. 2.

[6] Parent, *Ellen Glasgow*, 146.

tion from his charity work in the Bowery than from his sermons to a wealthy congregation. Although Algarcife, like Akershem, is himself not a politician, the political theme is rather solidly sounded by settings and incidents of the second part of the novel—the half Miss Glasgow wrote following her return to a Richmond embroiled in the "Free Silver" controversy—then left undeveloped. But in her first novel written in its entirety after the 1896 election, *The Voice of the People*, politics would be a central concern.

REBELLION AND ART

Midway into her second book, however, Ellen Glasgow became intensely aware that originality, timeliness, and even boldness of theme did not compensate for deficiency in craft. This was the lesson of reviews which followed publication of *The Descendant*. Regarding the "sensational" subject matter there was the predictable split in opinion between genteel critics and critics who generally applauded tendencies towards naturalism; a greater number than Miss Glasgow might have expected joined the latter camp. Conservative critics thought the author "unduly oppressed with the doctrine of heredity," or found that Michael's "selfishness poisons all that might have been sweet to him," or, more simply, that the book left a "nausea" in the mind. The more liberal critics thought it a "novel of the strenuous kind" with "considerable power." One called for a more orthodox pessimism; he regretted that "the anonymous author had left man a free moral agent in his world, so much so in fact that 'the essential sweetness of life remains unimpugned at its close.' " Regarding Miss Glasgow's style, however, critics of both camps agreed: her writing was forceful but untrained.[7]

The critic who offered constructive help where Miss Glasgow most needed it was Hamlin Garland. Although his review did not appear until August, it was, at once, one of the most critical and

---

[7] *Dial*, XXII (May 16, 1897), 310–11; *Literary World*, XXVII (May 15, 1897), 164; *Independent*, XLIX (July 29, 1897), 980; *Outlook*, LV (March 27, 1897), 885; *Chap-Book*, VI (April 1, 1897), 403–404. These reviews have been epitomized in Kelly, "Struggle for Recognition," 10–11.

most flattering, for Garland was a writer exceptionally qualified to judge a novel about reformers: during the nineties, he had become "the spokesman for the young radicals gathering in Chicago and New York." Like Miss Glasgow, he had sought to apply the teachings of popular science to life and literature.[8] Garland had read the novel just after publication, and had known at the time (apparently through his own connection with Harper's) that its author was a southern girl. He was disappointed therefore when he detected a "marked unreality" about the Virginia setting of the early chapters; the "surroundings seemed shadowy and sometimes artificial." The same feeling arose when Akershem escaped to New York: the boy seemed far more real than the setting. The author did not know how to select the "significant details." But, Garland went on, the author found herself when Akershem met Rachel, for this novelist's genius "delights to deal with spiritual combats." At that point "the narrative became a novel, bold, fearless, and unconventional, dealing with emotions and concepts with which the youth of this day are characteristically concerned": Michael's vacillation between rebellion and respectability, on the one hand, and Rachel's hesitancy to accept the bondage of marriage, on the other. While her male characters seemed very masculine, it was with Rachel's "inner struggles and defeats" that Miss Glasgow spoke with "the certainty and precision of genius." Garland attributed the novel's "most singular and original results" to the author's "scientifico-emotional interpretation of life" based on an obviously "intimate knowledge of Spencer, Darwin, Huxley, Haeckel, and other evolutionist leaders." In short, Miss Glasgow shared the "intellectual imagination" that Garland thought was producing the foremost literature of the day.

Garland's only nearsightedness may have been in assessing the effects of the "evolutionist" science on Miss Glasgow's control of diction and point of view, but even here he pointed room for improvement. While noting a vagueness of diction, he felt it was, for the most part, a strong adaptation of scientific phraseology. Al-

[8] Robert E. Spiller et al., Literary History of the United States (New York, 1953), 1017.

though he found her "moralizing" neither offensive nor tedious, her best moments came when she ceased to "comment upon her characters." Garland concluded that, despite its "grave faults," *The Descendant*'s achievement entitled Miss Glasgow to a "very high rank among the novelists of America. I consider *The Descendant* one of the most remarkable first books produced within the last ten years." [9]

Here perhaps was the friendly critic Ellen Glasgow needed. While praising her general view of things, Garland had made it clear that riding smoothly along the crests of contemporary science would not make her a great novelist; the novel had to be more than a potpourri of modern ideas and rebellious emotions. Garland had also indicated what, in Miss Glasgow's case, this *more* should consist of: intensification of her sense of place, greater exactness of diction, adherence to the dramatic point of view, and, perhaps, greater emphasis upon female characters. In response to these and similar suggestions, Miss Glasgow undertook a concentrated program to achieve a "firm foundation" for her fiction, a "steady control" over her ideas and material. She sought an art, a "philosophy of fiction," a "technique of working." Above all, she felt the "supreme necessity of a prose style so pure and flexible that it could bend without breaking" (*Woman,* 123).

Ellen Glasgow tells in her autobiography of inaugurating this project with the works of Henry James—which she read from beginning to end with great wariness because James was so popular as the model for other writers of her generation. Then, "tracing Henry James to his source," she immersed herself in Flaubert and Maupassant. Flaubert seemed a flawless realist, but his art was too apparent; it destroyed the life of his novels. She found Maupassant's *Une Vie* "the most beautiful novel in all literature." In this period between her first and second novels, she regarded Maupassant as "a supreme craftsman" and "yearned to write a novel as perfect in every sentence as *Une Vie*." When Maupassant's trick endings began to bore her, she settled on the Russians. In Chekhov, art had

[9] Hamlin Garland, "*The Descendant* and Its Author," *Book Buyer,* XV (August, 1897), 45–46.

been "used by life for its own purpose, and because it had been so used had become living." Most importantly, Tolstoy taught her that she could find universal human truths in the ordinary life of Virginia as easily as in the extraordinary lives of the big city; *War and Peace* seemed to say, "Touch life anywhere . . . and you will touch universality wherever you touch the earth" (*Woman*, 124–28). This universality included Tolstoy's structural device of using seasons of the year as silent poetic commentary on novelistic events.

Tolstoy's advice would also inspire her to use a Virginia setting for her third novel. In the meanwhile she produced a few poems and short stories. The poetry was primarily for the entertainment of intimate friends when they visited the private second-floor study she had recently furnished and then filled with scientific books and works on political economy. She did not consider herself a poet, for her poems were simply a way of "giving vent to the emotion of the moment." [10] It was in short fiction that she experimented with the techniques to control her rebellious ideas. By the fall of 1897, Miss Glasgow was offering the magazines several stories, two of which drew on her trip of the previous summer for details.[11]

"Between Two Shores" [12] recounts a shipboard romance in which chance and passion struggle with reason for control of the will, themes central to her second novel. Mrs. Lucy Smith, about thirty, a frustrated, repressed, and worried widow of a loveless marriage, sails from New York to Liverpool to recover—not so much, apparently, from the recent death of her husband—as from the marriage itself. She shelters and becomes involved with a man fleeing the gallows for murder. The interest in will in "Between Two Shores" probably owes more to Miss Glasgow's reading of Schopenhauer[13] than of Darwin, but two facts—that the heroine maintains her faith in a confessed criminal because he has demonstrated the capacity for personal kindness and sympathy, and that the sympa-

---

[10] Wellford, "The Author of *The Descendant*," 458, 464.

[11] James B. Colvert, "Agent and Author: Ellen Glasgow's Letters to Paul Revere Reynolds," *Studies in Bibliography*, XIV (Charlottesville, 1961), 180.

[12] Both stories are reprinted in Meeker (ed.), *The Collected Stories of Ellen Glasgow*, 24–51.

[13] See *Woman*, 91.

thies solicited by the story from the reader seem to support her decision—suggest a moral framework based on Darwinian sympathy rather than a strict legalism. Apparently Miss Glasgow felt that because the hero-murderer is capable of tenderness, his act of violence, which was also a "deed of honor," can be expiated through shared human love; in other words, Smith's essential sympathies signify that he is not damned and can still be restored to the community of men. Miss Glasgow would explore this theme in greater depth in her fifth novel, *The Deliverance*.

"A Point in Morals" also explores the importance of sympathy in moral decisions, and, like "Between Two Shores," it centers about a fugitive murderer. This time the Darwinian context is clearly established. The specific issue is euthanasia. The scene of the present action is the captain's table aboard a liner bound for New York. An Englishman, a journalist, a lawyer, a distinguished alienist, and a girl in black are discussing an issue which obviously bothers the alienist: "The question," he asserts, "is whether or not civilization is defeating its own aims in placing an exorbitant value on human life." The story develops more in the manner of a dialogue or symposium than of a short story proper. The alienist interpolates an incident to clarify his question; the others then discuss his anecdote. Some years before, he was returning on a train from Glasgow to London after spending two weeks in Tighnabruaich, a small village on the Kyles of Bute, "treating an invalid cousin who had acquired the morphine habit." With her excess morphine, thirty grains, in his baggage, he was sitting opposite an emaciated and shabby but genteel man. The latter remained to himself until he noticed the narcotic in the doctor's bag, whereupon he struck up a conversation, actually a plea for the drug. He recounted the tragedy of his life which included bigamy, forgery, and, most recently, murder. Scotland Yard and hanging awaited him in London. Morphine would offer painless suicide. If the doctor did not furnish the drug, the stranger would swallow the carbolic acid he had with him. Although the doctor knew the acid to be "the most corrosive of irritants," he refused to be the instrument of the doomed man's self-destruction. Yet when the train reached his own stop, he left the package on the seat. The next day he read in the *Times* that a wanted murderer had been found dead of morphine on the Midland Railway.

Reactions at the captain's table to the alienist's decision amplify the meaning of the incident. The girl in black, stressing the subjective value of a life, believes the alienist did right to let the doomed man die painlessly. The Englishman contends that the girl's sympathy misses the ethical side of the question. But the Englishman's view, which attempts to raise ethics to a level where sympathy is irrelevant, cannot be taken seriously from the Darwinian point of view, in which sympathy is the essence of the moral sense. In this context, the Englishman's view is ironic, as is the lawyer's, which simply contends that the alienist should have taken both the morphine and acid from the murderer and left "him to the care of the law." The alienist, who acted from sympathy for the stranger, confesses that though he felt like a murderer, there is "such a thing . . . as a conscientious murderer." In other words, the girl and the alienist (or Miss Glasgow through them) have refined the Darwinian notion of the moral sense so that the ultimate human value against which conduct is to be measured is no longer simply "life" or "survival," but the "meaningful" life. The doomed life or the life of immense suffering ceases to be an unqualified good, a theme she returns to in her strongest short story, "Jordan's End." Yet the decision regarding the life of suffering remains with the victim. Euthanasia is moral only when the sufferer wills self-destruction. To Miss Glasgow and her alienist, even a murderer deserves the opportunity for an "easeful death."

In addition to such refinements of moral outlook, the two short stories demonstrate Miss Glasgow's newly achieved ability to control her materials. The settings, the diction, and the points of view indicate corrections of shortcomings Garland had detected in *The Descendant*. She drew on personal experience for the settings, which are economically and convincingly established. The diction avoids the excessive imagery and, except in dialogue, the awkward scientific jargon of *The Descendant*. There are signs of growth toward greater exactness and economy, but the diction remains flexible enough to permit subjective adjectives like "wistfully," "girlish," and "furtive." In both stories the point of view is completely controlled. In "Between Two Shores" the narrator limits his internal observations to the mind of Lucy Smith, perhaps thus obeying Garland's implicit recommendation that Miss Glasgow emphasize the feminine outlook. In "A Point in Morals" the point of view is entirely objective; aside from the physical actions of the principals, the story consists completely of dialogue. The influence most apparent in technical aspects of both stories is Maupassant. The reversal of "Between Two Shores" is patterned on the French novelist's "famous trick ending," which "at first excited, then amused, and finally bored" Miss Glasgow.[14] The diction has some of Maupassant's matter-of-factness. In tales like "The Story of a Farm Girl," Maupassant perfected the limited omniscience which Miss Glasgow uses in "Between Two Shores." He also employed frequently the objective method—in "The Double Pins," for example— with which she experiments in "A Point in Morals." Miss Glasgow's apprenticeship work in these two stories helps explain why the second half of her next novel, *Phases of an Inferior Planet*—the half written after she launched the campaign to improve her art—seems more controlled in diction and point of view than the earlier half.

ALIENIST AND AGENT

"A Point in Morals" raises an additional question of considerable importance to Ellen Glasgow's later work and life; for an alienist, or psychologist, like that in this story, appears in five of the thirteen short stories attributed to her. Besides the alienist of this early story, her short fiction published in 1916 or later contains: Dr. Roland Maradick, a famous alienist, in "The Shadowy Third"; Dr. Drayton, a Washington nerve specialist, in "Dare's Gift"; Dr. Carstairs of Baltimore, the leading alienist in the country, in "Jordan's End"; and Dr. Estbridge, an analytical psychologist, in "The Professional Instinct." Is it not likely then that there was a living model or models for the reappearing psychologist?

14 *Ibid.*, 125.

Ellen Glasgow's papers show that she knew two doctors similar to the alienist very well. They were Drs. Pearce Bailey (1865–1922) and Joseph Collins (1866–1950), who also wrote literary criticism from a psychological point of view. Close associates, both were distinguished New York neurologists and among the earliest defenders in this country of psychosomatic medicine.[15] The Glasgow papers indicate that she probably knew Bailey before Collins, for the earliest letter from the latter belongs to the middle 1920's while those from Bailey belong to 1916. One letter from Bailey refers to Miss Glasgow's posthumously published short story, "The Professional Instinct," about an analytical psychologist who almost leaves his authoritarian and estranged wife in order to marry, or live with, a more intelligent younger woman. This letter indicates, moreover, that Bailey was helping with the actual composition of the story.[16]

Otherwise there are few references to Bailey in the Glasgow papers. The earliest clue is a reprint copy of Bailey's article, "Gustave Flaubert: A Psychological Study," which appeared in the *Bookman* for November 1908. A 1916 letter from Henry W. Anderson to Miss Glasgow[17] implies that she was then staying at Dr. Bailey's "place"; whether Anderson referred to Bailey's hospital (the Neurological Institute of New York), his New York home, or the Bailey family's home at fashionable Bailey's Beach in Newport, Rhode Island, is uncertain.

The final allusion to Bailey in Miss Glasgow's papers occurs in a letter Dr. Collins wrote her in the last months of her life. Collins urged her to leave the Richmond doctors and come to New York where he might see that she received the best doctors to permit her "to live the next few years in comparative comfort free from pain

[15] For brief biographies of Bailey and Collins, see *National Cyclopaedia of American Biography*, XXIV (New York, 1935), 192–93, and XL (New York, 1955), 418–19. See also the brochure, "Joseph Collins Foundation, 1951–1953," published by the Joseph Collins Foundation, 15 Broad Street, New York 4.

[16] Cf. Meeker (ed.), *Collected Stories*, 239–53, and Dr. Pearce Bailey to Ellen Glasgow, March 8, 1916, Glasgow Collection, Alderman. The letter also indicates that Miss Glasgow helped Bailey write an article on the "Heroin Habit," which appeared in the *New Republic*, April 22, 1916.

[17] Henry W. Anderson to Ellen Glasgow, August 16, 1916, Alderman. Anderson became engaged to Miss Glasgow in 1917.

and anguish." In obvious desperation Collins added, "If you cannot tolerate the expense of hospitalization I offer to pay it for you, and I do that in memory of P. B. who loved you and of J. C., who admires you. . . ." [18] "J. C." is probably Collins himself. "P. B.," we infer, was Bailey, who had, in 1909, joined Collins in founding the Neurological Institute of New York. Collins' statement is of special interest because the tone of all his letters in the Alderman Library collection reveals that he gave Miss Glasgow both literary and medical advice with far greater authority than any of the novelist's other friends dared assume in their correspondence.

For the full significance Collins' letter may have, however, it is necessary to compare it with passages in Miss Glasgow's autobiography and with a statement in Blair Rouse's short study, *Ellen Glasgow* (1962). In *The Woman Within*, Miss Glasgow described her ecstatic affair with a married man estranged from his wife; she called him "Gerald B——, because this name will do as well as another" (*Woman*, 153–68). Blair Rouse, referring to an unspecified letter from Collins, asserts that Collins knew the man Miss Glasgow loved and that Collins said that the man was a physician, not the financier mentioned in the autobiography.[19] Blair Rouse, however, does not identify the physician. If Collins had Bailey in mind, as his pleading letter to Miss Glasgow suggests, it is not surprising that there are so few references to Bailey in Miss Glasgow's papers, for she confessed in a letter written to her literary executors during her last year that, at some earlier time, she destroyed her most highly prized letters "in a desperate resolve to escape from the tragedy of the past. . . . Those that I did not destroy meant less to me and awoke no heartbreaking memories." [20]

Therefore, only the one short story, "A Point in Morals," (plus, possibly, an unclear statement in a letter she wrote from England in 1896) remains to suggest that Ellen Glasgow knew Pearce Bailey as early as the fall of 1897.[21] The parallels between the fictional alien-

---

18 April 8, 1945, Glasgow Collection, Alderman.
19 Blair Rouse, *Ellen Glasgow* (New York, 1962), 142n.
20 January 6, 1945, Glasgow Papers, Alderman.
21 From England, Ellen Glasgow wrote Cary McCormack of a young fellow on the *Etruria* whom she had spoken to only twice, but who nevertheless wrote her a letter

ist and the neurologist are striking. First, the alienist is thirty-odd years of age; Bailey would have been thirty-one in the year Miss Glasgow first sailed to England. Second, the alienist "had made a sudden leap into popularity through several successful cases"; Bailey had, by 1896, acquired a similar reputation by publishing several studies of pathological states of perception;[22] he was also well along in an authoritative investigation of *Accident and Injury in Their Relations to the Nervous System* to be published in 1898. Third, the alienist studied at Heidelberg; Bailey attended the University of Heidelberg (as well as those of Paris, Vienna, and Munich). Fourth, the alienist is called in to treat a patient with the morphine habit; Bailey later wrote a series of articles on the drug habit.[23] Finally, that Bailey called himself a neurologist does not mean that he was any less interested in nonorganic mental problems than an alienist would have been. Half of his neurological study of 1898 is devoted to traumatic neuroses. Moreover, he later published essays on such purely psychical phenomena as autistic states of consciousness.[24] These parallels suggest at least the possibility that Miss Glasgow knew Bailey by 1897. And the suggestion of Collins that Bailey was the man she loved is a useful hypothesis to work with until concrete evidence to the contrary turns up. Their relationship would, for example, provide one explanation for the increased psychological insight exhibited in her subsequent novels, including *Phases of an Inferior Planet*. It would also explain her frequent visits to New York during the years which followed.

There was, in addition, a very practical reason for such trips

---

from Paris that began, "May I dare to hope that you will let me write you?" Undated letter [August 1, 1896] in Glasgow Collection, Alderman. Miss Glasgow would have had a third opportunity to speak to this gentleman when she herself visited Paris in September, 1896.

22 See Pearce Bailey, "A Case of General Analgesia," *New York Medical Record* (December 28, 1895); "The Diagnosis of Idiopathic Epilepsy," *American Medical Surgery Bulletin* (August 8, 1896); and "Simulation of Nervous Disorders Following Accidents," *Railway Surgeon* (February 8, 1896).

23 See Pearce Bailey, "Change of Masters," *Harper's Magazine*, CXXVIII (October, 1913), 752–59; "Heroin Habit," *New Republic*, VI (April 22, 1916), 314–16, and "Drug Habit in U. S.," *New Republic*, XXVI (March 16, 1921), 67–69.

24 See Pearce Bailey, "The Wishful Self," *Scribner's Magazine*, LVIII (July, 1915), 115–21.

north. For by October, 1897, Miss Glasgow had returned to New York, and, from her apartment at 400 West 57th Street, was attempting to sell her shorter works to the magazines. She had by then cultivated the friendship of Walter Hines Page, the associate editor of *The Atlantic Monthly* and, like Miss Glasgow, an emancipated southerner. To Page's magazine she offered "The Freeman," her poem proclaiming the paradoxical freedom one achieves when he no longer is burdened by hope—"the freedom of despair." With Page she discussed her future plans as a novelist. He reinforced her ambition to give up short forms and to "become a great novelist or none at all." [25] Page warned her against commercial forces which might tempt her to lower her goals; he urged her to save herself for "great pieces of work." [26] Shortly afterwards, Page would himself tempt Miss Glasgow away from Harper and Brothers to join his new firm, Doubleday, Page and Company.

In the meanwhile, however, Harper's had expressed the hope to publish all her fiction. When she considered submitting a story to *McClure's Magazine*, Henry Mills Alden, the editor of *Harper's Magazine*, sent a very cordial letter assuring her that his company planned on her short stories also. To maintain her independence, Miss Glasgow consulted Paul R. Reynolds, who had established the first American literary agency only four years before. Reynolds placed "Between Two Shores" with *McClure's* but allowed "A Point in Morals" to go to *Harper's*.[27]

The major use Miss Glasgow wished to make of Reynolds would be as an entrée to the English publishers, for Reynolds had started his agency as their representative. In November, 1897, she instructed Reynolds to discover whether William Heinemann would like the English rights for her new novel. Because she so strongly valued the opinion of British readers and critics, she was willing to accept the lowest terms from an English publisher. By February, Reynolds had succeeded in obtaining a contract from

---

25 *Letters*, 24–25.
26 Burton J. Hendrick, *The Training of an American: The Earlier Life and Letters of Walter H. Page, 1855–1913* (New York, 1928), 335–37.
27 Colvert, "Agent and Author," 180.

Heinemann which promised Miss Glasgow a 15 percent royalty.[28]
In all negotiations with Reynolds, Miss Glasgow was icily formal
and precise in her demands. Neither her outstanding business acu-
men nor an English publisher, however, could guarantee the financial or critical reception of her second novel. The success of *Phases
of an Inferior Planet* fell far below the modest sensation created by
The Descendant.

SHELTERS AND EVASIONS

The settings, characters, and incidents of *Phases of an Inferior
Planet* have least to do with the South of any in novels written by
Ellen Glasgow, a fact which partially explains why it is her most
neglected book. But if the Virginia garden is taken to be a state of
mind rather than an area on a map, we find that this novel plays an
important role in Miss Glasgow's general critique of evasive habits
of mind. Directly attacked, though in a New York setting, is the
Episcopal Church, an essential institution of the Virginia aristocracy, one preserved, along with history, tradition, and romantic fiction, by the "good families" of Virginia.[29] The ultimate target,
though, is the set of mind the Church represents: a sheltering illusion, a high-minded evasion of the struggle for existence.

The novel assaults an underlying quality of the sheltered mind,
North and South, its hypocritical complacency based in part upon
widespread acceptance of those aspects of evolutionary theory which
appealed to the American outlook. Spencer's belief in cosmic progress through social selection tied in neatly with genteel America's
faith in evolutionary meliorism directed by a benevolent deity.[30]
Miss Glasgow selected her epigraph from a source which in itself
must have embarrassed this genteel world view satisfied with its
synthesis of science, religion, and political economy; she uses Eccle-
siastes to refute Spencer: "I returned, and saw under the sun, that
the race is not to the swift, nor the battle to the strong, neither yet

28 *Ibid.*, 180–83.
29 See Ellen Glasgow's comment in *Barren Ground*, 5.
30 Cf. Frederick W. Conner, *Cosmic Optimism: A Study of the Interpretation of
Evolution by American Poets from Emerson to Robinson* (Gainesville, 1949), 4–5.

bread to the wise, nor yet riches to men of understanding, nor yet favour to men of skill; but time and chance happeneth to them all." This choice is the first of numerous ironies in a novel which throughout supports Thomas Huxley's perception that "goodness and beauty" are often destroyed in the struggle for existence, while "ugliness and evil" (and conformity, Miss Glasgow would add) survive. The book does not, however, go so far as to accept the garden existence which Huxley proposed as the shelter for goodness and beauty. More specifically, Miss Glasgow's second novel explores the conflicts which make survival difficult for a man whose moral sense has developed in the opposite direction from Michael Akershem's— a man who, in his capacity to live for others, belongs to the future of the human species, as Akershem belonged to its savage past.

The chain of events in *Phases* is so complicated (Hardy-like in this) that adequate development would have required a larger book. Mariana, a southern girl in revolt, has come to New York where she lives in the Gotham, another of those apartment hotels, like the Templeton of *The Descendant*, in which shabby gentility and bohemia mix. She meets instead her neighbor, Anthony Algarcife, an apostate Episcopal minister turned Darwinian scientist and teacher. The two stumble into a frustrating marriage which, after the death of their child and the loss of Algarcife's job, ends with Mariana running away to sing in a traveling comic opera. Left alone, Algarcife skids toward suicide—but ends instead back in the ministry.

Eight years later, Mariana, now the wealthy widow of a second marriage and adventuress of undefined social position, returns to New York to find Algarcife a powerful but disillusioned churchman. Attracted by Mariana once more, he determines to run off with her. But Mariana chances upon him as he is conducting a mass and, unaware of his false position, is so awed by its splendor that she cannot let him give it up for her. Confused, she walks rainy streets trying to reach a decision. It is made for her: she has a recurrence of pneumonia.[31] Her death brings Algarcife to the edge of

---

31 This unconvincing aspect of the ending is probably a concession to one, or both, of two literary conventions. It gives a degree of finality expected by nineteenth-century readers, although Algarcife's suspended situation represents a step towards

suicide once again, but he is distracted from the abyss when an assistant breaks in to say that Father Algarcife is needed to ward off violence in an ironworks strike.

At the start, Algarcife and Mariana embody remarkable opposites of character. He is excessively altruistic and devoted to concrete realities; she is egotistical and thrives on the illusion of transcendent mysteries. He desires to renounce false shelters; she depends on them.

Algarcife is Miss Glasgow's most blatantly Darwinian protagonist. Orphaned in the care of an outstanding High Church Episcopal minister who educated the brilliant boy to be his successor, Algarcife is driven by the lack of faith and a hunger for knowledge from the shelter of the church into science. Free of any religious feelings, he seeks to comprehend all realities, beautiful and grotesque.[32] He wills so strongly to create his own environment and govern his own behavior that he represses passions which might distract him from his work (43, 50, 75). If he seems dry, ascetic, irascible, and misanthropic (42, 112, 117), it is because he is devoted to the search for knowledge—rather than the search for pleasure. His grand project is to preserve a "strongly modified theory of pangenesis" [33]—to substantiate the biological transmission of acquired characteristics—by reconciling "Darwin's gemmules, Weismann's germ-plasm, and Galton's stirp" (51, 52). But most importantly, Algarcife is instinctively altruistic: his first impulse when he hears Mariana, still a stranger, sobbing from hunger in the room adjoin-

---

the more modern open ending. Next, to a certain mentality (that of F. N. Doubleday for example, who later objected to Sister Carrie's unending successes and had publication of Dreiser's novel suspended), it would be a "happy ending," in as much as the "wicked" (Mariana, the adventuress) are given their "just" punishment. Miss Glasgow, however, should be applauded for not having conceded the second half of the "happy ending"—the reward of the virtuous, for Algarcife's apparent reward, his success, is, in fact, a living hell. A double irony arises from his "virtue"—i.e., his return to the church—being only apparent, at which point the very idea of "rewards and punishments" becomes absurd. Much later Miss Glasgow noted how great a burden the convention of the happy end, reinforced by the "artificial glow of . . . American idealism," had been to her early novels; see Measure, 118–19.

32 Phases, 45, 48, 65.

33 Pangenesis is the much criticized concept which Darwin introduced in Variation of Animals and Plants Under Domestication; it includes a now discredited explanation of the biological transmission of acquired characteristics.

ing his, is "to hasten in the direction from whence the sound came."
From sympathy, he violates "the artificial restraints of society" and
invites Mariana to his room for supper (43–45).

Later, talking with Mariana, he states his anti-garden attitudes
towards conventions, evasive idealism, sympathy, and civilization:

> "True, we have a thin layer of hypocrisy, which we call civilization.
> It prompts us to sugar-coat the sins which our forefathers swallowed
> in the rough; that is all. It is purely artificial. In a hundred thou-
> sand years it may get soaked in, and then the artificial refinement
> will become real and civilization will set in. . . . And then we will
> realize that to be civilized is to shrink as instinctively from inflicting
> as from enduring pain. Sympathy is merely a quickening of the
> imagination, in which state we are able to propel ourselves men-
> tally into conditions other than our own" (46–47).

Algarcife's notion of sympathy parallels closely that of Darwin,
while his emphasis on propelling ourselves mentally into the situations of others echoes Leslie Stephen's Darwinian view of "secondary emotions." His negative estimate of convention as a "thin layer
of hypocrisy" may owe a good deal to Miss Glasgow's familiarity
with Walter Bagehot's stress on breaking the "cake of custom." Presumably artificial conventions are to be broken when one responds
to the demands of the sympathies.

Miss Glasgow gives the impression that Algarcife's "peculiar sen-
sitiveness of sympathy" is a foretaste of a truer civilization than
presently exists. Mariana has never met a man of his type before. She compares him with the "fox-hunting heroes of her childish days." Those fearless hunters of the South would have regarded
Algarcife's concern "as a mark of effeminacy" and would have
"ruthlessly laughed to scorn." Algarcife has no place for the semi-
barbaric virtues of Mariana's childhood. Miss Glasgow implies that
although Algarcife is the "priest of the coming generation," he is
the "pariah of the present," and will be "trampled into nothingness." He is a moral mutant, out of time and place (74–75). As such
he lacks survival value.

Miss Glasgow makes no to-do over the question whether the
source of Algarcife's "moral sense" is Nature or Nurture. Com-

pared to most of her characters, he is noticeably without a heritage. When very young, he was sent as an orphan to the care of Father Speares (105). Perhaps Algarcife retains subconsciously Father Speares's belief in "the existence of a vital ethical principle in nature" even though he has rejected the priest's God (69). The implication, however, is that his sympathies are "instinctive," which in 1898 generally connoted innate patterns of behavior. This "instinct" is most likely Algarcife's inheritance—biological or learned —from his mother, a New Orleans Creole who married a New Yorker and "died because the North was so cold" (99). His sole memory of her in the novel is of maternal sympathy; her delicate hand on his forehead when he went crying to her "seemed to him . . . the only touch of love with the power to console" (182).

In contrast, the best to be said of Mariana is that she has the sensibility of an artist: she has ambitions to sing Wagner. But the concrete results of this artistic temperament are her blind idealism and her evasion of unpleasant sensations (8), marked contrasts to Akershem's positivistic pursuit of all experience. Although she has revolted against the South and come to New York, she has not managed to free herself from its ideology. She still exists "in a maze of the imagination, feasting upon the unsubstantial food of idealism" (20–22). She has a southern-bred longing for self-transcending, infinite mysteries. From her "unsatisfied restlessness of self" and "complete submergence of soul in idea" developed her devotion to the least substantial of fine arts, music. Her response reeks of repressed sexuality and religiosity: sitting in the fifth gallery of the Metropolitan Opera House, she sometimes "grasped the railing with her quivering hands and bowed her head in an ecstasy of appreciation. It was the ecstasy with which a monk in mediaeval days must have thrilled when he faced in a dim cathedral some beautiful and earthly Virgin of the great Raphael. It was the purest form of sensuous self-abnegation" (28). This mystical thrust expresses the same craving for pleasant sensations that in part motivated her earlier conversion to the Episcopal Church.

The human results of her idealism and longing for infinites are: self-seeking, self-pity, condescension toward the supposedly unwashed classes (40), and a willingness to exploit others—her father, her friends, and both her husbands—to shelter her ideal of a colorful existence (92, 94–95, 275). Mariana's growth in the novel is away from this self-seeking, evasive idealism toward a less egocentric appreciation of the inherent worth of others (236–37, 314).

But her transformation takes place separate from the events of the novel, which focus instead upon Algarcife's struggle, outside all shelter, for economic and psychological existence. While mediocre minds thrive on all sides of him, he slides into the abyss. The stages of his descent—the relinquishment of volition before unconquerable forces (134–35); a complete sense of isolation from the chain of humanity; an ironic view of the absurd treadmill existence of others (176–77); a shocked perception of the ludicrous shape of the human body (183); alienation, physical disgust, nausea before the naked facts of life and the struggle to be born, marry, propagate, and die; total estrangement from the self and the personal past (177)—will seem familiar to readers of our contemporary literature of despair, especially Sartre's *Nausea*. Similar stages occur in *Barren Ground* during Dorinda's descent into despair. The explanations for this remarkable record of despair (more often asserted in *Phases* than dramatized, unfortunately) are probably biographical ones plus the fact that by this point in her career Miss Glasgow knew Schopenhauer's *The World as Will and Idea* (1818).[34] From Schopenhauer's conception of will and nothingness, she possibly borrowed an intellectual interpretation of despair to give shape to her personal understanding of it. Algarcife's crisis leads him beyond all protecting illusions to a gnawing sense of the void that surrounds him. After the will has been abolished, social laws have dropped away, and the real world has become nothing, there is, before Algarcife, to use Schopenhauer's phrase, "certainly only nothingness." In Algarcife's own words: "It was as if he had reached the ultimate nothing, the end to which his pathway led. Though he dashed his

---

[34] *Woman*, 91. Cf. her allusion to Schopenhauer in her short story of the same period, "A Point in Morals," and the statement by her nephew Carrington C. Tutwiler in "Excerpts from 'Ellen Glasgow—the Writer as Reader,'" 218. Cf. also the quote from Schopenhauer among the epigraphs of *The Descendant*.

brains into the void, not one breath of the universal progress would swerve from its course" (181–82). Schopenhauer suggests vaguely that in nothingness "the saint sees something positive which other men do not see"—an implication which Bertrand Russell, however, asserts is merely rhetorical and insincere.[35] Certainly Algarcife finds nothing positive in nothingness; he is free, but freedom is anguishing. Even freedom for suicide becomes a stale prospect. To have no hope of life and yet to be unable to die for lack of will is, of course, to be totally in despair. In this condition, he slips, through no effort of his own, back into the hands of his childhood protector, Father Speares, and, consequently, in good *fin-de-siècle* fashion, into the shelter of the Church. But after his vision of the ultimate void, the lies other men live by can have no power to convince him.

Algarcife's return to the Church introduces the recurring theme of many of Ellen Glasgow's novels, which she later called the "sheltered life," an essential goal of genteel existence. The Church here is Miss Glasgow's earliest literary approach to Thomas Huxley's "garden," or "state of art": a "small patch of soil" where the belligerent "state of nature" has been brought to an end "by the intervention of man." [36] Algarcife, the harbinger of a new morality who could not survive in natural competition with mediocrity, prospers in the artificial world created by an ancient tradition of clergymen. In this environment free from the struggle for existence, conditions have been adjusted to meet the needs of such selfless individuals as Algarcife. It is artificial selection on the grand scale.

Ironically, Algarcife can return to his shelter only when he is volitionless, passionless, indifferent to the pursuit of knowledge; these seem the traits for which the garden selects him. But there are other needs besides security, needs once felt by Algarcife, that the Church cannot satisfy: the hunger for realities, which drove him originally from the Church for it violated the conventions from which his shelter derives; or, again, his genuine concern as a man of the Church to devote himself to charity cases in hospitals and the Bowery. These deeper drives lie dormant or must wait while he

---

35 Bertrand Russell, *A History of Western Philosophy* (New York, 1945), 755–58.
36 *Evolution and Ethics and Other Essays* (New York, 1896), 9.

counsels wealthy, love-hungry wives of men who reserve their passion for mistresses. Fortunately his High Church duties are formal with little content; the methodical rituals and rites make possible his unfeeling ministry and his continued annihilation of self in a faith in which his void-ridden mind has no interest (241). His wealthy congregation mistakes apathy for humility; the women find his indifference attractive (210, 240).

Algarcife makes no effort to dissimulate his lack of emotion, nor is he in bad faith; he has not tried to deceive himself about the falseness of his position. Consequently, the price he pays for shelter is the sense of inadvertently deceiving others, the guilt of having sold himself to the Church as payment for Father Speares' kindness (200–201, 217, 298–99). Weighed with guilt, lethargy, and self-disgust, he has no prospect but to work himself into exhaustion and death (196).

Perhaps Algarcife should have been left in this state of despair, but the return of Mariana gives Miss Glasgow an opportunity to experiment with a subject then becoming popular in scientific literature—hysteria. If she knew the discoveries of Charcot, Janet, and Breuer in this area, it must have been through summaries appearing in such early American works in psychology as William James's *Principles of Psychology* (1890), or Pearce Bailey's *Accident and Injury, Their Relations to Diseases of the Nervous System* (1898), which uses ideas of Charcot and Janet in analyzing forms of hysteria similar to the emotional anaesthesia through which Algarcife passes. Otherwise, in her own family, in the sufferings of her mother, Cary, and herself, there was ample authority for Algarcife's traumatic state. She knew from experience that the awakening of personal will in such cases depends first on the recovery of emotion, and that the one state worse than complete despair is hope burning at the heart of despair but powerless to fulfill itself. Mariana becomes the device for turning this final screw on Algarcife (cf. 257, 294, 303, 307).

Ironically, Mariana could not have accomplished this end without having matured out of her former evasive idealism. As she says after eight years, "I don't idealize any longer. . . . I have lopped off

an ideal every hour since I saw you." In sloughing off the false consciousness of her southern childhood, she has learned to adjust to
things as they are and acquired an "imaginative sympathy for humanity" (80–82, 236–37). Consequently, she will not let Algarcife
sacrifice his luxurious life as a priest. She imagines he belongs
within the chancel, not on a worthless farm in the South. From
this position of misunderstanding, she ironically discovers the de-
terministic assumption of the novel: "that it is not given one to
begin over again for a single day; that of all things under the sun,
the past is the one thing irremediable." She comes to the right insight, but for the wrong reason: "This was his life, and what was
hers? What had she that could recompense him for the sacrifice of
the Eucharistic robes and the pride of the Cross?" Thus, Algarcife
is imprisoned inextricably in the hell of his own false position
(314–16).

The remainder of the novel bears out Mariana's pessimistic view
of the remedy of time; her regret that there is no way to undo what
circumstance has determined sets the mood of the ending. The notion that Algarcife might have survived the escape to the farm does
not stand up. Algarcife, who has had no rural experience, holds to
a naïve Jeffersonian fantasy that he will "till the land and drive the
plough and take up the common round of life again—a life free from
action as from failure, into which no changes might ring despair"
(307). In this fantasy there is no comprehension of the great struggle he would face, as a yeoman, against the always changing forces
of nature. Algarcife stands a more realistic chance of survival within
the shelter of the chancel; it is the reward of conformity to social
conventions. Furthermore, in the reversal which follows Mariana's
visit to the cathedral, there is the suggestion that, because a man
depends to a large extent upon the way others view him for his
image of himself, he is what he *does*, rather than what he *thinks*;
that the human reality is action; that the private self is simply an
alibi man fabricates to keep from seeing himself as he, in fact, is for
others; and that, consequently, any false role or compromise with
evasive idealism is fatal. Algarcife has become that man whom
Mariana beholds in Eucharistic robes, protected by the altar. He is

a man of sympathy. He has become also a man who dreams of escape to a farm, who toys with the promise of suicide; but who does neither, and hurries instead to stop strikes, hoping perhaps to have his false situation ended by a stray bullet.

Algarcife's extraordinary capacity for altruism makes him, in an important sense, the opposite of Michael Akershem, who was helplessly egocentric. Inasmuch as each character dominates the novel in which he appears and draws the reader's sympathy, it might seem that Ellen Glasgow had, in turn, embraced opposing views of human nature. This inconsistency is only apparent, and can be more accurately explained as an indication of Miss Glasgow's critical detachment. Algarcife, as a student, sometimes played a similar trick: in his complete freedom from dogma and orthodoxy, he made a practice of alternately taking both the negative and affirmative sides of a given argument, "detecting his own weaknesses as ruthlessly as he had detected those" of his teacher (66). Later, as a priest, he published a volume of sermons to refute a series of anonymous magazine articles attacking religion from the scientific point of view (205), articles which were, in fact, the earlier products of his own pen (288–89). In the same way, Miss Glasgow first polarized the two instincts joined in tension by Darwin's image of man, and then isolated each for careful study in a separate novel.

The driving self-interest of Akershem fitted him for the fiercely competitive universe described by Spencer, Sumner, and Kidd. Miss Glasgow showed, however, that the limits of such fitness arise when the egotist violates certain conventions which, however hypocritically they may be held, make possible the community of men. In Algarcife she embodies the opposite pole; to a man of his profound altruism social conventions are themselves an encumbrance to social feelings. She presses Algarcife's pure moral sense, as she had Akershem's egotism, to its extremity; the crisis arises when the former can no longer make necessary assertions of self, when he can no longer restrain Mariana, when he no longer wills to live. The man who lives for others can only flourish, it turns out, in an artificial environment sheltered from the struggle for life. In both novels, the attack upon the sheltered life is implicit—in its failure to domesticate Akershem and in the negative values it encourages in Algarcife. Because the "best" cannot otherwise survive, Miss Glasgow judges this an inferior planet.

FAILURE

The Descendant was a publisher's success, while *Phases*, which appeared in March, 1898, sold miserably and reaped abuse from the critics. Well over two-thirds of the reviews were decidedly unfavorable, charging that Miss Glasgow was so obsessed and "hardened by her scientific knowledge" that she neglected character motivation and development. The English reviews and sales were in no way better than the American.[37] It is difficult to say how much this defeat affected Miss Glasgow's estimate of her own work; in September, before the English reviews appeared, she reassured her agent, and perhaps herself, that "the kind of success I prefer most now is that which comes from a discriminating public—which is never large."[38] The reasons for the failure of her second novel have to do with the author's view of it, with the publisher's view of it, and with the ways it violated the world view of American readers.

At some point during the creation of *Phases* Miss Glasgow's interest in its theme and setting began to stray. She had been well along in it before her European trip, during which it was dropped completely. When she returned to America and her novel, she found the nation and even Richmond deep in the controversy of the 1896 Bryan–McKinley campaign. Perhaps as a consequence, the first half of *Phases* is unified around the relationship of Anthony Algarcife and Mariana Musin, while the second half is marred by several not-very-well-integrated episodes having to do with Tammany politics. A further reason for her waning interest in *Phases* shows up in her letters of 1897 to Walter Page. Prior to October,[39] during a period when she was "studying the ground work of *Phases*"

37 Kelly, "Struggle for Recognition," 23–25.
38 Colvert, "Agent and Author," 187.
39 *Letters*, 24. The date Blair Rouse assigned to this letter, October 28, 1897, seems a little late since "The Freeman," a poem she returned in it to Page after some revisions, was published in the October, 1897, *Atlantic Monthly*.

(probably restudying the unity of the action at Page's suggestion), she found herself "getting most impatient for its completion." She already was planning "a bigger and more ambitious work" and wanted to get *Phases* off her mind so that she might put her whole strength into the new book. Perhaps under the spell of Tolstoy's novels, which seemed to her to discover the universal in the most ordinary materials, she was preparing to reject the advice of "an English literary man . . . that I should go abroad to develope [*sic*] my work, that the life I have chosen to portray is more interesting when taken from a French or English standpoint." The scene for her third novel would be laid—not in France, England, or even New York—but in Virginia.[40] She was anxious to explore the brave new literary world, and *Phases* suffered in art from her divided interest.

A second reason *Phases* failed may, in fairness, be attributed to the financial position of her publisher, Harper and Brothers. Since the passage of the international copyright law of 1891, Harper's, an old house, had had to cut corners to compete with the many vigorous firms created in response to copyright protection. Harper's gained support from Morgan's bank and finally adjusted, but in 1898 "only the more established authors were given extensive publicity." Publicity for *Phases* "appeared only in large advertisements containing notices of several authors." [41]

The third and most important cause of the failure of *Phases* to sell well and to attract critics was its obvious affront to the American outlook. As reviewers noted, it showed that the author was not after the popularity accorded "cheap romances" and other easy, painless fiction, especially romantic colonial novels.[42] Instead, Miss Glasgow's second novel ran counter to major religious, literary, and philosophic traditions of the day. Akershem, as an agnostic scientist of whom circumstances make an extremely successful priest without, at the same time, correcting his deficient faith, seemed incredible to a nation which has often been as naïve about religion as

---

[40] March 26, 1898, *Letters*, 26–27; *Woman*, 128.
[41] Kelly, "Struggle for Recognition," 26–27.
[42] *Ibid.*, 25–26.

about sincerity. It is possible that many Americans had found their romantic image of themselves in rootless, ruthlessly individualistic Michael Akershem and missed entirely Miss Glasgow's criticism of his naïve egotism. It is possible also that Americans found nothing they understood in Anthony Algarcife's imaginative sympathy—nor in his failure. It is certain that they found the notion of an entirely insincere priest repugnant.[43] The North and West were too wrapped up in success and Edenic innocence to appreciate Miss Glasgow's notion of the nature of things, while the South—the only region to which (in Toynbee's phrase) history had happened—had retreated into its own project of self-deception where complementary, self-deceiving fables of the Lost Cause and a New South allowed one to dwell on glories imagined for the past and future rather than face the painful failures of the present.

As a result of her second novel's failure to find an audience, Miss Glasgow seems to have learned that she could not continue presenting such depressing philosophical realities in her books; she would write a number of novels before she again looked as directly into nothingness as she had with Algarcife. In 1898 she obviously did not desire, despite her earlier assurance to her agent, to take shelter by writing only for a coterie. She wished to keep her novels in the main arena of competition, even if she had to find, somewhere between Akershem and Algarcife, protagonists who embodied less precisely than they the extremes of the question that perplexed her: whether man is necessarily a self-seeking animal, or whether, under some circumstances, he is capable of what Darwin had described as moral behavior. With this shift in perspective, she was eager to attack the garden of southern civilization head-on.

---

43 *Ibid.*, 23.

Chapter V

The Survival of the Clannish, 1898–1900

The Voice of the People

AMERICA'S OLDEST GARDEN

The failure of *Phases of an Inferior Planet* seems to have lowered temporarily the demand for Ellen Glasgow's writings, for although she had earlier planned to follow *Phases* with a small volume of poetry, Reynolds, her agent, found it impossible to place individual poems in English or American magazines, and publication of the collection was delayed four years. Determined not to repeat this failure, she planned to devote two full years to her "long novel upon modern conditions of life in Virginia." [1] She spent a good part of the spring and summer of 1898 exploring the face and spirit of the state. She selected as the primary setting of the novel Williamsburg, colonial capital of Virginia, site of the second oldest college in the English colonies, and a small community redolent with tradition and names like Washington, Jefferson, Marshall, Madison, and Monroe. Miss Glasgow and her sister, Cary McCormack, spent the month of May at the Colonial Inn in Williamsburg in order to study its college, its ancient Courthouse and Courthouse green, and its best families.

In her autobiography she points out that she also received in Williamsburg an unexpected lesson in the "mob spirit," which may have influenced her forthcoming novel. This unpleasant experience

---

1 Colvert, "Agent and Author," 186–87; "Chronicle and Comment," *Bookman* (New York), V (July, 1897), 370.

involved the indifferent neighbor of her childhood who would become the confidant of her old age, James Branch Cabell. Cabell, according to Miss Glasgow's account, in his final year at the College of William and Mary, was unjustly implicated by gossip in a scandal that arose when a literary associate of his, "the leading middle-aged intellectual of the village," was charged with sexual perversion. Miss Glasgow found herself repelled by the amusement the best people of Williamsburg found in distributing the rumor by "innuendo and parenthesis." A "refined mob with a character on a pinpoint" was as pernicious as a vulgar mob of the French Revolution showing off a head on a pike; both crowds displayed the same psychological malady—a compulsion to inflict pain and remain anonymous.[2] The mobs which were to distribute the rumors and provide the violent conclusion of her next novel would share this sickness.

To gain firsthand details for another pivotal episode of the novel, Miss Glasgow and one of her sisters (probably Cary) convinced a family friend to smuggle them into the Democratic State Convention at Roanoke. The only feminine observers in a crowd of more than a thousand men, they were hidden, the anecdote goes, on a hot day in late summer, in an obscure corner behind the stage. Miss Glasgow found the flood of southern oratory and the response of the delegates exciting, amusing, and usable.[3] Then, the month of September Miss Glasgow and Cary spent "stranded afar off in the mountains" at Crockett Arsenic–Lithia Springs near Shawsville, Virginia. Photographs record that the two sisters, in long full dresses, explored this backwoods section of Virginia. One pictures Cary balancing on a one-log bridge; another catches a farmer hauling logs through a stream on a cart drawn by oxen.[4] Perhaps Miss Glasgow reasoned that the mountains preserved rural life as it had been near Williamsburg twenty-five years earlier, when the poor whites of her next novel were alive.

2 Cf. *Woman*, 130–34, and *Measure*, 61–62.

3 Cf. *Measure*, 62–63; Marcosson, "The Personal Ellen Glasgow," 619–21; Mildred Rutherford, *The South in History and Literature, a Hand-Book of Southern Authors from the Settlement of Jamestown, 1607 to Living Writers* (Atlanta, 1907), 738.

4 Cf. Colvert, "Agent and Author," 187, and two photographs from the possession of Miss Eliza Huger Dunkin (Mrs. Percy Gamble Kammerer) now deposited in the Glasgow Collection at Alderman.

In October she was back in Richmond, hard at work on the book, when Hamlin Garland paid a visit. Garland noted in his chronicle that he was surprised to find a girl so young, "tall and fair, with a childlike roundness of cheek and chin." He added, however, that her mind was "very far from being childish." He talked with her about Spencer and Darwin and was encouraged by her "alarming candor of statement": "She frankly confessed that she didn't like happy people." She showed him a collection of her poems, "all dealing with the dignity of despair, the splendor of hell, and the stern decrees of fate—many of them succinct and powerful of diction." Garland recorded a prediction of Miss Glasgow's career: "The order of her progress seems reversed. She is beginning with the bitterness of age. She is likely to be a marked personality in Southern literature. Her work will not be pleasant, but it will be original and powerful." [5]

Miss Glasgow later explained that she was unusually bitter at the time of Garland's visit because her ears troubled her; her portion of the conversation was conducted in an "agonizing tension because his voice was not clear enough for me to understand what he said." If circumstances had been more conducive to open communication, a closer relationship, which would have profited Miss Glasgow, might have developed. She later noted, however, that New York and association with Howells had unfortunately tamed Garland of his wildness and his originality and had civilized out of him the "almost savage fidelity to life" of *Main-Traveled Roads*. She was unwilling to establish a permanent association with any disciple of the "dull gentility" which weakened Howells' realism (*Woman*, 137–41).

The middle of November found Miss Glasgow back in New York for medical and literary reasons. In a steady background of city noise she seemed to hear better. She had now begun her endless "pilgrimage all over the world" seeking specialists who might end her deafness, caused, apparently, by a "hardening in the Eustachian tube and the middle ear." In New York she also paid more visits to the Authors' Club and met the "various authors who would soon

[5] Hamlin Garland, *Roadside Meetings* (New York, 1930), 349.

become, by self-election, the Forty Immortals of the American Academy." She thought them guilty of having "created both the literature of America and the literary renown that embalmed it." They impressed her as soft with benevolence and an "evergreen optimism." In her memoirs, though, she gave them credit for an unequaled amount of "sheer mental energy" directed toward the commendable goal of creating a fairer social order. "Many of them worked, without reward, to make living conditions more tolerable for the dispossessed of society. If there were robber barons in industry, there were, as well, giants of good will in philanthropy." [6]

Her brother Arthur showed in a small way the symptoms of this industrialist-philanthropist complex when he visited America (apparently in 1898): he felt sorry for Ellen, Cary, Rebe, and Frank, because the old gray house on Main Street in Richmond seemed a tomb. He prescribed an ocean voyage and a change of countries to seal off unpleasant memories (*Woman*, 145). By the end of December Miss Glasgow planned on an eight-month journey, financed by Arthur, through Europe and North Africa.[7] Rebe and Cary would come along, but Frank, who perhaps most needed the therapy, could not break loose from "his tedious round in the Tredegar Iron Works." On February 4, 1899, the three sisters sailed from New York for Egypt aboard an old ship, the *Aller*, of the North German Lloyd Line. Miss Glasgow's autobiography gives the details of their visit to the Pyramids, then to the coast of Asia Minor, Smyrna, the Aegean Sea, the Isles of Greece, Athens, Corfu, the Alps, Italy, and Switzerland. By May they had reached Paris; from there they passed on to England and Scandinavia.[8] From Constantinople, at the end of March, Miss Glasgow wrote a lengthy letter to Richmond describing their visit to the Old Seraglio, the palace of the early Sultans. She was dazzled by the "suits of mail wrought of gold and silver, glittering with diamonds," by "emeralds the size of eggs," by "tapestries embroidered in a sheet of pearls," and by the dagger, with a "hilt formed of three huge emeralds," carried by Mahammed,

---

[6] Cf. Colvert, "Agent and Author," 187, and *Woman*, 137–44.
[7] Colvert, "Agent and Author," 187–88.
[8] Cf. Colvert, 188, and *Woman*, 145–51.

the conqueror of Constantinople. She could not escape the thought, however, that such beauties could be commanded only by an old eastern despotism. She thought of the real life that had been destroyed to create this oriental fairy tale—"the lives of thousands of workmen and the fortunes of several kingdoms." Later, enjoying the April sun at Hadrian's Villa near Tivoli, in the Roman Forum, and among the ruins of Pompeii, Miss Glasgow read and reread *The Thoughts of the Emperor Marcus Aurelius,* underscoring this time passages on the inevitability of change and the absence of anything new under the sun.[9] In England, the sisters Glasgow made a special visit to the village of Haworth (near Leeds) "because of our feeling for the Brontës, especially for Emily." Finally, in late August they sailed homeward on the *Kaiser Wilhelm* and reached New York the first Tuesday in September.[10]

The return to America meant renewed work on her novel put aside for eight months, and increased worries about publishers. She warmed to the job of writing and seemed to enjoy the "change of literary base" which the use of Virginia materials involved. In December she wrote Page that if the book "should chance to find a wide reading public, I should probably work upon a series of Virginia novels as true as I believe this one to be." [11] Page asked to see

9 "Richmonders in Constantinople," Richmond *Dispatch*, April 23, 1899, p. 7; Tutwiler, *Ellen Glasgow's Library,* 12–14.

10 *Woman,* 149–51, and Colvert, "Agent and Author," 188.

11 This quotation from December 2, 1899, has, it seems, some significance for the rather artificial controversy which has raged since Miss Glasgow's death as to whether she did, in fact, *plan* and execute a social history of Virginia or whether the idea of a social history arose after the fact of her having created it—cf. Daniel W. Patterson, "Ellen Glasgow's Plan for a Social History of Virginia," *Modern Fiction Studies,* V (Winter, 1959–60), 353–60, and Oliver L. Steele, "Ellen Glasgow, Social History and the 'Virginia Edition,' " *Modern Fiction Studies* (Summer, 1961), 173–76. The chief cause of the debate was James Branch Cabell's comment in *As I Remember It* (New York, 1955), 219—published a year after Miss Glasgow's posthumous autobiography, which alluded to the scandal of Cabell's last year at William and Mary—that he had given her the idea for the social history in 1925 to unify the collected edition of her novels. It is not surprising that Cabell made such a charge—whether for revenge or just to stir up the sort of satanic controversy for which he was once famous and which endeared him to Miss Glasgow. But it is odd that any one should take the statement of so infamous an ironist—he titled a late book, *Let Me Lie*—to have a simple historical meaning. It is not likely that Miss Glasgow could have had any more exact notion in 1900 of her total work than to intend a "series of Virginia novels as true" as *The Voice of the People.* Whether the idea existed before or after the fact is of little prac-

the book, which Miss Glasgow was very glad to have him do, though she warned that she intended for "Messrs. Harper to continue to be my publishers." [12] Page, who rose from a middle-class farm family in Piedmont North Carolina to be the editor of *The Atlantic Monthly* and went on to become an adviser to Rockefeller and Wilson's ambassador to Great Britain,[13] would take a special interest in Nick Burr, Miss Glasgow's poor-white protagonist who becomes governor of Virginia. Before he saw the novel, however, he initiated a campaign to draw her away from Harper's. He warned that the present manager of her publishing house was not "Harper and Brothers at all, but merely a business conducted by a receiver to pay off his creditors" and that the receiver might sell any of her books without consulting her. At the same time, Page notified Miss Glasgow that F. N. Doubleday and he were about to convert Doubleday and McClure into Doubleday, Page and Co., which would be able to do more for her novels than Harper's. Miss Glasgow wrote Reynolds for advice, assuring her agent that he would be allowed to handle negotiations with Heinemann for the English edition though she herself would make arrangements for the American publication. Then she dedicated a winter of very fine weather to concentrated work on the book she now called *The Voice of the People* and described as "not historical in the conventional sense, . . . not romantically exciting, but . . . a good, sound, solid, true-to-life kind of novel." By the end of February, 1900, the manuscript was in the printer's hands—at Doubleday, Page, and Co., Page having written Miss Glasgow that this book was "much the strongest" she had ever done.[14]

---

tical significance. After all, Balzac, her chief model for a unified social chronicle, did not get the idea of *La Comédie Humaine* until he collected his novels in 1842— Stefan Zweig, *Balzac* (New York, 1946), 326. It is still not certain whether her chief successor in this area, Faulkner, planned the saga of Yoknapatawpha County in advance, although Harold Eads of the manuscripts division of Alderman Library contends that there has recently been discovered among the Faulkner papers an *as yet undated*, waterlogged, rat-chewed manuscript—long lost by Faulkner himself—which lists the major interrelationships of characters, settings and incidents in his novels. No such written plan by Miss Glasgow is known to have existed.

12 *Letters*, 29.

13 For Page's rise see Hendrick, *The Training of an American*, 5–8 et *passim*.

14 *Letters*, 29–30, and Colvert, "Agent and Author," 188–90.

OLD FAMILIES AND NEW MEN

Foremost students of both subjects have called *The Voice of the People* the pioneer novel about southern poor whites and small towns, two important themes of twentieth-century fiction. But as one of these authorities, Shields McIlwaine, has admitted: Miss Glasgow "is concerned . . . with the lower or primitive levels of folk [and with the village] only as they represent a relation to or progress toward the goal of all society: a culture of social justice and gentle living." [15] Her third book was the first in which Miss Glasgow fully developed the tension between civilization and biology she came to call her major theme, for it was the first in which she knew the setting with sufficient intimacy to create a strong sense of ethos—culture interacting with character. Here the basic egotistical and social instincts of both major characters must adjust to the demands of a complex culture, the garden of southern life. The novel gracefully touches on several important social questions—the absence of public education in the South, the tyrannical power of railroad interests in Virginia politics, the emergence of Populism. But it focuses upon the family-class system so that the perverse power of family pride emerges as the key aspect of the southern tradition explored in this novel. Using the stock situation of the novel of manners, the difficulties of a lonely newcomer fighting for a position in a perniciously smug society, Miss Glasgow converts the pattern into an effective though ironic tragedy of manners. At the same time she provides new vitality for the romantic plot, the element of the novel of manners which had grown hackneyed in the historical romances of Thomas Nelson Page and Joel Chandler Harris fantasying the reconciliation of the North and the South. Like Henry James, who had made serious use of a similar pattern in his tragedies of international misunderstanding, she demonstrates that, in a metaphysical, religious, and political milieu which will sustain no further Socrates, Saint Joan, or Prince Hamlet, the fate of

[15] Shields McIlwaine, *The Southern Poor-White from Lubberland to Tobacco Road* (Norman, Okla., 1939), 184–85; Ima H. Herron, *The Small Town in American Literature* (Durham, 1939), 331.

a Daisy Miller, a Christopher Newman, a Milly Theale, or a Nicholas Burr is, indeed, among the most significant events. The influence of a book like James's *The American* is apparent in the role family pride plays in *The Voice of the People*; the differences between the French and Tidewater aristocracies are little more than accidents of geography.

But up to the final catastrophe, the incidents follow a thoroughly American mythic pattern: the rise in politics of the Jacksonian hero, a man of the people, born in a log cabin. Nick Burr, at twelve (in the early 1870's) turns against the complacent life of his overworked father, and talks his way into the patronage of a Kingsborough aristocrat, who sees him through to a law degree. But Burr also falls in love with a childhood classmate, blue-blooded Eugenia Battle, and, on returning to practice in Kingsborough, he asks her to marry him. When Eugenia accepts, a false rumor (one voice of the people) which links Burr with a pregnant girl causes them to split up in anger. Burr goes to the state legislature in Richmond, and Eugenia marries their childhood schoolmate, Dudley Webb, who is of her own social class.

Fifteen years later, having earned popularity in the Democratic Party, Burr wins the governorship. His subsequent administration earns him the ambiguous title, "The Man of Conscience," and a chance to progress to a national Senate seat, for which he is opposed by Webb. Thus he meets Eugenia again, but the passion seems dead. The race for the Senate is close and, in the last week, dirty. Just prior to the election, Burr, who seems above politics per se, returns to Kingsborough to protect a Negro in danger of lynching. The mob kills Burr by mistake. Dudley takes all.

From the start, the chief barrier between Burr and his success is the patronizing attitude of that class of Virginians united as a tightly closed family by the aristocratic tradition. Miss Glasgow prepares early for this conflict. When Nick begins to borrow books from his lifelong patron, Judge Bassett, the first he selects is Sir Henry Maine's *Ancient Law* (1861). Maine is difficult reading for a twelve-year-old with only three short winters of schooling, so Miss

Glasgow has him spell his way through the opening paragraphs.[16] In this manner she works into her text Maine's familiar first sentence: "The most celebrated system of jurisprudence known to the world begins, as it ends, with a code." This skillful authorial maneuver (a "free choice") serves a triple purpose. First, as an allusion to the Twelve Tables of Roman Law which aided the rise of the plebeians of Rome by fixing for the first time their rights vis-à-vis the aristocratic oligarchy that formerly ruled by custom and fiat, it sounds the theme of the rise of the poor whites of Virginia. Second, the allusion to the Justinian Code ("as it ends") implies the passing of a great tradition, another theme. Most importantly, inasmuch as the Roman law was a cornerstone of Roman civilization, the quotation from Maine stresses, by analogy, the importance to Virginia culture of the still unwritten "code of manners" which Miss Glasgow elsewhere called, with double-edged irony, the "finest creation" of modern civilization (*Woman*, 140). It is with this "cake of custom" that Burr must contend. Burr's ascent becomes not only a threat to the chivalric code of manners, but a gauge of the code's value and viability in a changing society. Measured in relation to Burr (the "hopelessly modern"), the code and the traditions supported by it (the "helplessly past") have, as Miss Glasgow's objective and dramatic method demonstrates, several things that one can say for them, but many that must be said against. The novel provides a spectrum of the tradition's favorable and unfavorable qualities.

The most commendable product of the code is Judge Bassett, whose imperturbable affability derives from a sense of family security (4). When, in a moment of instinctive generosity, he promises to help little Nick train to be a judge, his fine home becomes a shelter wherein the boy can acquire the learning he will need to compete and succeed (7). Miss Glasgow, borrowing directly, perhaps, from Huxley, uses the judge's carefully cultivated garden of vegetables and scarlet poppies, of lilacs and syringa, to symbolize

---

16 Ellen Glasgow, *The Voice of the People* (New York, 1900), 21. Hereinafter cited as *Voice* or simply by page.

the sheltering function of the tradition. The ruined state of the garden at the end of the book connotes the moribund aspect of that tradition (314, 433). Even embodied in the judge, the tradition cannot cope justly with Burr, for at the back of the judge's consciousness lurk the automatic traps of the class-ridden mind. The judge assumes that Nick *should* grow up to be a farmer rather than a judge and finds the boy unbearably stubborn for a man of his class (5, 11), a less than democratic attitude; Burr, as he himself learns, is finally "Amos Burr's son—we must give him a chance" (434). The judge's helpless and half-conscious arrogance of class represents, as Miss Glasgow deftly suggests, the underside of benevolent paternalism: when, just before his death, Burr as governor needs a man to share a problem with as a fellow statesman and equal, he finds only a senile benefactor, a practitioner of specious *noblesse oblige*.

Generally, though, the pernicious aspects of the tradition are less veiled with benevolence. Much can be learned about the absurd condition of southern education in this period from the opinions of Mrs. Jane Dudley Webb, a war widow, who lives on the past of the Dudley family. In the initial phase of Reconstruction, August 1865–67, which the Confederates themselves controlled, the white southerners had instigated a system of public education which they carefully restricted to "the superior race of man—the White race." At the same time, they remained hostile to efforts of the Freedman's Bureau to educate former slaves. After the Congressional challenge to this clearly unjust system was crushed by the Redeemers, white southerners saw to it that all public education, black and white, was crippled, ostensibly to protect the public debt, and thereby ensured the existence of an illiterate and manipulatable majority of southern voters until after 1900.[17] A contributing cause of the educational policies in the retrenchment period becomes transparent in the activity of Mrs. Webb, for she expresses the same received ignorance about class as her historical contemporaries did about race. Although her own son owes his education

17 Cf. Franklin, *Reconstruction*, 38–39, 46, 52; Woodward, *Origins of the New South*, 61–64.

to the benevolence of the judge, as soon as she learns Nick Burr has been admitted to the judge's private school, she rushes to inform the judge of her outrage that her boy is associating "with his inferiors." According to Mrs. Webb's theory of blood, "It is folly to educate a person above his station" (114–18).

Her son Dudley, like his father, is a stereotyped embodiment of traits that novels of the period commonly associated with aristocratic southern blood. His class-derived ability to dissimulate fellow feeling makes him a popular politician, who puts party above the people (44, 116, 117, 196, 342, 400); he regards those of Burr's class as "common"; he exhibits a cavalier disregard for the affection of his wife (380, 411, 416). Yet, when he has the choice between a sure but devious path to the Senate (by reviving the rumor associating Nick with Bessie Pollard) and saving Burr from a political smear, chivalry delivers him from littleness: "The instinct of generations was stronger than the appeal of the moment—he might sin a great sin, but he could never commit a meanness" (430).

The other major representatives of the tradition, the Battle family, are, with the exception of Bernard, more likeable than the Webbs—but less effective. A class-determined doubleness characterizes General Tom Battle's treatment of women, poor whites, and former slaves, a pattern which shows convincingly that sexual arrogance, class prejudice, and racism are cut from the same threadbare cloth—a state of consciousness that depends utterly upon simpleminded hierarchies supported by blood and masculine privilege. For example, beneath the sheltering and generous aspect of the general's view of woman there lurks, Miss Glasgow shows, an unquestioned assumption of masculine superiority which cannot imagine a woman capable of looking at things as coolly as a man (119). The same ambivalence appears in Battle's handling of his former slaves, who, like their historical counterparts, have come back to the old quarters following a taste of freedom and necessity off the plantation. One moment the general threatens to run them off; the next, his sense of responsibility causes him to share his skimpy supplies with one or another of them (58–59, 74–76). Thus Miss Glasgow makes fun of *noblesse oblige*. The assumption of class, sexual,

or racial superiority cuts both ways; privilege carries the responsibility of maintaining the artificial garden for those deemed less able
to compete in the natural state, and, as the bourbon-addicted general admits, his garden is in poor condition (20). Superiority can
become burdensome. So long as such gentlemen as the judge and
the general continued to block—or, at least, to control—the votes
and other freedoms of their blacks, their ladies, and their poor-
white neighbors, they had also to shelter and support their Mrs.
Webbs, their Nicholas Burrs, their black Caesars and Moseses (271).
This is one of the amusing but serious ironies Miss Glasgow's continuing exploration of *noblesse oblige* achieved. The sickness of the
system is obvious.

But the most pernicious effect of the aristocratic tradition is seen
in the power it exerts on Eugenia Battle who grows up within its
overprotective confines. Because her mother is dead and the discipline of her father lax, she enjoys in her early years a freedom to
develop sympathies not generally encouraged by her father's tradition, especially an intense social instinct or need for affection directed beyond her clan toward her puppy, the servants, Negro girls
and boys, and especially her classmate, poor-white Nick Burr, whose
special defender she becomes (19–20, 49, 62, 99–107, 117). Although
her sense of fellow feeling is strong enough that she will not let
Dudley call Nick "common," her consciousness is so permeated to
its depths with the traps of class-thinking that she automatically
takes Nick to be common despite her own protests to the contrary.
With this little perversity, Miss Glasgow indicates that Eugenia's
extra-familial sympathy is innate, or at least prior to her sense of
class, while the latter has been given to her, like the word "common," by her environment—primarily her family. But family conditioning is sufficiently successful that Eugenia is torn apart at the
instinctual or pre-conscious level by two, often-opposing sets of
drives: family feeling and the social instinct. Family affection in-
terferes with the instinctive sympathy or compassion which Miss
Glasgow considered the source of a larger and more viable guide to
social conduct than the former. Family feeling does not always, as
John Fiske, Alexander Sutherland, and several other Darwinists

theorized, prepare the individual, Eugenia Battle in this case, for participation in the broader human community. Eventually, values acquired from her family restrict her sense of community to her family, or, at best, her "clan."

Her schizoid conflict becomes most intense in crises which involve Burr, stimulating her fellow feeling, and her brother Bernard, confirming the family feeling. In each case, it is the familiar southern syndrome, the quasi-incestuous fear of outsiders, which triumphs. The structural crisis or turning point of the novel, the collapse of her romance with Burr, focuses precisely upon this inner conflict. At this point, in the early 1880's, Eugenia's family feeling, still unformed, is scarcely distinguishable from the echoes of her family's class prejudice lingering unwelcomed in her mind. She happens to see Burr talking with "round, rosy" Bessie Pollard, significantly the *merchant's* daughter, and finds herself "vaguely offended and sharply irritated." Then hurrying home from this unpleasantness, she encounters Nick's father, Amos Burr, who stands before her the full man, "hairy, ominous, uncouth," a potent challenge to her false consciousness about Nick himself, whose poverty and people she has always conceived of "only in the heroic measures that related to his emancipation from them." Now, her encounter with Amos means the end of her romantic evasion: she realizes "for the first time the full horror of the fact" that Amos is "father to the man" she loves (243–44). Afterwards, Nick himself refuses to confirm her desire for pleasing illusions. He forces her to look beneath the idealized mask he knows he wears in her mind; she must become fully cognizant of all exterior differences between the class of her birth and that into which she intends to marry. She must accept as reality that her brother Bernard is the womanizer who got Bessie Pollard pregnant and refuses to take the rap. But the logic of Eugenia's mind is the illusory variety of evasive idealism; she falls back on the old class axioms: Nick's indignant defense of the painfully real confirms the rudeness of his class. She can more easily accept the rumor linking Nick with Bessie's condition than believe his word (and Bessie's) implicating Eugenia's own kind in such a "dastardly piece of work." For the first time Eugenia's family or racial instinct has hardened: all the implications regarding Burr's origins and his nature are less painful than the reality about her brother and family: "It was in the clash of class, after all, that their theories had crumbled." Nick's pride was "the pride of caste," she decided, and her own strongest instinct, that for blood and clan (249–52).

But Eugenia's subsequent career shows that the conflict of her heart (or psyche) with itself is not so easily settled: her social instinct, her need for affection, for the "assurance of human companionship," remains exceedingly intense. She throws herself into Dudley's arms, sobbing, "I must be loved. . . . I must be loved or I shall die" (282–83). Marriage to Dudley is in fact a retreat from reality, from uncertainty over the future, deeper into the secure shadows of class and family; for fifteen years their union lacks passion but survives on some force "like the claim of kinship—quiet, unimpassioned, full of service" (382).

To evade unpleasant challenges to the tight complacency of family loyalty, she becomes fanatical in defense of the institution. When Bernard's wife, for example, refuses to fight to have her husband pardoned for embezzlement charges so that he can return to Virginia and his family, Eugenia is incensed: "Hush," she commands Lottie, her sister-in-law, "you are one of us, and you have no right to desert us. . . . I am only his sister, and I have stood by him through it all. Do you think, if his sins were twenty times as great, that I should fall away from him now?" Lottie's reply, free of familial illusions, represents the real: "Oh, but I am not a Battle. . . . Battle sins are just like other people's sins to me." Eugenia responds with the regulation defense mechanism of aristocratic minds: "Lottie was common—hopelessly common": the simplistic class-dictated solution to all discomforting situations. Eugenia realizes that she has placed family loyalty and "Battle breeding" above "Battle virtue" and all other questions of right-and-wrong or true-and-false, but she is sunk into false consciousness so deeply that struggle is as futile as panic might be to a poor swimmer (370–73).

And when, after fifteen years away from the Webbs, Burr, now a distinguished governor, attends a formal dinner at which Dudley's

easy sense of humor is the enlivening spirit, the governor, an outsider, withdraws into an embrasure to observe Eugenia, her husband, and their friends: "It was," he recognizes, "as if she were in
the midst of a great family party, held together by the ties of blood"
(342). But this tight family security, even though it keeps Burr at
a distance, cannot fill Eugenia's deepest emotional need. Earlier
she tried charities, and for a few months tranquilly waiting for her
first child to be born she believed she was happy. But the child died
after a week, and "the fulfillment of her nature . . . withered in the
bud" (383). Following her second child, she becomes obsessed with
maternalism, perversely possessive and protective, thus ensuring
another sheltered generation of Virginians (405–11).

In the end, Eugenia has only her son, and her Dud-ley, now a senator, somewhat distinguished, in his wife's eyes, for having squashed
the lie about Burr. The day after Burr's death, Eugenia reconciles
herself to this state of things: "she was merely resting from emotion—as she would rest for the remainder of her days" (443). The
final image of the novel is a family portrait: mother and the senator
bending over their son: " 'Yes, he was a great man,' repeated Eugenia. She looked up at her husband as he stood before her—buoyant with expectation, mellowed by the glow of assured success. He
smiled into her face, and she smiled back again with quick tenderness. Then she bent above her child and kissed his lips, and the
sunshine coming from the day without shone in her eyes" (444).
The ironies which turn up like ghosts in this tableau (fully as ambiguous as the similarly "happy" ending of *The Damnation of
Theron Ware*) are quiet but malicious ones: Eugenia's warm reference to Burr; Webb's always ready, empty smile;[18] Eugenia's (too)
quick tenderness; the husband's expectation followed by the wife's
ambiguously placed kiss (almost surely on her son's lips, though
just uncertain enough to lead the romantic mind where it will);
and, finally, the external radiance picked up by Eugenia's eyes.
Thus Miss Glasgow as ironist revitalizes the romantic ending.

18 Cf. Webb's affability with the smile on the face of all the judge's ancestors (8–9);
this is the decorous show of teeth that saves embarrassing situations.

Thus "the Battles" lick their wounds and shelter their young.

The question may arise: why would a man of Nicholas Burr's class wish to work his way into such a "family," with all its blindness of tradition and prejudice? The answer, as we shall see, is simply human nature.

But, first, let it be admitted that Burr, the protagonist, is the least convincing character in the novel. He seems to exist on at least three levels of imagination: first, as a realistic ("low mimetic," as Frye uses the term) male character mirroring the political corruption of Virginia in the nineties; second, as an archetypal Populist-leaning hero; and, third, as the embodiment of those aspects of human nature, the social and self-preserving instincts, with which Miss Glasgow was experimenting in her early books. Because he fails to materialize at the first level, he is unconvincing at the second; he succeeds only in the most abstract mode, the third. Whereas Miss Glasgow probably relied on introspection and intuition for Eugenia's intricate psychic ambivalence, and upon familiar "types" from literature and Virginian life for the Webbs, Battles, and Bassetts, there seems to have been no precise model in reality upon which to build Nicholas Burr. He remains no more than a shadowy desideratum which had to be purely imaginary because Virginia politics of the period provided no one who combined his class, character, and stature. He seems to be all successful Populist and quasi-Populist leaders—Tillman, Watson, Leonidas Polk, Bryan, even Honest Abe—rolled into a splendid archetype purged of pitchforks, racism, hayseeds, and Christian pietism. By contrast, Virginia's Populists were generally patrician by birth and out-defrauded at the polls by Democrats.[19]

For the closest parallel to Burr's career we must look west of Virginia to the seemingly still untamed politics of Kentucky which provides the sensational story of Democratic reformer, William Goebel. Son of a German immigrant cabinetmaker, Goebel, like Burr, had to break with his father's ambitions for him in order to study law. His benefactor (his "Judge Bassett") was a Senator

[19] Woodward, *Origins of the New South*, 245, 261.

Stevenson, called "the very Ultima Thule of the patricianism of Virginia and Kentucky." Goebel rose to prominence (and the attention of W. J. Bryan) as an outspoken defender of agrarian interests ("the people"), especially against the Democratic and Republican machines of his state, both apparently controlled by the powerful Louisville and Nashville Railroad Company and its representatives, including August Belmont. A bachelor politician like Burr, Goebel was plagued in his campaigns by opponents circulating the rumor that he was a murderer—he once killed a man in a politically motivated duel—a detail which roughly parallels Nick's trouble with the Bessie Pollard lie. Selected governor only after the Democratic legislature threw out unfavorable election returns, Goebel, not yet sworn in, was shot from ambush as he approached the State Capitol. In the indignant mob reaction to the assassination attempt, a Negro was also shot by a full round of pistol bullets, for having crowded against a white man. Goebel himself died five days later, February 3, 1900[20]—less than a month before Ellen Glasgow delivered her manuscript to the publisher. (The ways Miss Glasgow transformed each incident in transferring it to Virginia would be the subject for a separate study.)

From the strictly Virginian point of view, then, Miss Glasgow's novel is not, in fact, realistic since it mirrors no existing reality; rather it is more nearly (as all her early books, in some sense, are) a *novel of possibilities*, a speculative experimental novel which attempts to explore (and perhaps shape) the present-future by projecting present possibilities into a still nonexistent but possible future. Burr is the largely hypothetical ingredient in an experiment, every other element of which is dictated by present reality. Mark Schorer, who has discussed the use of the novel form as an "imaginative test of theoretical abstraction," [21] points out that in such experimental novels, the unity of the work hinges upon the

20 Urey Woodson, *The First New Dealer, William Goebel* (Louisville, 1939), 3, 231, *et passim*; Thomas D. Clark, "The People, William Goebel, and the Kentucky Railroad," *Journal of Southern History*, V (February–November, 1939), 34–48; and Woodward, *Origins of the New South*, 374–79.

21 Mark Schorer, "Introduction," in D. H. Lawrence, *Lady Chatterley's Lover* (New York, 1959), 12.

author's honesty and willingness to reject abstractions or hypotheses which are "wrong"—that is, "merely abstract" and incapable of being worked by the imagination into the real world. The failure of a novel is obvious to readers when the author, unable to prove an abstraction right, is unwilling to let "the lives of the characters, in the actualities of the plot," prove it wrong and uses his ending, instead, to negate the impetus of the story itself. This pattern does more than the concept of the tragic plot to explain the accidental sacrifice of the "politician with a conscience" in a novel about a state where the word "politics" was, until very recently, synonymous with the Byrd machine.

As an imaginative re-creation of the Virginia political ambience in the Populist period, *The Voice of the People* is less a revelation than a confirmation; one must know the period in order to see the significance of issues raised by Burr's candidacy—issues mentioned only incidentally or, at least, with greater restraint than in any naturalistic exposé or protest novel. For example, there is unfavorable mention made in passing of Mahonism, referring to William Mahone, the self-made railroad executive and Machiavelli of Virginia politics during the late seventies and the eighties; but the speaker is Judge Bassett, who as a Bourbon is hardly a reliable person to comment on Mahone (316). The force of other references to the control of Virginians and their politics by corporation and railroad lobbies in the nineties—probably J. P. Morgan's monopoly which eventually included the Southern Railway, the Seaboard Air Line, and the Atlantic Coast Line[22]—is dissipated when the reader takes into consideration either the character of the speakers or Burr's own effort to be "fair to both" railroads and the people (302–304, 346). Unqualified critiques are usually directed against more generalized targets. Burr, as a candidate of the people, stubbornly opposes the machine of his own Democratic Party, with its overriding commitment to party loyalty (in a decade of the powerful third-party Populists) and its placing of patronage above the welfare of the people (328, 330, 400). In a region where it is often enough for one politician simply to insinuate that his opponent

22 Woodward, *Origins of the New South*, 121, 122, 292ff.

would "accept" votes from the black community, Burr actively seeks both the lower-class white and black votes (as Populists had done in the early nineties but not often after 1896); he resists efforts to restrict the suffrage of either poor whites or blacks and seems to have no part in blatant techniques of Negro disenfranchisement, such as the ballot-box abuses, poll taxes, grandfather clauses, and constitution-interpretation clauses which, between 1897 and 1904, reduced the registered voters in some southern states by more perhaps than 60 percent.[23]

But the author's indignation in mentioning such abuses is thrown into question by her inability to transcend either her distaste for her father's sexual interests or the Anglo-Saxon racism of the period, which by 1900 had spread to the increasingly empire-minded North and, in the process, taken on the vocabulary of Darwinism.[24] The narrator's unmasked observations (a mulatto, for example, is "the degenerate descendant of two races that mix only to decay," 309) make it difficult for the reader to take racist slogans assigned to obviously unreliable characters with complete dramatic detachment: " 'And he died for a damned brute [Negro],' was what [the sheriff] said" (442). That Miss Glasgow omitted the first of these racial slurs in the revised editions of her novels and changed the second slur to the less stilted "damned nigger," underscores the embarrassing aspect of the passages.

In a narrative context so lacking either in political sophistication or partisan zeal, it is impossible to accept a character whose mind should be filled more with the destiny of his people than with the party arrangements at the Webbs' house. Perhaps it is an unfair reaction, but class conflicts seem too often in this book to come down to problems of romance and manners rather than political issues. Male characters must exist in a male context—or in violent opposition to a female one. Things here are not in the proportions one expects in important American political novels, which, right or wrong, assume political (public) solutions for all social (at base, individual and private) problems. Miss Glasgow's contextually un-

23 Cf. 345, 401, 422; Woodward, *Origins of the New South*, 321–49.
24 Woodward, *Origins of the New South*, 324, 334.

supported public hero never measures up to the archetypal role he seems created to play.

The portrait of Burr's private self has sufficient unity, however, to make the public self seem almost coincidental, accidental, and intrusive by contrast (although, in the end, the two Burrs come together just long enough to destroy him). In its concern for Burr's essential or private self lies the continuity between this and Miss Glasgow's earlier books written without *The Voice of the People*'s complexly realized sense of tradition. The essential Burr represents a fusion of the best qualities of Michael Akershem and Anthony Algarcife.

Burr possesses in full measure Akershem's instinct for self-assertion, his success drive, his energy, persistence, and stubborn will, his native brightness and retentive memory (40, 41, 147, 161, 303). He is, as his resigned father says, "plum full of grit" (5). While it is clear that Nick inherited none of his forceful characteristics from his father (126), their source is not immediately apparent. Certainly his early worship of Jefferson's democratic theories created in him a sense of openness about his own future which his crushed father lacked, and a confidence in the underlying goodness, worthiness, and improvability of the common people (84–85, 217, 305). Some of his drive and intelligence also derive, whether by nature or nurture, from his mother's side of the family. She is dead, but clues to her character survive in her sister, Nick's stepmother, Marthy Burr, a woman of indomitable energy (wasted on potatoes), loving kindness, and prominent skull bones (33, 264, 318, 395). In addition, his maternal uncle, Nick Sales, was a man of great native intelligence, "all book larnin' an' mighty little [common] sense," one of Gray's "mute inglorious Miltons" twisted by plough and mire into an Andersonian grotesque (263–65).

Burr also shares Akershem's seemingly instinctual tendency to revert to violence in order to protect his ego, as in his two quarrels with Eugenia about Bernard (251, 358). But Burr's environmental conditioning, especially his "wilderness period" of hard, sacrificial, demeaning work in a general store and as a poor dirt farmer, enlarge his spirit and reduce his ego (148, 152, 160). For this and other reasons, including the kindness of Marthy, Burr's ambition and will to power are tempered, like Algarcife and not Akershem, by an instinctual feeling for others. As an only brother and son, Nick sacrifices his career to raise his family from debt (147). As Eugenia's lover, he is arduous, strong, and gentle (234, 236). Eventually he learns enough about himself, his pride, and his rage, to absorb the chronic hatred for Bernard (359–65). Here is the desired mean between Akershem's destructive egotism and Algarcife's too vulnerable altruism. As a private man, Burr is clearly ready for and worthy of, Miss Glasgow would have us know, anything the people of Virginia (poor whites, blacks, *and* aristocrats) can possibly offer.

But Virginia is not mature enough to accept Burr. It is too narrow, too stultified, too static to provide a suitable public role and satisfy his personal sympathies for others at the same time. The public niche, the governor's office, is a lonely place, for he distrusts and is misunderstood by his patronage-minded advisers, and finds himself ill at ease with the class a governor is expected to meet socially, chiefly because this class has no more profound concerns than a graceful dinner party (343). On the latter occasions he takes solitary shelter in a womanless governor's mansion where he listens, figuratively, for the voice of the people. He comes to the sad recognition "that beyond that uncertain abstraction which he [calls] 'the People,' he [is] an alien among his kind," that he has no emotional ties to humanity, no "common claim of kinship which" belongs "to all mankind." His public context provides no justification for his private existence; there is only a nothingness at the center of his being (394–95).

It is in part this essential need to overcome the isolation of public office—this desire to relate somehow to "the people" and thereby justify his continued existence—that draws Burr to Kingsborough for his final visit. Here his public role, the defender of justice, coalesces with the private need. At midnight, after a disappointing approach to Judge Bassett, he goes out to meet the people—the lynch mob, largely "good country people" who have violated the quiet shadows of Kingsborough as though stealing into an unkempt garden. In the moments before the single catastrophic shot, the people, who have given in to "lawless rage," are savages, while Burr himself—hearing one of the mob call out, "We'll be damned, but we'll get the nigger!"—sees red and feels "the old savage instinct [blaze] within him—the instinct to do battle to death" (440–42). It is the most terrifying irony of the novel that Burr finds his longed-for union with the people as much in his own reversion to savagery as in his frustrated public sympathy for the unseen condemned criminal. A sharing of sympathies with Eugenia would have been the preferred solution—had all other things been equal. But racism and easy violence are too much accepted by southerners, and the determinants molding the attitudes of Burr and Eugenia, especially the perverted class and family forces working on Eugenia, prove irreversible. Thus the author's imagination finds itself unable to work the theoretical abstraction embodied in Burr into the dream garden of southern society, which is in Virginia the "real" world.

In the context of this novel alone it is not possible to say whether Burr's failure to win Eugenia's hand and the acceptance of her class results entirely from psychological and social forces portrayed in the novel or is caused in part by a residual class arrogance in Miss Glasgow herself. No doubt Eugenia's rejection is convincing, given her social and psychological blind spots, because Miss Glasgow channeled her own residual and perhaps unacknowledged class feeling into Eugenia. An argument for social bad faith on the author's part gains credence if similarly romantic situations between the classes are traced through Miss Glasgow's novels, for it is not until her eighth, *The Romance of a Plain Man* (1909), that an affair between a nonaristocratic male and an aristocratic female comes to its logical culmination, marriage. Although Betty Ambler in *The Battle-Ground* accepts Dan Montjoy and wealthy Maria Fletcher in *The Deliverance* accepts impoverished Christopher Blake, the male character in each case bears at least half aristocratic blood, while Maria, whose father was once an overseer on the Blake estate, is genteel only through education. Even in *The Romance of a Plain Man*, self-made Ben Starr, conscious that he lacks genteel graces, senses an alienation from his wife and her coldly aristocratic family.

In all cases, the nonaristocratic male must *transcend* his own class before he is acceptable. No doubt Miss Glasgow's purpose in each situation included the description of the blind stodginess of self-styled aristocracies, but had her will to fuse the classes been free of all bad faith she probably could have found a way to do so—before 1909—without blunting her social criticism. The likelihood of authorial self-deception is at least as great when Ellen Glasgow treats lower-class male protagonists as when William Styron takes a black revolutionary for hero or James Baldwin a white homosexual: her effort should be viewed, like theirs, as an imperfect but pioneering attempt to transcend self by sloughing off the prejudicial limitations of one's own consciousness, in a period when the nation glorified surrender to "authentic selfhood." What her intellect wished to accept, some strong part of her emotions resisted. And Eugenia is the imaginative expression of this residual emotion.

In *The Voice of the People*, there is none of the awkward scientific apparatus or clumsy evolutionary jargon which made *The Descendant* a curiosity. The words "race," "instinct," "sympathy," "code," and "tradition" appear frequently, but the general reader may take them solely for their non-Darwinian and emotional values. Miss Glasgow, rather than relinquishing her earlier interest in the bearing of modern scientific knowledge on social and individual problems, has learned, through technical discipline, to body forth her ideas with greater art than pretense. Perhaps one might wish to say that by nature Akershem and Burr are much the same and differ only by nurture, especially the care shown Burr by Marthy, which is lacking in Akershem's career; but this assertion is an indefensible one, for it remains ambiguous whether part of the instinct for sympathy Burr shares with Marthy is not innate. Miss Glasgow has quietly prepared for this ambiguity—implicit in the science of the 1890's—by having the stepmother's blood, as well as her example, work in Nick, since she is also his aunt.

If Burr shares Akershem's will, Eugenia is closer to the quick vulnerable sympathies of Anthony Algarcife. Her family affections, unlike her perhaps innate sympathies, are tied, though, to social class and preserve its boundaries when the latter are in danger of dissolving. The family affections seem both the source and result of the code which unites the Battles, in fear and almost incestuously, with other older families against interlopers like Burr. It is in the grasp, portrayal, and criticism of this rich complexity of family, code, and class—especially as these cultural forces pervert and twist essential human nature—that *The Voice of the People* surpasses Miss Glasgow's earlier books. At one time, perhaps, clannishness helped preserve the species. Now it only prolongs the decay of the Old Order. In the modern era of changing possibilities, when such admirably endowed individuals as Nicholas Burr present themselves, a larger moral sense, Miss Glasgow implies with her mind if not her emotions, is essential—one based on wider sympathies. For, in smothering her inherent social instinct, family feeling only leads Eugenia to turn an (almost) deaf ear to the one voice she wishes to hear—that of Nick Burr, the voice of the people.

LOVE, SUCCESS, AND THE SECULAR CONVERSION

With the completion of *The Voice of the People* and until at least the last months of 1906, the important events of Ellen Glasgow's private life are generally difficult and perhaps finally impossible to document, for they belong to that poignant period which she later, "in a desperate resolve to escape from the tragedy of the past," sought to blot out—primarily out of memory and incidentally out of literary history—by destroying all relevant papers and mementos.[25] If the hint of Miss Glasgow's friend and adviser, Joseph Collins, is correct, the interval covered by this gap in our knowledge probably included a crisis (or crises) in her relationship with the neurologist Pearce Bailey.[26]

According to Miss Glasgow's own retrospective account, however, it was during the winter of 1899–1900 that she met and fell immediately in love with a tall, thin, slightly graying financier who, during the following five years, transformed her from a gloomy in-

[25] Ellen Glasgow to her Literary Executors, January 6, 1945, Glasgow Collection, Alderman.

[26] See pp. 103–106 above.

tellectual hardened and brittle beyond her years into an adaptable woman aware of the new possibilities available simply by yielding a bit to the impulses of life (*Woman*, 153ff.)—much as the life of Lucy Smith, the heroine of "Between Two Shores," had opened when she fell in love. Although there are serious objections to the details Miss Glasgow provides in her account of the affair with "Gerald B——," [27] her version does have a psychological truth verifiable by studying the change in her handling of the Darwinian themes in the three novels which presumably followed her most complete capitulation to passion. Because it has this sort of validity, Miss Glasgow's probably fictionalized record of her major love affair must be taken into consideration, in lieu of a more reliable account.

Briefly then, Miss Glasgow and "Gerald B——" met in New York, in the drawing room of a mutual friend, one evening following a matinee at the opera or the theater. The attraction was immediate—and mutual. B. "had been married for years and was the father of two sons," but "it was common knowledge" that he and his wife "were barely more than strangers to each other." For her own part, Miss Glasgow, now in her late twenties, was determined, after eight years of bitterness, to hold tenaciously to her chance at love.

[27] For example, Miss Glasgow says that the meeting with "Gerald B——" occurred in New York; yet there is no evidence to suggest that Miss Glasgow misled Paul R. Reynolds when she wrote him (December 10, 1899): "I am afraid I shan't be in New York this winter—I am working too hard, and the weather here is too glorious to forego" (Colvert, "Agent and Author," 190). Instead, by late February, 1900, she had devoted sufficient time to *Voice* to have it in the printer's hands; moreover, the nine available letters by her from that winter were addressed from Richmond. Furthermore, Miss Glasgow's account of how the joy of loving B. caused her finally, after years of mourning her mother and Walter McCormack (as was the southern custom), to put off black for vivid colors accords with her transformation during the first visit to England in April, 1896 (cf. *Woman*, 160, with Ellen Glasgow to Cary McCormack, April 28, 1896, Alderman). Personally, I must agree with James Branch Cabell that Miss Glasgow's autobiography contains some "of her very best fiction," at least regarding the "Gerald B——" episode (See Cabell's *As I Remember It* [New York, 1955], 127). But in denying Miss Glasgow's own story, I do not have a better one to offer. Of Miss Glasgow's close acquaintances, only Dr. Joseph Collins provided an alternate interpretation; in Chapter 4, I have described the evidence available in the Alderman Library to support Collins' implication that his colleague, Pearce Bailey, was the man Miss Glasgow loved. If Bailey was the recipient of her affection, the winter of 1899–1900 is perhaps the least likely date for the relationship to have got underway, for in November, 1899, Bailey married Edith Lawrence Black of New York City.

To her great joy, she found that B.'s clear, crisp voice was understandable without straining, an ease which dissolved tremendous anxiety. B. knew, too, how to repeat himself, when it was necessary, without showing pity or impatience. It seemed, as Miss Glasgow later wrote, that "out of the whole world of men, I had met the one man who knew, by sympathy, or by some other instinct, the right way of approach, who could, by his simple presence, release me from my too sensitive fears." The two shared a "kind of intimate laughter" which sprang from a "kindred sense of humor" and a "compelling physical magnetism." B. restored Miss Glasgow's lost faith in herself. She discovered "that my own identity, that I, myself, could triumph over brute circumstances," triumph over "what I had regarded as an insurmountable impediment." She resolved to make herself well, happy, beautiful. She adopted a regimen of cold baths, long walks, and golf, and thus "won back at least moderate health and nervous equilibrium." [28] In psychological terms the love of B. effected a "conversion" of Miss Glasgow's view of herself in relation to the external world; [29] in her words, it "destroyed and then recreated the entire inner world of my consciousness" (*Woman*, 153–60). An upheaval so complete in her set of mind would be expected to affect her fiction, and a change is detectable when the earlier novels are compared with the later: whereas the protagonists of the first three books struggle with heredity and circumstances and are defeated, the protagonists of the three following novels manage to endure and, in one case at least, to master such determinants.

Romance, however, was not the only force working in the spring of 1900 to restore Miss Glasgow's faith in herself, for the April publication of *The Voice of the People* attracted the most widespread and favorable attention yet accorded one of her books, and gave her for the first time a temporary position on the best-seller lists. Suc-

28 Therapy similar to Bailey's prescription for traumatic hysteria in *Accident and Injury, Their Relations to Diseases of the Nervous System* (New York, 1899), 394–418.

29 For this use of the word "conversion," see Kenneth Burke, "Secular Conversions," *Permanence and Change: An Anatomy of Purpose* (New York, 1965), 125–47, and Jean-Paul Sartre, *Being and Nothingness* (New York, 1956), 412n. Cf. William James, "Conversion," *The Varieties of Religious Experience: A Study of Human Nature* (New York, 1961), especially 163–68.

cess in 1900 was especially significant for a novel of its realistic emphasis, because *The Voice of the People* appeared in the midst of a great spate of very popular historical romances. It had to compete with Thomas Nelson Page's romance of Reconstruction, *Red Rock*, with Mary Johnston's historical romance, *To Have and To Hold*, with Charles Major's *When Knighthood Was in Flower*, and Winston Churchill's *Richard Carvel*.

The reaction in the South was milder than in the North or in England. The Richmond *Times* thought the depiction of Virginia politics was exaggerated out of proportion, and noted that the romance between Eugenia and Nick Burr was highly improbable "in view of the great difference in their social position." [30] Otherwise, as Miss Glasgow described in a letter to Page, the reception of Virginians was not overly critical: "People are saying very pleasant things about it. From Williamsburg I have received invitations to visit and letters headed 'Kingsborough'—they—or some of them—are delighted that I showed them to be not progressive. The political part appeals to the Richmond people I have seen or heard from—among them one of our governors wrote me a private note—I imagine, however, that the politicians generally won't care for it" (*Letters*, 31). The northern reviewers, however, agreed that the novel was the "best picture of Southern life" they had "ever seen in a work of fiction." [31] In England, the *Bookman* preferred Miss Glasgow's book to the latest novels by Mary Johnston and Thomas N. Page and placed it with the local color stories of George W. Cable.[32] Miss Glasgow's new publishers advertised the novel tastefully, and for several months it ranked high in the sales lists of individual northern cities. In the end, however, it did not stand in the top ten books for the year and "its total sales probably did not exceed fifty thousand—a good number, but not exceptional for the day." [33]

It has been suggested elsewhere that Miss Glasgow's "refusal to

---

[30] Richmond *Times*, April 15, 1900, p. 8; quoted in Kelly, *Struggle for Recognition*, 32–33.
[31] Kelly, *Struggle for Recognition*, 37.
[32] *Bookman* (London), XVIII (September, 1900), 167–68, and XIX (October, 1900), 29; quoted in Kelly, "Struggle for Recognition."
[33] Kelly, *Struggle for Recognition*, 40–41.

compromise with public taste was holding back" her success and
that even after *The Voice of the People* "she was determined to go
on her own way," although that way meant continued despair.[34]
More accurately perhaps, Miss Glasgow, under the influence of her
affection for B., was moving away from her former alienation from
public taste and towards a frame of mind that made a partial compromise with popular taste completely natural, a frame of mind to
which despair was temporarily alien and unwelcomed. This, at
least, is the inference to be drawn from the course of the conflict
between human nature and tradition in Miss Glasgow's next novel,
The Battle-Ground, where the destruction of an entire social order
is considered "worth the price" because it liberates finer possibilities of human nature.

34 *Ibid.,* 41.

Chapter VI

The Destruction of Class, 1900–1902

The Battle-Ground

THE HISTORICAL METHOD

Composition of *The Battle-Ground* involved a challenge Ellen Glasgow had not previously encountered, for in it she had to re-create an era which had ended before she was born. Although her memoirs give the impression that she spent the spring and summer of 1900 ecstatically chasing around Manhattan in B.'s small racing car—from tiny taverns, out to Coney Island, and back to a special obscure Hungarian restaurant (*Woman*, 160–62)—letters from the period show that she actually spent a good deal of that time in or near Richmond carefully laying the groundwork for her new book. Presumably the idea for her fourth and fifth novels was as old as that for *The Voice of the People* (*Woman*, 129); the three are, in fact, chronological sequels, with *The Voice of the People* using the most recent events of Virginia history, those falling entirely within a period of Miss Glasgow's life when she was aware of public events. The composition of the other two novels was necessarily postponed because, for Miss Glasgow (though not for her parents), they were "historical" stories and required a special sort of research. For this reason, at the end of March 1900, she was planning to devote at least two or three years developing a plot she already had in mind, which would be "laid before and during the late war."

Realizing the popularity of such stories, she inquired of Reynolds, her agent, whether the book could be placed with a magazine to begin in serial form as soon as she finished. An offer of serialization Miss Glasgow could accept did not materialize, and soon after Heinemann heard what she planned he refused the book, perhaps because he had originally been attracted by her less popular, more rebellious subjects. Though shocked by Heinemann's decision, Miss Glasgow did not feel threatened, for she knew that Doubleday, Page and Co. had representatives abroad who could easily find another English publisher. Through Page's company the book was placed with Archibald Constable and Company for a royalty arrangement of better than 15 percent, and Miss Glasgow went confidently about her historical studies.[1]

The Battle-Ground is a conscientiously researched novel. Of all the novels of the Civil War written between 1885 and 1924, it is generally considered the first and best realistic treatment of the war from the southern point of view, and stands, with Stephen Crane's *The Red Badge of Courage,* as an outstanding war novel of the period.[2] For it, Miss Glasgow "read innumerable diaries and letters," gathered incidents and tales from close relatives and actual participants, and kept by her the "complete files, from 1860 to 1865, of *The Richmond Enquirer, The Richmond Examiner,* and *The New York Herald*" (*Measure,* 21).

But when one considers Edmund Wilson's *Patriotic Gore,* that catalog of the rich written resources on the Civil War, Miss Glasgow's achievement in research must be judged only partially complete. In general, the novel supports Ralph Ellison's opinion that "fiction isn't written out of history, it's written out of other art forms." [3] The best chapters, those describing battle behavior, are de-romanticized, a realistic attitude toward war that she may have borrowed from memoirs by Grant and Sherman but which more likely comes from earlier novels and stories such as John W. De

1 Colvert, "Agent and Author," 191–92.

2 Cf. Sheldon Van Auken, "The Southern Historical Novel in the Early Twentieth Century," *Journal of Southern History,* XIV (May, 1948), 171, 186; Ernest E. Leisy, *The American Historical Novel* (Norman, Okla., 1950), 162; Robert A. Lively, *Fiction Fights the Civil War* (Chapel Hill, 1957), 33.

3 "The Uses of History in Fiction: Ralph Ellison, William Styron, Robert Penn Warren, and C. Vann Woodward, A Panel Discussion," *Southern Literary Journal,* I (Spring, 1969), 89.

Forest's *Miss Ravenel's Conversion*, Albion Tourgée's *Figs and Thistles*, Ambrose Bierce's *Tales of Soldiers and Civilians*, Joseph Kirkland's *The Captain of Company K*, Stephen Crane's *The Red Badge of Courage*, or the nonheroic war novels of Stendhal, Zola, and Tolstoy. Her protagonist, his dependence on his slave, and the slave's dialect echo Joel Chandler Harris' story, "Balaam and his Master" (1891). In order to titillate the "predominantly female audience" for which most historical fiction in America has been written,[4] Miss Glasgow borrows from popular novels of the period the "romantic plot" of infatuation and contrived obstacles to love, an approach she had used but transcended in previous books. For her picture of antebellum life she might have spent less time with magazines of formal fashions and more with Frederick Olmsted's *The Cotton Kingdom*, which would have shown her how unrepresentative her little band of gay Virginia planters were of the dreary South at large. Had it been available, Mary Chesnut's candid *Diary from Dixie* would have given her material for behind-the-lines romance and encouraged a franker appraisal of the planter's wife's distressed reaction to opportunities for promiscuity, incest, and miscegenation afforded males by the slave system. In short, the novel is sometimes lacking in what Georg Lukács says matters most in historical novels: "fidelity in the reproduction of the material foundations of the life of a given period"; it is, however, strong in the portrayal of "manners and the feelings and thoughts" derived from such material foundations.[5] Finally, Miss Glasgow shows no knowledge of the numerous scholarly arguments produced by southerners to justify their region's political rebellion. For her, the war is less an irrepressible conflict between competing economic and constitutional positions than a needless misunderstanding between an unrepresentative group of perversely hotheaded southerners and certain unnamed, uninformed northern politicians who misjudge the depth of southern loyalty to soil and state. Like T. N. Page and Harris, she has played down serious regional differences in order to hasten the postwar reconciliation of North and South.

[4] *Ibid.*, 65.
[5] Lukács is quoted in *Ibid.*, 67.

For all her sources, she was interested, not in a detailed historical interpretation, but only in the events and scenes that impressed themselves upon her characters. To get more completely into their point of view she planned to spend the summer or fall of 1900 in the lower and northern areas of the Shenandoah Valley near the scenes she had chosen, and then to begin writing in the autumn.[6] The trip to the Valley did not materialize in 1900, for in May and June, Cary was not feeling very well and went for her health to Virginia Beach, and by the fall, Miss Glasgow was herself in poor health. Nevertheless, in June of the next year, by which time she had written twenty-five of the book's predicted forty chapters (primarily those dealing with plantation life before the war), she and Cary went "to the Valley to take the drive over some of the battle grounds and country" (Bull Run Creek, Antietam, Winchester, Romney, Appomattox) that would be used in the war scenes. Later in the summer, they retreated to Nova Scotia for a period of steady writing.[7] Then, after a possible interruption for Christmas with the Pages in Englewood, New Jersey, Miss Glasgow put on the finishing touches, rejected an opportunity for serialization in a newspaper, and had the novel ready for April publication (*Letters*, 36, 40).

THE FOP AND THE JOB EXPERIENCE

Despite *The Battle-Ground*'s reputation, it is hard *not* to agree completely with Louis D. Rubin, Jr.'s verdict that today the book seems a "conventional love story" and that Miss Glasgow's "prewar society is properly romantic, her plantation belles glamorous, her Confederate soldiers cavaliers all." [8] Much of the novel is of exactly this sort. There are, however, several aspects which seem to suggest that

[6] Ellen Glasgow to Walter Hines Page, April 18, 1900, in *Letters*, 30.

[7] Coralie Johnston to Mary Johnston, May 1, May 10, June 7, 1900; January 7, June 14, 1901, Mary Johnston Collection, Alderman. Coralie Johnston's letter of January 7, 1901, suggests that during this period Miss Glasgow had taken a new interest in Balzac, as one British reviewer had suggested she do; cf. Kelly, "Struggle for Recognition," 40.

[8] Louis D. Rubin, Jr., "The Image of an Army: The Civil War in Southern Fiction," *Southern Writers: Appraisals in Our Time*, ed. R. C. Simonini, Jr. (Charlottesville, 1964), 58.

Miss Glasgow at least intended to do otherwise: the plantation romance is overripe and sometimes riddled by ironic diction, the real heroine is respected less for her glamour than her fortitude, and the central cavalier turns out to be an ineffectual, passive foot soldier who earns respect only when he sloughs off his class-given behavior.

The popularity of *The Battle-Ground* was no doubt due, as Miss Glasgow certainly knew it would be, to its war fire and glory, its romantic plot, and its evocation of a courteous serene antebellum South. These subjects and scenes it shares with the innumerable books on the Civil War that flooded the American market with the flowering of historical fiction at the turn of the century. These, however, were not Miss Glasgow's personal interests in the story, as she made clear in a letter to Page before she began writing: "I may say just here that the usual war novel of our country is detestable to me—I want to do something different—to make, as it were, a picture of varied characters who lived and loved and suffered during those years, and to show the *effects of the times upon the development of their natures*. The war will be merely an effective setting for a story of life." [9] In concentrating upon the effects which events have upon the development of human nature, Miss Glasgow was changing the focus of her interest, for in her previous three books she had been concerned primarily with the tragic influence of events on fairly static types of characters; in *The Battle-Ground*, she recognizes the possibility that an extremely drastic alteration in a character's situation can produce an equally important change in his behavior—provided he is resilient enough to survive and adapt to the changing conditions themselves. In addition, the novel considers the possibility that the major effects of heredity may sometimes be purely imaginary; it criticizes the failure of excessive convention to permit fellow feeling beyond a single class or race, and depicts the inability of the sheltered life, founded on class-protecting, class-deceiving lies, to stand up against the realities, not only of the battlefield, but of human nature. How completely Miss Glasgow adheres to the task she has appointed herself in the letter to Page becomes obvious from considering the conflict Dandridge

[9] April 18, 1900, in *Letters*, 30 (italics added).

Montjoy experiences between the voice of tradition and the demands of his own nature when he faces the holocaust.

The early events of *The Battle-Ground* are romantic clichés from the Anglo-American literary tradition. Dan Montjoy, sixteen years old (about 1854), arrives for the first time at Chericoke, the plantation of his maternal grandfather in the southern Shenandoah. He has begged his way over two hundred miles from the unidentified city where he recently buried his mother. Major Lightfoot welcomes his grandson, though the former still nurses the hurt caused years before when Jane, his only child, ran off with that "dirty scamp," Jack Montjoy. Dan takes easily to life at Chericoke and eventually falls in love, as is fitting, with Virginia Ambler, a young belle from Uplands, the neighboring plantation. However, after two years at the University of Virginia and the summer of 1859 in Europe, he returns to find Virginia still pretty but somewhat simple and falls in love with her more energetic and independent sister, Betty, who has worshipped him for five years. Then following a duel defending the honor of a barmaid, Dan is jailed overnight, expelled by the university, and disinherited by his grandfather. He takes up residence at a tavern ten miles from Chericoke, and becomes a stage driver in order to survive.

After Virginia follows the lower South in secession, Dan goes into the infantry. Here the novel becomes more realistic. Between chapters describing the women's ordeal at home and in Richmond, the story takes Dan in detailed fashion through the course of the war, from before the victory at the first battle of Bull Run Creek to Appomattox. In the final skirmish Dan wraps himself in stars, bars, and glory and, inflated by heroism, is bitterly let down three days later when his company wanders across the assembly at Appomattox. After several days of food and rest, Dan starts west toward the Valley, only to find Chericoke burned to the ground by raiders, Major Lightfoot and his wife living in the overseer's house, and the former slaves wandering about the place caught between freedom and necessity. But Betty is also there and ready to cure him of war, if it takes twenty years (a cautious estimate, it seems).

Dan Montjoy's problem is the inverse of Nicholas Burr's. Burr was an alien to the social tradition dominant in his environment, whereas Montjoy is too much a member of the great family of the chivalrous; his problem is to survive when the protective walls and foppish adornments of the tradition have crumbled before savagery—and not only to survive, but to discover what sort of man he is. Montjoy's girlfriend, Betty Ambler, defines his situation, and that of the novel, in a scene before the war begins. Speaking of the way her coyness riles him, Dan warns Betty, "When you treat me like this you raise the devil in me. . . . As I told you before, Betty, when I'm not Lightfoot [i. e., polite], I'm Montjoy [i. e., violent]." More amused than frightened, Betty spins Dan a riddle: "When you're neither Lightfoot nor Montjoy, you're just yourself, and it's then, after all, that I like you best." Dan's response betrays his ardor: "When you like me best, . . . Betty, when is that?" Betty replies, "When you're just yourself, Dan . . . ." [10] Montjoy's battle, then, though he does not realize it, is for maturity: to find this man Betty sees in him. As it develops, he succeeds by divesting himself, haphazardly, of both the moribund chivalric tradition he has inherited from the Lightfoot family and the sense of inferiority which derives from his awareness that he is the heir, not only of Jane Lightfoot, but of Jack Montjoy, who beat his wife until she died and then deserted his son (30). The battlegrounds of northern Virginia become the external scenes of Dan's internal struggle. The self he finds belongs not to the exclusive family of the chivalrous but to the greater community of all men.

Miss Glasgow devotes over 260 pages (more than half the novel) to her re-creation of the tradition Montjoy carries into war. By contrast, Stephen Crane had used a few paragraphs to sketch in the cultural elements Henry Fleming took with him: some moralizing from his mother about alcohol and about reading his Bible, and an inner fear that "secular and religious education had effaced the throat-grappling instinct," thereby reducing his chances of "witnessing a Greeklike struggle." [11] Cultural tradition, however, plays

[10] Ellen Glasgow, *The Battle-Ground* (New York, 1902), 188–89. Hereinafter cited as *Battle-Ground* or simply by page.

[11] Stephen Crane, *The Red Badge of Courage*, ed. R. W. Stallman (New York, 1960), 13–16.

a much larger role in Montjoy's response to war than in Fleming's. Miss Glasgow's evocation of the South's mythic past is a distillation of those elements which she knew Virginians imagine to be most representative of the period, a distillation purified of all ostensibly disagreeable ingredients. The gentry she describes is not entirely mythic; Olmsted concedes in *The Cotton Kingdom* that there were perhaps a "dozen or hundred . . . old families . . . in Carolina and Virginia in their colony days . . . which, with some sort of propriety, could be termed a gentry." [12] There is nothing in Miss Glasgow's book, however, to give the sense, so strong in J. K. Paulding's *Letters from the South* (1817) and in Styron's recent antebellum novel, that Virginia in its postcolonial period was already an economic backwash trying stubbornly to raise its single money crop, tobacco, in soil exhausted by the reckless use of slave labor, and breeding slaves chiefly for the flourishing trans-Appalachian cotton states.[13] Of the possible literary attitudes toward the plantation system, along a continuum from adulation through mimesis, irony, satire, and polemic to invective, Miss Glasgow usually employs the most gently critical, irony. A touch of irony turns up occasionally in the diction to deflate the romance. For example, when Dan rides off in the moonlight with "the vision of Virginia" floating "before him at his saddle bow," there is the following comparison: "he might have been a cavalier fresh from the service of his lady or his king, or riding carelessly to his death for the sake of the drunken young Pretender" (137). It is the historically accurate word, "drunken," that punctures the balloons of southern chivalry and related Scotch-Irish nostalgia. But there are not enough such touches, especially in the boy-girl scenes, to keep the tone from turning saccharine. Although the narrator attempts, unsuccessfully, to keep the love scenes realistic by reminding the reader that what Betty finds sublime about Dan is actually his "inherent recklessness," it is Betty who eventually has to take over and tell Dan (and the reader) that their love-talk parodies the Homeric epic! As a parody of the plantation

---

[12] Quoted in Wilson, *Patriotic Gore*, 224.
[13] *Ibid.*, 439–40.

imitations of Scott's imitations of Homer, however, *The Battle-Ground* is far less successful than J. P. Kennedy's *Swallow Barn.*

If it succeeds at all as a critique of antebellum life, it is because it allows the planters to put themselves forth as a superfluous class, the result of a socioeconomic structure with a powerful system of production, slavery, but totally inadequate means of distribution. Everything about the aristocrats is superfluous; there are too many compliments and gaudy neckties, too many roses, fish, and "fat lands," too much preserves, Madeira, port, and Latin elegance. The major is "always" polite—when he is not angry (82). Ambler's "smooth white hand" has "about it a certain *plump* kindliness"—even holding a riding whip (45). As such, the aristocratic life style has the air of too many magnolias left overnight in a closed room, or the perhaps intentional mockery of life found in waxworks museums. The Lightfoots and Amblers form a tight family, divided only by an occasional, forgivable difference of opinion, but knit together by an unending exchange of dinners, toasts, sons, and daughters, and the tedious invention of innocuous, gallant flattery.

The moribund quality of this society is clear long before the discordant elements become visible when, halfway through the novel, news of the Harpers Ferry incident reveals that this little social island of Amblers and Lightfoots floats innocently along in a sleeping volcano of black unrest (243–47). Later still, Miss Glasgow informs the reader that the private Eden of Uplands and Chericoke is possible only because such poor whites as Pinetop, an illiterate mountaineer, are held in check (442). (But there is as yet no pressure on families of the Amblers' and Lightfoots' social rank from the classes below, classes which became mobile thirty years later in the era of *The Voice of the People.*) While Miss Glasgow fills in Montjoy's chivalric heritage, she also draws her readers (those of 1902) into what seems to be nothing more than a popular romance of the Lost Cause, saving her critical realism for the later incidents.

Although there is no overt recognition of the tenuous southern union Miss Glasgow knew in her own household between the Scotch-Irish and the older English families of Virginia, the passionate Major Lightfoot and even-tempered Mr. Ambler embody the two sometimes conflicting positions. The Lightfoots are the most important source of the tradition Dan inherits. Not only are they related to the Fitzhughs (31), but the major is an admirer of William L. Yancey (86). George Fitzhugh was the "most influential pro-slavery propagandist of the decade before the war" and Yancey one of the South's most extreme "Fire-Eaters." [14] The major follows their radical line when he claims the right to own slaves is a divine institution (biblically precedented) and the foundation of the South's aristocracy (63, 89). Originally attracted, like many wealthy planters, by Whiggish pretensions to gentility (59, 133), he becomes a Breckenridge Democrat when the southern wing of that party endorses the Dred Scott doctrine that Congress has no right to bar slavery from the territories (272). Emotionally anti-Union, he uncompromisingly boasts that Virginia made the Union and can unmake it if she wishes (86), but is so governed by sympathy that he invests his own money to rescue beaten slaves from their cruel masters (88). In the years which lead to the war, the major stands with the most volatile war hawks. Having fought (for the Union) in the War of 1812 and the Mexican War, he predicts it will take two weeks for the South to run the Yankees back where they belong (279–80). Yet in 1861, the major is down with the gout and too old and senile for the war (275–76); Dan, his grandson, and Governor Ambler, the Unionist, bear the brunt of the major's irresponsibility.

Dan becomes a copy of the cavalier major, whom he dearly loves (64). Whether by nature or nurture, in his adolescent phase he displays the same savage fighting spirit (41), the same romantic patriotism (299), the same gallant defense of ladies (54), the same paternalistic attitude towards slaves (67, 371), and the Lightfoot pride of family and class (30, 38). But the major, in his affection for the boy, overindulges him, and the qualities which were sometimes amusing in the major go to seed in Dan. Quiet, determined, disdainful, and vindictive when he arrives at Chericoke, Dan grows progressively more insolent, arrogant, selfish, and wild (28, 65–66). Basically of a kind heart, he is, nevertheless, full of himself and

[14] *Ibid.*, 341.

takes to lording it over the slaves and overseer (64). He restricts his loyalties to his slave, Big Abel, and his horse, Prince Rupert—both gifts from his grandfather (65, 123). His first two years at the university are given over to directionless, complacent hedonism (168); rumors reach Chericoke that he has been losing at cards and generally "sowing his wild oats," as the major proudly puts it (84). He returns to Chericoke with the title, "Beau" Montjoy, and with the affectations of a ladies' man and dandy, a foppish collection of imported red cravats (127, 132–33), and pomade for his hair (285). He finds his identity as a Lightfoot in such external properties (321).

For all such symbols, Dan is troubled by his Montjoy blood, which he sometimes regards as a barrier to a Lightfoot future and, at other times, uses as an alibi for devilish behavior. But Betty is all too certain how he will turn out—wholly like a Lightfoot: a "well-fed country gentleman," with rich fields and too many servants, who grows stout, red-faced, and dull (171). This seems to be Ellen Glasgow's version of the Southern Dream in its everyday variety, and it suits Dan's expectations better than the only other life-style he can imagine, a fat-souled, thin-bodied beggar who sits in the dust by the roadside and eats his sour grapes (172). He has no desire to imitate Job, and it is improbable that he ever will. Even when the major turns him out for shaming the Lightfoot name, it seems a temporary arrangement, for Dan is joined by his servant Big Abel, who brings along Dan's expensive clothes and toiletries so that his master may remain a gentleman—even in exile (232–33). Certainly, if Dan is not to be restored to his Lightfoot inheritance by his grandfather's repentance, as was the convention in English novels, he will make it there on his own, as in American plots: he has an offer to read for the law (260). But the unforeseen war transforms the hedonist into an unwilling Job, divested one by one of his family, his fortune, his servants, and his future—reduced, ironically, to the beggar he once scorned.

In fairness to Montjoy, it should be pointed out that, had the war not intervened, he might have matured into a man less like his grandfather and more like Governor Ambler, a man embodying the reasonable eighteenth-century statesmanlike qualities of Miss

Glasgow's Southern Dream at its pre-Calhoun best. For Betty, who inclines toward her father's view of things, sees something admirable in Dan that is neither Montjoy nor Lightfoot (82, 189). If Dan had married Betty and become, by imitation, an "Ambler," he would have restricted his foppishness to a bother about his elaborately tucked shirtfronts and a vanity, perhaps, about his lack of height (17, 46). He might have developed the governor's good humor and hospitality (20), provided a rose garden for the amusement and shelter of his and his wife's old-maid relatives (20), served Virginia as her chief executive, and then retired with distinction to his plantation (17). His views on slavery might have developed, like Ambler's, along the more reasonable mainstream of Virginian thought than the South Carolina and deep-South aberration of his grandfather. Apparently, Ambler's alarm at the sinful injustice of slavery, his love of the Union, his sense of a wild justice in slave insurrections, and his plan to free all his slaves in his will (247, 269, 417, 450) are more representative, than Lightfoot's attitude, of the position taken by the Randolphs, the Lees, and other "pre-war Virginians of most intellectual or moral stature," who by 1850 had freed almost 55,000 blacks; in 1832 the Virginia legislature had come within a few votes of abolishing slavery.[15] On this point extant histories and southern apologetics, such as the novels of T. N. Page, seem to concur. But war destroys this set of possibilities for Dan and gives him another—more modest—the opportunity to find himself.

The tradition Dan inherits also includes rigid roles for women, blacks, and nonaristocratic whites. As with the contrast between Lightfoot and Ambler, Miss Glasgow is interested here in portraying tensions within each role by showing the resistance of individuals to stereotypes imposed upon them. Even the southern belle ideal embodied in Virginia is undercut, for Dan, as he matures, finds her increasingly simple, possessed by a beauty that is precious but specious. The females of greater depth, Molly Lightfoot, Julia Ambler, and Betty, have more capacity for endurance than delicate Virginia. The ladies, especially Julia and Betty, are the chief prac-

15 *Ibid.*, 350–51.

titioners of redeeming compassion for slaves in the novel, but the pragmatic effect of their sympathy and common sense is constrained by their unquestioning loyalty to the pernicious authority of their master-husbands and the Bible. Although Julia Ambler is the source of her husband's plan to free his slaves in his will (19), much of her active will to struggle against this social crime is sapped because her superstition-ridden mind cannot transcend the "timid wonder that the Bible 'countenanced' slavery" (69). In general, women retreat as wives or spinsters into some quiet, chivalry-protected corner of the rose garden where, like Miss Lydia and Aunt Pussy, they tend the fruits and flowers (20).

The chief role slaves play in the novel is that of cheerful faithful retainers. Slaves who have just been sold are childish in their excitement and, of course, singing (4). House servants imitate the white master in dress (23); cooks are vain about their cooking (100). Young slaves are petty thieves (6), the grinning butts of practical jokes (94), and sloppy about their work (200). They include superstitious conjurers (3). They have no desire to be liberated by northern Republicans, display no militancy, do not aid John Brown after Harpers Ferry and do not leave the plantation when freed (87, 244, 253, 450); they prefer to remain passive recipients of paternalistic benevolence (175). Free blacks are objects of pity from the whites and contempt from the enslaved blacks (148). Even to a supposedly reasonable man like Peyton Ambler, slaves are ultimately expendable; in a choice between slavery and the Union, he would "ship the negroes back to Africa, and hold on to the [Union] flag" (152)— a stance characteristically taken by aristocrats in Virginia novels at the turn of the century. In the racial atmosphere of the period, with Anglo-Saxonism at its height and the mania for national reunion demanding the scapegoat sacrifice of the black, the demeaning stereotype projected above, even by Ambler, accorded with popular expectations.

But there is an undercurrent in the novel which goes deeper than this stereotype prevalent in fiction by southern novelists, like Page and Mary Johnston. Slavery, even in the most benevolent and paternalistic form, is inhumane. Although a member of the owner's family, a slave has no marriage rights of his own; some are shown weeping in heartbreak or growing bitter over their broken families (6, 149). The depth of the master's paternal responsibility is measured by the fact that even Ambler does not know his property by name and face (249). Other blacks prove themselves more capable of independence and dignity than the stereotype suggests. Free and compassionate Levi, who toils as a blacksmith to eat each day's bread in freedom, becomes a symbol to Dan of emancipation from the plantation system (222). When a white overseer joins the army, black Hosea rises "to take his place" (434). And Big Abel, though a flat comic surrogate father in the Uncle Remus tradition, is the embodiment of resourcefulness in extricating Dan from the traps into which military fervor precipitates the youth (368, 400, 402, 404). Although it is not dramatized, the novel sees some justication for slave uprisings. In place of a hothead's claim that blacks are damned by God and the Bible to endure Ham's curse of eternal servitude (227), Ambler, like Jefferson before him, fears that it is the white man who has transgressed—against natural laws, not Biblical authority—and that the black man, who has shown himself capable of rebellion in the 1831 Southampton uprising of Nat Turner, would have a wild, natural justice on his side should he go forth to kill in a "pitiable and ineffectual struggle for . . . freedom" (245–47). The narrator later concurs that slavery was a shadow upon all southern whites and worth any price to have lifted (485). Thus Miss Glasgow's view of blacks is more complex here than in her previous novel. But in a period like the early 1900's when the legal, political, and economic resources of the nation were cynically used to protect "white supremacy," a view of the black man as rebel was probably interpreted less as an argument in behalf of his dignity as a man than as an alarmist position underlining the need to stretch the law of the land to keep blacks in their place; pathetically, even the black's blow for freedom could be reforged into the chain to bind him tighter. Indeed, it would probably be an error to interpret Miss Glasgow's attack on slavery—not at all uncommon in the sectionally conciliatory novels of the period—as an assault on racism as well.

Lower-class whites receive only sketchy treatment. Miss Glasgow's portrait of plantation life would have been a better likeness of the antebellum South had it drawn upon Olmsted's *The Cotton Kingdom* for details of the other 99 percent of the southern planters, who did not live in gaily lighted mansions with Doric columns like Uplands and Chericoke but in windowless log cabins in which a fireplace was the only source of light and receptacle for spat tobacco juice. Class standing is treated, both by characters and narrator, less as an economic category than a moral one. For example, although Rainy-day Jones is a slaveholder, he is *déclassé* because he beats his property (73, 89). The merchant class and performers of services are shown as a pig-lazy, Godridden, alcoholic group dependent on aristocratic benevolence (227, 231–32, 237–38). Because the lower class itself lacks dignity in this novel, the only way a nonaristocrat can gain respect in the eyes of the characters, the narrator, and even the author, is by transcending his class; thus, a tavern-keeper's wife, Mrs. Hicks, is *raised* through suffering "from the ordinary level of the ignorant and the ugly into some bond of sympathy with [Dan's aristocratic] dead mother" (241). The only large group of nonaristocrats in the book, the Yankee privates who feed and advise Dan after Appomattox, are also transcendently generous and sympathetic and, therefore, more one-dimensional than Mrs. Hicks. The only nonaristocrat given a full-sized portrait (actually a series of static snapshots) is the nonliterate mountaineer, Pinetop, who transcends his class to become a yeoman in the Thomas Jefferson tradition. Although lithe, hardy, quick-witted, and educable, he is lacking in class awareness: when it dawns on him in mid-battle that this is a slaveowners' war, that he owns no blacks and has no interest in the outcome, he allows superstition to get the better of common sense and stays to fight for the honor of some occult presence called "ole Virginny" which has been sullied by the feet of outsiders (323). It is this superstitious regard for the soil (currently called the territorial instinct), Miss Glasgow shows us, that sent most Virginians to the defense of the Confederacy—not the combined pressures of boredom, public opinion, cynical politicians, and conscription. Pinetop's presence, however, permits Miss Glasgow to attack Fitzhugh's once popular argument for slavery, that the institution was beneficial to poor whites because it provided society with a bottom rail to which no white man sank; through Dan's consciousness Miss Glasgow filters the more realistic opinion that the inability to compete with free or lowcost black labor "degraded the white workman to the level of serf" (442). Pinetop fills what, in this novel, seems one of the chief functions of lower classes in an aristocratic society: his nonliteracy qualifies him as an object for the chivalric paternalism of Dan, who teaches the farmboy to read with much the same benevolence as he had earlier supported a poorer classmate at the university (73, 444–45). It is Miss Glasgow's failure to deal realistically with blacks and nonaristocratic whites that leaves the reader of *The Battle-Ground* with a deficient sense of the material foundations upon which Dan's superfluous early way of life rests.

The divestment of this inherited lifestyle is a gradual process which proceeds both externally and internally, for war does not precipitate young Montjoy immediately into a state of nature; he carries with him, even as a private in the infantry, the attitudes and conveniences of a gentleman, not the least of which is Big Abel. There is, before the first engagement, the scene—probably more accurate than believable—of green but merry foot soldiers sitting in the shade eating green apples while their black servants do the woodcutting and ditchdigging assigned the masters. These are young gentlemen "who embraced a cause as fervently as they would embrace a woman; men in whom the love of an abstract principle became, not a religion, but a romantic passion" (283–84). The boys beg and loan hair ointments, worry about their fine clothes, and complain about the impudence of officers who have forgotten that their privates are gentlemen and that they (the officers) are not (288).

In short, Dan carries a class-determined view of war which belongs to another age; he thinks of "an old engraving of 'Waterloo,' which hung on the dining-room wall at Chericoke. That was war. ... He saw the prancing horses, the dramatic gestures of the generals with flowing hair, the blur of waving flags and naked swords. It was like a page torn from the eternal Romance; . . . it was white blood, indeed, that did not glow with the hope of sharing in that picture; of hanging immortal in an engraving on the wall" (296–97). Consequently, whereas Crane's Henry Fleming has difficulty discovering a lie through which he can deceive himself into courage, Montjoy's courage is barely in question, for the necessary lie has been an essential part of his aristocratic education—or reflex conditioning. Indeed, when he thinks of "Waterloo," "the Major's fighting blood" stirs in the grandson's veins and "generations of dead Lightfoots" scent "the coming battle from the dust." At the start of perhaps the most psychologically percipient episode of the novel, Dan associates the impatience of his officer's horse with the ordinary thrills of childhood blood sports: "He had an odd feeling that it was all a great fox hunt . . . that they were waiting only for the calling of the hounds. . . . The suppressed excitement of the fox hunt was upon him, and the hoarse voices of the officers thrilled him as if they were the baying of the hounds. He heard the musical jingle of moving cavalry" (296–97). Thus aroused, Dan supposes that his life is "a little thing to give his country." He thinks of blood determinism, but his behavior suggests a conditioned reflex combined with simple atavism. He reacts to words of patriotism as he does to the stimuli of the hunt; the former appeal to his southern ardor: "The sound of the bugle, the fluttering of the flags, the flash of hot steel in the sunlight, the high old words that stirred men's pulses—these things were his by blood and right of heritage. He could no more have stifled the impulse that prompted him to take a side in any fight than he could have kept his heart cool beneath the impassioned voice of a Southern orator. The Major's blood ran warm through many generations" (299–300).

With this conditioning, the recovery of the savage brute within him is no problem. His heroics are passive, mindlessly animalistic. At the first sound of fire, he finds himself exhilarated, "stepping high above the earth" (306). Something "like a nervous spasm" shakes his heart; he is "no more afraid" (311). When the "smell of the battle—a smell of oil and smoke, of blood and sweat" comes to his nostrils, the "hot old blood" of the ancestors rallies to the call of the descendant. He moves forward in a golden dust, and then, "as he bent to fire, the fury of the game swept over him and aroused the sleeping brute within him. All the primeval instincts, throttled by the restraint of centuries—the instincts of bloodguiltiness, of hot pursuit, of the fierce exhilaration of the chase, of the death grapple with a resisting foe—these awoke suddenly to life and turned the battle scarlet to his eyes" (312). The reversion is complete. The restraints of civilization are just this easily lost for the young aristocrats, the veils covering the realm of the brute just that thin.[16] With courage no problem for Montjoy, there is little for Miss Glasgow to say about the battles he fights; after this initial naturalistic account, which compares favorably with similar descriptions of battle euphoria by such war veterans as John W. De Forest, Ambrose Bierce, and the son of William Sherman, battles do not much interest her.[17]

The effects of battles do interest her, however, for it is in the aftermath of savagery that Dan finds the self which is neither Lightfoot nor Montjoy, and the veils hiding him from his humanity are thick. After the drunkenness of battle, he experiences a nausea among the dead and dying until his aversion is partially relieved by the sardonic remarks of Governor Ambler, the most humane man Dan has ever known. Ambler considers Manassas a "glorious victory" and assures Dan "that after the first fight it comes easy, . . . it comes too easy" (315). Because the public requirements of war are mechanically achieved, Miss Glasgow focuses upon the private experiences of her characters. But the attempt to maintain the sense of time passing in a public or historical dimension *and* private dimensions (plus the cycles of natural time) gets the author into difficulties; she has a four-year war on her hands with only a few historical incidents (Bull Runs I and II, the invasion of Maryland, the retreat, the sieges of Richmond, the Wilderness campaign, and Appomattox) to fill those years. She pads out the historical time scheme with summarizing chapters in which seasons change at Uplands and Chericoke; a more effective approach would have been a

---

16 For a typical Confederate romance, which uses the same external events without any psychological understanding of atavism, see John Esten Cooke, *Surry of Eagle's-Nest* (New York, 1894 [1866]), 88, 188–89.

17 Wilson, *Patriotic Gore*, 214, 621, 736

suprareal condensation of time such as Crane had used in Chapter XVII of *Maggie* to suggest, through a single stroll from Broadway to the river, the direction of Maggie's entire career as a prostitute.

More intense and germane to her theme are the private chapters in which Dan passes most of the four war years between battles, hungry, freezing, or fevered, on forced marches, or wounded, hiding in stables. Here he relinquishes his identity as a Lightfoot along with his clothes and cleanliness (284, 286, 462, 487). Here he learns he can wear rags, eat green corn, Pinetop's uncooked fat bacon, and what Abel calls "nigger food" (381, 386, 402, 470).

Moving parallel to such external transformations is the unfolding of his attitude toward his Montjoy blood, the romance of war, and interclass relationships. When during an episode in a makeshift Richmond hospital, Dan, wounded himself, sees his father die with great dignity, he realizes his hereditary inferiority is totally imaginary, a revelation which brings his first modest pride in his father (375–77). Simultaneously, Dan's image of war (and the novel's) moves from his class-determined concept, the glory of the "Waterloo" engraving, to the pathos of fragile Virginia, wandering, fevered, exhausted, and very pregnant, through crowded Richmond warehouses and churches, looking for her wounded husband, before she returns to her rooms in a boarding house to die of a miscarriage, while the high magnolia blossoming outside her window, like Virginia a symbol of the romantic South, gives off a perfume so heavy that, mingled with the hot dust of the city, it is sickening (357–67, 373). Dan comes to feel only shame about the war, a "vulgar affront" against "the dignity of earth—of the fruitful life of seasons and crops" (401–402). And at Appomattox he perceives, in a devastating epiphany, that he has given everything for a country that no longer exists: his body is wrecked, his mind blighted, his spirit dead, his hands maimed, his youth wasted, his energy sapped, his soil ruined, and his future decayed (477–78, 492). A memory of Chericoke's warm halls, like a star, guides him home, but he finds there instead "a heap of ashes," "a cold mound of charred and crumbled bricks"—more "relics of a hot skirmish" (495, 502). The only compensations for his lost possessions and romantic idealism are his new respect for his father and his broadened awareness that the various classes, races, and sexes are mutually dependent upon one another and can survive such massive determinants as war only through the sort of sympathetic understanding which binds Dan initially to Mrs. Hicks and later to a plodding mountaineer, a thieving slave, several small-farm families, and generous Union soldiers at Appomattox (241, 389, 403–404, 470, 479–81).

Dependence on Betty, a member of the supposedly sheltered sex, is the most difficult humility Dan has to accept. A surgeon has told him, "You may take ten—you may take twenty years to rebuild yourself." Dan does not see "by what right of love" he may dare make Betty's "strong youth a prop for his feeble life": "because she loved him, did it follow that she must be sacrificed" for a beggar, an utter failure? As it turns out, Dan's hesitancy to accept Betty's aid is so much self-deception, for when he tells her the way he feels, and she, playing gently with the comic mixture of pride, male self-importance, and bad faith in Dan, turns to leave him, he crumples up beside the ruins of Chericoke, thus drawing Betty back, with all the curative powers she is willing to provide (510–12). (Here Miss Glasgow is toying with the expected happy end of a romantic plot much as she undercut the end of *The Voice of the People*.)

Wherein does Betty's own resilience lie that she can absorb this "broken-down soldier from the ranks" and hold out to him the promise, "We will begin again, . . . together" (512)? The narrator compares her solicitude for Dan to a mother's care for a tired child (511), but her curative power goes beyond maternal instinct: she has "her father's head and her mother's heart" (82), plus a will which shows up nowhere else in her family except in her father's vain determination to add "a full cubit to his stature" by holding himself severely erect (17). In all these she exceeds her pretty, prim, bashful belle of a sister, Virginia (4, 70, 77, 109, 163)—a contrast that anticipates the tension between Virginia Pendleton and forceful Susan Treadwell in an important novel of Miss Glasgow's middle period, *Virginia*. Besides being resolute, defiant, assertive, competitive, saucy, spirited, and independent, Betty has, as is needlessly reiterated in the novel, an exceedingly highly developed sense of compassion (2, 7, 8, 67, etc.), which she received from her mother (19, 25). During the war Betty takes charge of the battered plantation (434–35); and by the end she seems to be managing both Uplands and Chericoke and caring not only for her mother, but for the major and Molly Lightfoot as well (505–508). Somehow she seems adequate, in compassion and will, for all her burdens—including, now, Dan himself.

It is consistent with Miss Glasgow's general position that the South, having suffered the destruction of the Old Order plus the epical disorder of war itself, looked afterwards to women like Betty Ambler as the mainstays of a new order. In her books, the postwar South is a matriarchal society devoted to worshipping two feminine ideals, the Old South and the purity of southern women; one in which figurehead "colonels," "generals," "judges," and "governors" are propped up by puritanically hard and industrious women; the war was sexual suicide for the southern male. Thus Betty not only looks back, in the gallery of Miss Glasgow's creations, to Eugenia Battle's intense sympathies (Betty is more intelligent), but points forward to heroines of equal determination, if less compassion: Gabriella Carr *(Life and Gabriella)*, Dorinda Oakley *(Barren Ground)*, Ada Fincastle *(Vein of Iron)*, and Roy Timberlake *(In This Our Life)*. It is as much Betty's compassion as her passion which motivates her to take on destitute Montjoy; it is her intelligence and fortitude that enable her to do so (509).

Two curious aspects of Betty's sympathy raise provocative questions regarding Miss Glasgow's evolutionary beliefs in 1902 and the metaphysical dimensions of the Civil War as southerners saw it. Betty's sympathetic imagination, her "dual consciousness," so intense that on several occasions she believes she has had extrasensory contact with Dan (119, 328), can perhaps be explained as wishful thinking. More difficult to explain, however, is the way Betty's compassion goes out, not only to the human and animal realms, but to supposedly insentient vegetable life and inorganic nature, including a path and some "poor naked elms" (99, 123). When one of the big trees is blown down, she cries "half the day, just as if it were a human being" (182). Like Miss Glasgow as a child, Betty is a "believer"—in conjurers, and in mind or spirit as an attribute of nature. Most important, she has faith that a benevolent deity—God, "supreme, beneficent, watchful in little things"—is on the South's side (332).

Edmund Wilson has shown that America's metaphysical understanding of the Civil War was as primitive as the medieval view of the crusades. Abolitionists and defenders of the Union, including the Stowes, Garrison, Francis Grierson, John Trowbridge, and many others, believed their cause represented the will of a Calvinistic God in a Manichean struggle of liberty and human advancement against barbarism and the dark ages. Even Lincoln, a free thinker, clothed himself in a mantle of divine righteousness and occasionally applied the word "God" to his "conception of history as a power which somehow takes possession of men and works out its intentions through them" in a semi-religious manner "most familiar today as one of the characteristic features of Marxism." And Lee, his mind formed by the Church of England and West Point, envisioned God as a benevolent feudal benefactor who, "in His all-wise providence" and through "His almighty will," intervened continuously as the "only hope and refuge" of the southern army. Betty's position probably echoes sources similar to Lee's.[18]

Miss Glasgow plays Betty's providential theory off against the seemingly rational metaphysics shared by Dan and Governor Ambler, a position in line with Virginians of the Enlightenment as well as with scientific thinking at the end of the nineteenth century. Ambler sees the ultimate order in human affairs as that embodied in "natural laws" which might someday require a just recompense for the wrongs of slavery (243)—a position taken by Jefferson in his discussion of slavery in *Notes on Virginia* (1784). Ambler later associates the "orderly working out of natural laws" with the cycle of birth and death, with "events as seasonable as the springing up and the cutting down of the corn," and with the responsibility of one man for the welfare of another (250). Dan too sees a moral or, at least, ultimate dimension in the natural order of seasons and crops and in the "dignity of earth" (402); the hills which guard his

18 *Ibid.*, 102, 235 *et passim*, 330.

ruined valley are themselves immutable, untouchable (499). The narrator goes even farther than Dan's perception that the war is a shameful affront to the earth by asserting, as we have seen, that slavery too offends the natural order of man (485).

References to the immutable cycles of nature introduce a third temporal dimension of the novel, one that transcends both the historical and personal time schemes in structuring the book's episodes. *The Battle-Ground* is a chronicle in which events occurring, it seems, accidentally in time and space are ultimately unified by their relationship to the universal cycles of birth, growth, maturity, death, rebirth—or spring, summer, autumn, winter, spring.[19] Book One, "Golden Years," emphasizing Dan's welcome at Chericoke, his youthful innocent relationships with Betty and Virginia, and his early education, is basically summer in setting and Edenic in tone. Book Two, "Young Blood," describing the confusions of young love, the fall of Dan from the major's favor, the raid on Harpers Ferry, and South Carolina's secession, is set at the end of the year 1858, in September, 1859, through the autumn of 1859, and in December, 1860. In Book Three, "The School of War," young southerners go to war and experience initial victories in the summer of 1861 and learn by Christmas and New Year's the hard realities of war; fragile Virginia is sacrificed on the "altar of the war god" in the ironic spring of 1862; and Dan transcends his shame of the Montjoy blood in July. Book Four, "The Return of the Vanquished," includes the doomed September invasion of Maryland, the winter quarters of 1862–63, the successful May–June Wilderness campaigns of 1864, and the ironic spring of 1865—doubly ironic because the South's military defeat is its victory over slavery and disunion.

Tying selected historical events and private crises to significant rhythms of the year as a structural principle might have been one aspect of the earth-connected universality Miss Glasgow had earlier discovered in *War and Peace* (perhaps in Meredith, as well). The willingness to show a sympathetic correspondence between private destinies and the seasons, a structural device she had first used

19 Edwin Muir, *The Structure of the Novel* (London, 1963), 112.

gropingly in *The Voice of the People*, implies a growing rejection of the Malthusian-Darwinian sense of natural warfare which dominated her first two works wherein chance, struggle, and alienation characterize man's relationship to the natural order. Perhaps, by 1902, Miss Glasgow had herself recovered what Dan felt on the road to Romney: a "sense of kinship with external things," a "passionate recognition of the appeal of the dumb things" which replaces one's "old childish petulance" with "a kindly tolerance" and softens "even the common outlines of . . . daily life" (347). Only the comparison of *The Battle-Ground* with her subsequent works can determine for certain whether she had, in fact, undergone this conversion of consciousness.

Despite its possible departure in this one area from Miss Glasgow's earlier views, her fourth novel further develops the interest of her earlier books in the conflict between human nature and tradition. In it she gives her fullest statement to date of the pernicious aspects of the sheltered life, for in an important sense Dan Montjoy's problem is the reverse of one difficulty faced by Miss Glasgow's three earlier protagonists. Michael Akershem, Anthony Algarcife, and Nicholas Burr were strangers to any sheltering social traditions; they were outsiders looking in—whether with distrust, indifference, or envy. Dan Montjoy, by contrast, is a foppish young man with a cut-and-dried future—until the war frees him of his protective cultural inheritance. During his years as a dandy, Montjoy, perhaps, resembles Mariana Musin more than he does any of Miss Glasgow's early protagonists; he shares Mariana's longing for color, though he is better able to satisfy his desires than she was. As Mariana's suffering transformed her character, so war gives Montjoy a chance to learn he can survive without the ornaments of tradition, including Big Abel; to discover, too, with considerable increase of humility, that he is greatly indebted to individuals both in and out of his own class. Not only is Montjoy the polar opposite of Miss Glasgow's previous traditionless protagonists, but in him she has found, for the first time, a protagonist capable of surviving with others—if only because he admits that he needs them. In addition, Montjoy at his father's death is Miss Glasgow's first character clearly to demonstrate that the most important consequence of heredity as a determinant of behavior may, under some circumstances, be entirely psychological. The psychological consequence of heredity would be a central theme in Miss Glasgow's next novel. Finally, Montjoy is the first of her heroes with sufficient resilience to adapt to a major alteration in his environment. The possibility that new attitudes and patterns of behavior might be induced in a character by a change in external determinants would become the source of deliverance in the novel which followed.

Like Dan, Betty Ambler is an extension beyond Miss Glasgow's earlier characters. She is, with Anthony Algarcife and Eugenia Battle, an individual of intense sympathies. But Betty has the common sense, drive, and saving humor (151) without which the latter two characters failed to triumph over oppressive forces. Because she is realistically assertive, Betty transcends the great belle tradition that determines the behavior of her sister Virginia, a tradition which makes the latter too flowerlike to outlast the war. Fortunately, Betty, unlike Eugenia, never experiences a conflict between her family-class feeling and her wider sympathies—probably because in 1865 the boundaries of class were still too sharp to permit it.

The Freeman: CONVERSION IN MINIATURE

The Battle-Ground substantially nourished the appetite for success which the reception of *The Voice of the People* had created in Ellen Glasgow two years earlier. Within two weeks *The Battle-Ground* sold twenty-one thousand copies; it maintained third or fourth place on the sales lists through the summer and fall, behind the indomitable, if not unfair, competition of Owen Wister's *The Virginian* and Alice Caldwell Hegan's *Mrs. Wiggs of the Cabbage Patch*. In all, two hundred thousand copies of Miss Glasgow's only Civil War novel were printed. Out of twenty or so reviews, only two—those in the *Critic* and the *Literary Digest*, which saw simply one more wartime story—were unfavorable. The Richmond *Times* said little of importance but stressed the book's "sincerity" and "charm." In the North, William Morton Page of *The Dial* found it "one of the best novels of the South during the period which precedes and includes the Civil War that has ever been written." Other northern critics recognized it as an historical novel of character rather than of melodramatic claptrap and pointed out that Miss Glasgow was a writer of "human life," not of provinciality. The novel was received more enthusiastically in England than her earlier books. The *Athenaeum* compared it favorably with Stephen Crane's war novel, while the *Spectator*, impressed by the realism, acclaimed it an important and essential book, though not for those who disliked "minutely realistic accounts of the horrors of war." In short, Miss Glasgow had written her first novel in a popular genre, had "done it with artistry and good taste," and, in the process, had managed, like Crane, to expand the genre toward greater character analysis.[20]

This wave of popularity did little to dampen Miss Glasgow's and Walter Page's plan to follow her fourth novel with her first book of poetry. When, late in January, 1902, Page inquired whether she had enough poems to make a book, she wrote that there were "enough to make a small volume" and that she would "like tremendously to have them come out." She warned him that they were "rather unconventional," then hurriedly assured, "But if you don't mind this, I don't; and they are certainly strong besides being good verse." She proposed that he look them over and "suggest any to be left out." They were published the following August, but the important reviews did not begin to appear until October. In the meanwhile, Miss Glasgow, having declined an invitation to visit the Pages at Englewood, set out, with Rebe, Cary, and an Irish terrier, to spend late July, August, and early September in the Adirondacks—presumably near B.—as the doctor had ordered.[21]

The Freeman and Other Poems contains verses written over a period of at least six years. Some, including "The Master Hand," "To a Strange God," and "England's Greatness," are clearly from the time of her first visit to England in 1896. Miss Glasgow seems

---

20 Richmond *Times*, March 30, 1902, p. 20; *Dial*, XXXII (June 1, 1902), 385; *Athenaeum*, I (June 28, 1902), 812; *Spectator*, LXXXVIII (June 14, 1902), 922. These reviews have been epitomized in Kelly, "Struggle for Recognition," 47–53.

21 Ellen Glasgow to Walter Hines Page, *Letters*, 36–39.

to have considered poetry a form of intense statement, not of condensed suggestiveness. And her occasional masks are not difficult to get behind. Consequently, the poems can be taken as statements of Miss Glasgow's outlook over a period of years; as such they reflect the major change in her state of mind during that time.

The majority of the poems seem to express her bitterness during the late nineties. The attitude of conflict is rife. The poet masks as an emancipated slave who stands upright and free amid scourgings, chains, arrows, thunder, and rain: while others "fight and fail" on the cosmic battlefields and "crouch in prayer," the freeman stands unfettered because he is not encumbered with hopes: "I know / The freedom of despair" ("The Freeman"). In a more Poe-like vein, the poet is a lunatic pursued by a shadowy presence (perhaps the wolf of deafness) that steals on his heels "as the bridegroom to the bride." The lunatic must keep constant vigil against the shadow; he cannot sleep, for:

> While I sleep
> It will creep
> Till I lie beneath It dead.

Resistance is futile; eventually weariness will triumph; the shadow will fly into "my heart," and

> will gloat
> O'er my throat
> As Its length upon me lies.
> ("The Shadow")

The poet sees herself as a hunter rummaging through the charnel house for "the secrets of the night," trying to pry "Eternal Mysteries" from "skeletons with toothless jaws" ("The Hunter").

In this struggle the poet expects no help from others. She poses as a warrior waging a losing fight alone against Fate, never asking succor, content to fall alone at last ("Battle Cry"). Others lack wisdom; they resemble a nation which lifts victory ribbons high and sounds its thanks to God while all about are images of a devastating war: blood, smoke, fire, cannon, dust, vultures, ravished women, "the death-cry of a wounded horse," and the cries of hungry children ("War"). When the poet thinks of others, she imagines "the blasphemy of human wills" evident in "man's bloody footprint" left on "the smiling mask that Nature wears" ("The Vision of Hell"). It is impossible to relate to others, for love itself is a failure. Love is arid; it is the "weary round" of a woman who faces unending sunrise and sunset while her "stillborn hopes" lie "buried in / The desert of her heart" ("Aridity"). Love is desperate; it is the frantic desire of a woman to be held fast by her lover, though the "sun be dead" and the "flames of hell be cast" for them ("Reunion"). Love cannot escape death; it is the anguish of a woman who waits for her heart finally to break and be done, while she shudders by a "corpse upon the bed" ("Love Has Passed Along the Way"). Love leaves one longing for the unnatural—for the return of a dead bride, whose embrace has to her lover the tempting appearance of life ("Death-in-Life").

The idea of God offers even less assistance than man; indeed, he is an unthinking tyrant—a bully. The poet imagines herself as a dead man called to life by heaven, who resents the need to endure more life, and cries to God, "Couldst Thou not leave me Death?" ("Resurrection"). She poses as an individual whose pious life has earned him the eternal reward but who refuses God's offer, in one case, because a loved one has been damned ("A Supplicant") or, in a second, because animals—especially a faithful dog—are not also allowed in heaven ("To My Dog"). The God of the Western world is a god of flesh, war, lust, and imperialism ("To a Strange God"). The poet curses God for giving man life, a "lying travesty," for marring the lives he has made, for gambling with a "million worlds" as stakes, and for choosing only "the stronger for salvation":

> "The stronger finds your heaven; the weaker finds
> An endless pain."
> ("The Vision of Hell")

Saddled with a god so cruel, the poet can only pray that the former will give her the courage and measured freedom to live her life of pain and, finally, to meet his "judgment with a laugh" ("A Prayer").

Cosmic irony often seems the only posture for the freeman vis-à-vis the injustice of the universe. The poet masks herself as a traveler riding alone against a barren background of snow, but harassed by storm clouds, a black hawk, sharp blasts, howling wolves, and hands beckoning from open graves. To resist the will of so many sirens of Death, the rider laughs and journeys "to my own"—that is, to his own will or to his own Death ("The Traveller"). The poet, in this cosmic mood, recommends that he who is sick of poisoned arrows, the "bold burlesque of Fate," and the parodies of love and hate should "stand aside to grasp / The humour of the whole" ("The True Comedian").

There are, however, a minority of poems in *The Freeman* which, in as much as they affirm beyond cosmic irony, seem to belong to Miss Glasgow's period of measured acceptance of the universe after 1900 (or possibly to some time before 1892, for Miss Glasgow had been scribbling verses since she was seven). In these, she affirms a type of quiescent acceptance of life, compassion towards man and beast, the kinship of man with beast and vegetable, and the courageous penetration of the barriers of the known. She poses as a Stoic who takes refuge in a "world within my breast" from the lightning and thunder without; "all that Life or Death contains" exists within, and "all the joys I count of worth / Become my own at will" ("The Sage"). In a mood of Eastern mysticism, she imagines she is a lone pine set in the mountains and surrounded by vultures and the void. For the tree, "there is no time, no space, no depth, / No love, no hate, no passionate despair." There is, finally, not even death for the pine, for "Decay cannot unmake me, I am part / Of an eternal whole" ("The Moutain Pine"). In this mood, she turns to the heathen god overthrown and caged in glass by the British Museum; he (presumably an image of Buddha) is a god of "insuperable peace" who greets scoffing tourists with a smile carved in stone ("To a Strange God"). Mary, "Mother of all the Sorrows" and "Daughter of dreams and visions," is a being of more active compassion; the poet calls her "blessed" because she has absorbed so much of the world's woe, including the anguishing memory of her heart nailed to the cross ("Mary"). The poet, however, is capable of only a bitter compassion—sympathy less than divine. In the supposedly God-created conflict between the weak and the strong, she chooses to side with "the damned":

> "I take my stand upon the weaker side,
>   I grasp the sinner's hand, I share his fate;
>   The hell of those who failed, I choose, or those
>   Who win too late."

But, as God informs her, in doing so, she has sided with those now living, for "the earth is hell" ("The Vision of Hell").

Furthermore, the poet would, in Darwinian fashion, extend her sympathies, though embittered, to the lower animals. She imagines a dog showing affection for a dying woman while indifferent mankind passes her by; but, for its show of feeling, the dog is stoned ("Justice"). She states that her respect for her pet is such that, had she to choose between it and eternity, she would elect the former ("To My Dog"). This sentiment would be patently silly in most contexts—and may, finally, be so in this—but there is a logical, if not satisfying, explanation for its occurrence in Miss Glasgow's poetry. Her sustained study of evolutionary theory and her growing interest in Eastern thought had both led to the same conclusion: that man is so closely kin to other animals—either because he evolved from them or because the same cosmic power (the Godhead) is present in each—that anthropocentric value assumptions, including that of man's superiority, stand on rather boggy grounds. The situation of "To My Dog" is not actually as absurd as it seems since it has a precedent, Yudhisthira, in *The Mahabharata*, where the royal saint's faithful dog is an incarnation of Dharma. In "A Creed," she affirms her broad belief "In fellowship of living things,/ In kindred claims of Man and Beast"; she then extends the brotherhood to include the vegetable realm, for it is her belief "That weed and flower and worm and man / Result from One Supernal Cause." Although kin, these living beings can exist in peace only through sympathy and compassion—a "pity, measured not nor priced"; therefore, the poet puts her faith in "all souls luminous with love,/ Alike in Buddha and in Christ," and in any rights that correct wrongs. It is the instinct of sympathy which finally dissolves the poet's attitude of conflict without demanding her withdrawal, like the sage or mountain pine, from passion, space, and time.

In short, these poems, largely written between 1896 and 1902, reflect the conversion of consciousness that Miss Glasgow speaks of in her memoirs and that is noticeable when the intellectual limits of her early characters (Michael Akershem, for example) are compared with the less limited possibilities of her later ones (Betty Ambler, for example). *The Freeman* stands as a bridge between the pessimistic materialism of Miss Glasgow's first three novels and the extreme mysticism and idealism of her sixth, *The Wheel of Life*; here, the two contradictory ontological options are suspended in a tension. The reader of the poems finds Miss Glasgow moving, it seems, away from the simple positivism towards an increased interest in the strange power of the human consciousness to "make its own world." To be sure, the external world probably remains the same, but there is a good deal to be said for how one sees himself in relation to it. If one assumes the Malthusian-Darwinian attitude of conflict, it is one sort of universe; if, on the other hand, one comes to the universe with modest expectations, and a measured acceptance of whatever it may offer, it is an entirely different place to live in.

The final poem of the collection, "The Hunter," best reflects this transformation in Miss Glasgow's attitude. There are four stanzas of eight lines each; the first two stanzas depict the poet searching in a charnel house for "secrets of the dust"; she plunges her "hands among the dead" to discover "Eternal Mysteries." Then, in the first line of stanza three, she comes "forth into the light of day," and wherever she passes, like Blake and Whitman:

> A grain of sand, a blade of grass,
> Smite me to silence as I pass.
> In living men and worms I trace
> Old allegories of the race;
> In weeds put forth from out the sod
> I read the Scriptures of my God.

Then the poet pauses to watch the vultures on the mountains ahead; she glances behind to survey the harvest of her past, from the house of death and morbid sorrow and from the contemplation of the

unity of man and nature: "My tottering feet have paused alone /
Before the barriers of the known." It is only a pause, for she will
press on, "a hunter of the Truth."

In 1902 Miss Glasgow could not of course say what new knowledge lay beyond those barriers; she could not see that the mountain
ahead might be a less modest version of the charnel house. What is
important, however, is that she had made an initial transformation
of consciousness—from the morose set of mind suggested by the
poet's search of the charnel house to that implied by the poet's
emergence into the light of day. The poet found both experiences profitable and was ready to repeat either if necessary. The
protagonist of Miss Glasgow's next novel would undergo a similar
conversion of consciousness, but, for him, the years of morbidity
were so costly that emergence into the light would come as an unquestionable deliverance. In his case, as in Miss Glasgow's, human
sympathy—love, perhaps—would be the catalyst of conversion.

The critical reception finally accorded *The Freeman and Other
Poems* must have provided Miss Glasgow with a respectable test of
her newly acquired capacity to make her own world. The book did
not sell, nor was it reviewed, widely. The reviews which spoke of it
sometimes did so harshly. The *Nation*, for example, alarmed apparently by the book's insufficient idealism, found it "almost wholly
painful" and saw in it the "tendency to exuberance and cheap trag-
ical utterance . . . so long charged upon the poets of our Southern
States." The *Critic*, more cogently, found the same seriousness, defi-
niteness, austerity, and intensity as in her novels—then added that
her poems have power but lack flexibility and melody. It has been
suggested elsewhere that Miss Glasgow probably did not think the
volume of poetry would advance her reputation.[22] If she did not
expect good reviews—and so modest a view of her own work would
have been out of character for Miss Glasgow—then her new state of
consciousness was indeed genuine and deep. Unfortunately, however, any unambiguous evidence of her reaction to such harsh reviews as the *Nation*'s seems to have been destroyed in her lament-
able attempt to blot out the painful past.

22 *Nation*, LXXV (October 9, 1902), 290; *Critic*, XLII (January, 1903), 89; epitomized by Kelly, "Struggle for Recognition," 71–73.

Chapter VII

The Transcendence of Class, 1902–1904

The Deliverance

ROOTS OF THE NOVEL

Whether in response to the critical failure of her poems or to a crisis in her relationship with B., identifiable now only in the fictionalized account in *The Wheel of Life*, Ellen Glasgow came to the end of 1902 in unusually low spirits. During Christmas, she used that "season when one may speak sincerely from the heart" to excuse the "doleful letter of good wishes" she addressed to Walter Page. In it, she looked back over her association with Page and his firm and thanked him for his "personal friendship"; he had given her saving "encouragement, even when you did not dream that I needed it, when you did not know how bitterly I wanted to throw it all away—and life with it." Then she alluded obliquely to the recent crisis, to something that had occurred during her last visit to New York—either in September on the way home from the Adirondacks, or on an unspecified trip in November or December: "The years have brought a good many things to me, but they have taken them all away again except my work. . . . When I left New York it did not seem to me within the remotest range of probabilities that I should see the New Year in upon this planet." She had, as she said, "come to the final choice that some are forced to make. . . . Yet here I am." She had been saved, as in the year of Walter McCormack's death, by her work, the idea for a new novel, "another big, deep, human document which no one will understand because it is wrung from life itself—and not from sugared romance. I doubt much if even you will care for it, but . . . it was this or death for me. . . . The idea saved me, and I can now sit down quietly since the storm is over." The book, she hinted, would flow out of her own suffering: "Whether my own life goes into my books I do not know, but such as are in me I must write, and it will be the quiet, happy souls who turn out the popular romances, and we others, who have never been able to forget our . . . cross, will continue to inflict upon our publishers the books that go down into the heart of things and appeal to those few that have been there before us." [1]

As the novel stands, however, there are two equally important germinal ideas. The latter half of the book is dominated by the notion of love as conversion, for love changes the protagonist's morose revenge compulsion to acceptance, as love for B. had altered Miss Glasgow's attitude of conflict. But the first half of the novel is dominated by the idea, or image, of an old lady, stately, blind, and paralyzed, sitting sternly erect in a massive Elizabethan chair of blackened oak, and entirely unaware of the poverty-stricken cottage in which her chair has been placed. The story of a similarly sheltered lady had been related to Miss Glasgow by an elderly friend, Miss Etta Munford, when she was no more than nine or ten. If, as Miss Glasgow reports in her preface to *The Deliverance*, the latter image was the seed from which the book flowered (*Measure*, 26), then perhaps she had written parts of the book and had been unable to go further until the saving idea she referred to in the letter to Page came to her. At any rate, in little more than a year after that letter, Miss Glasgow's longest, most complex, and, perhaps, best novel to date was ready for publication. The speed with which it was written is more surprising in light of Miss Glasgow's delivery of the manuscript to an illustrator in July, 1903, before she departed for a European vacation (*Letters*, 43).

Following two days with the Pages at Englewood, she, Cary, and Rebe sailed Saturday, July 18, for Antwerp. After spending a "few precious moments" there "before the Rubens in the Cathedral,"

---

[1] December 26, 1902, *Letters*, 40–41.

they went straight to Switzerland. She "conceived a hatred for Lucerne," presumably because there they "chanced upon the largest hotel in Switzerland and . . . one of the most costly in all Europe." But in Interlaken at the Riegenhotel, things were more to Miss Glasgow's taste. They found themselves "sitting at the feet of the Jungfrau, . . . the first real mountain" she had ever seen. It is likely that B. accompanied Miss Glasgow to Interlaken or met her there. This is perhaps the occasion she speaks of in her autobiography when she and B. walked "together over an emerald path" in the Alps. More than thirty years later she would recall the moss, the Alpine blue sky, and the path which went "through a thick wood, in a park," and then, in what seems a thinly veiled sexual allusion,

> wound on and upward, higher and higher. We walked slowly, scarcely speaking, scarcely breathing in that brilliant light. On and upward, higher, and still higher. Then suddenly, the trees parted, the woods thinned and disappeared. Earth and sky met and mingled. We stood . . . alone with the radiant whiteness of the Jungfrau. From the mountain, we turned . . . to each other. We were silent, because it seemed to us that all had been said. But the thought flashed through my mind, and was gone, "Never in all my life can I be happier than I am, now, here, at this moment!"
> (*Woman*, 164)

If Miss Glasgow was, as she seems to suggest here, more fortunate than Goethe's Faust, it was not because she had had more experiences of passion than Faust—but fewer and, consequently, read more meaning into them. It was a trick of consciousness similar to that of her next protagonist, in whom loneliness had created a "brooding habit of mind" which caused him to conserve his emotions, whether love or hate.[2]

After a week or so at Interlaken, the Glasgow sisters planned to "go on a little trip and then to Mürren" where they intended staying. Where they went from Mürren and when they returned to America remains uncertain. Miss Glasgow's novel, *The Deliver-*

2 Ellen Glasgow, *The Deliverance* (New York, 1904), 241. Hereinafter cited as *Deliverance* or simply by page.

ance, was finished, however, in time for publication in January 1904; she spent the winter in New York—ostensibly "seeing her book through the press." [3]

NATURE, NURTURE, AND *The Deliverance*

The Deliverance is Ellen Glasgow's only novel before 1913 about which it might be claimed that somewhere in the thickets there lurks a failed masterpiece. For all the rhetorical analysis of motives, unconvincing dialogue (especially in man-talk passages), and feminine fussiness, there is a power in the symbolic conception, the heightened interiority and complexity of the characters, in the control of themes, structure, and imagery which place the novel above any she created before *Virginia* (1913)—perhaps before *Barren Ground* (1925). It is the first of her books to operate upon readers geometrically (affecting several faculties of comprehension simultaneously) rather than linearly, chiefly because here Miss Glasgow manages, as Hardy often did, to tie her characters' behavior to elemental passions which are tied, in turn, to the primal powers of the earth. It is possible to argue that *The Deliverance* should have been built upon the two-phase, elevation-and-fall structure of revenge tragedies like *Hamlet* but tries instead to imitate the elevation-fall-and-rebirth pattern of a romance like *The Winter's Tale*; this argument, however, mistakenly assumes revenge to be the theme of the novel. It is not. The true theme is that of all fiction with naturalistic tendencies, the conflict between determinism and freedom. The ultimate failure of *The Deliverance* lies partly in the reader's expectations, partly in the book itself; for the wish-fulfilling third phase of a romance traditionally depends upon a religious vision of time—such as the Vedantic vegetation myth or "perennial philosophy" underlying Whitman's "Song of Myself" and Wolfe's *Look Homeward, Angel,* or the displaced Christian ritual of rebirth and the related "perennial philosophy" supporting the final act of *The Winter's Tale.* But to support the third phase of *The Deliverance,* in which her hero is redeemed by a change in determinants, Miss

[3] "Portrait," *The Critic,* XLIV (March, 1904), 200.

Glasgow could fall back on no rituals, religious visions, and super-
stitions—only on the speculations of science, a demythologized view
of the vegetation cycle, and a great burst of sentimental desire.

Although covering some eight or nine years of calendar time, beginning in the middle 1880's, *The Deliverance* is structured upon
two full turns of the wheel of seasons with a foreshortened third. In
June of the first cycle we are introduced to morose, illiterate young
Christopher Blake, who seems dogged to an early grave by the necessity of feeding five people (two sisters, an uncle, his mother, and
himself) on a small tobacco farm of seventy acres while maintaining his blind mother's expensive illusion that the family still lives
in ancient Blake Hall, not the overseer's house. For fifteen years
Blake has been ridden by the compulsion to kill Bill Fletcher, and
thereby revenge the series of ambiguous incidents that after the war
put Fletcher, once the Blakes' overseer, in the Blake family home.
In July of this cycle Blake meets Fletcher's granddaughter, Maria;
the attraction is strong for both, though doomed by Blake's sullen
pride; she marries and moves to Europe. In September, Blake saves
the life of Fletcher's weak-willed but beloved grandson, Will, and
by November has begun shaping the latter as the instrument of his
revenge. The first cycle and Blake's success are complete in August
five years later when Will disappoints his grandfather's dynastic ambitions by marrying a promiscuous poor-white girl. In retaliation
Fletcher tries to destroy Blake's mother's false position, but she simply passes into a deep senile coma and eventually dies with her
illusions intact. Blake has had control of this first cycle and is actively responsible for what has happened.

In the second cycle, Blake, who no longer controls Will and has
no interest in revenge, is acted on by unfamiliar forces. His resurrection starts the following March when Maria returns from her
miserable marriage, her husband dead. In April she begins to educate Blake, and in June they pledge themselves to one another. At
this time Will, learning his grandfather intends to disinherit him,
kills the old man; when Blake assumes full legal responsibility for
the crime, the second cycle is complete.

The third cycle includes the autumn jailing of Blake, his physical

breakdown during the second winter of his sentence, his spring revival, and finally, in the third autumn of his sentence, his reprieve,
his reunion with Maria, and their new life in Blake Hall—begun
out of season like the damask rose Blake notices blooming beside
him. As in the earlier novels, the past is irremediable. Unlike the
earlier books, however, the past here can be absorbed and transcended—when it is accepted rather than evaded.

The Deliverance was Miss Glasgow's most penetrating look, to
date, into two important matters, the causes and nature of the sheltered life and the related question, whether nature or education,
biology or tradition, heredity or environment, is the stronger determinant of an individual's behavior. If, as Heraclitus said and
Christopher Blake comes to realize (541), character is destiny, what
precisely is character? Perhaps character, as the narrator of *The
Deliverance* asserts, is temperament and, as such, "plastic matter
for the mark of circumstance" (180). This, at any rate, seems to be
the thesis of the novel, for Miss Glasgow between 1902 and 1904
had reached the conclusion expressed years later in her preface to
The Deliverance: "that environment more than inheritance determines character. What it does not determine is the tendency of
native impulse nurtured by tradition and legend, unless tradition
and legend may be considered a part of environment." In her main
character, Christopher Blake, she was "trying to test the strength of
hereditary fibre when it has been long subjected to the power of
malignant circumstances" (*Measure*, 34)—and, finally, to the power
of human affection. In these terse sentences, Miss Glasgow has com-
pacted both a radical attack upon the aristocratic concept of tradition and an impressive understanding of the body of theory, today
called cultural anthropology, which comes down to us from such
nineteenth-century thinkers as Darwin, Walter Bagehot, and August Weismann. To understand the symbolic functions of characters in *The Deliverance*, we must digress a moment to clarify what
is implied when Miss Glasgow suggests that "tradition and legend
may be considered a part of environment."

The Battle-Ground described primarily a change in physical environments—from the external comforts of the plantation to the external adversities of war—with some attention given to changes in outlook caused by these physical alterations. In *The Deliverance*, this tangible external disruption has already occurred before the novel begins. This novel focuses instead upon much more subtle transformations in what naturalists today call the "conceptual environment," which includes tradition and legend. In order for a hereditary aristocracy to coerce the allegiance of the lower classes, it must, of course, convince them, and, perhaps, itself that it has the authority of tradition literally *in its veins* and that its tradition flows backward in time to some Golden Age (Eden, Sinai, Delphi, Rome or, for the American sense of time, Jamestown, Plymouth, and Philadelphia) when "ultimate values" were established. As we have already implied, Darwin, like the Enlightenment, reversed the temporal relations of culture: since civilization, like individual conscience, involves the conversion of the dictates of the moral sense into habitual convictions—not institutions based upon codes of conduct, given in the beginning—the Golden Ages, if they are ever to exist, will lie in the future. The problem then is not how to conserve established institutions (for the rage to hold on to any pattern of order once established is one of the most irrational instincts in any animal, including man) but how to insure progressive change. Solutions came from Bagehot and Weismann.

First, as Bagehot asserted in *Physics and Politics* (1873), a work which must have appealed profoundly to Ellen Glasgow, one must break the heavy "cake of custom," for customs, which are transmitted by man's imitativeness and conserved by his politics, eventually crush the finer possibilities of human nature. As one means of destroying old customs and diffusing new, Bagehot stressed the role of military victories, in which one culture (usually the victor) absorbs another. In *The Deliverance*, victory has already occurred; but although Bill Fletcher flocks, like Henry Grady and other enthusiasts of the New South, after the northern dream of money, money, money, he cannot clear his mind of southern views on class and race. Bagehot's second device for the diffusion of progress, one more powerful than military victory, was free discussion in government—the stimulation and education of the mind.[4]

Going beyond the arguments of Darwin and Bagehot on the subject of cultural change was August Weismann, who widened the gap they had opened between blood lines and cultural progress. In his essays of the eighties, Weismann distinguished two kinds of evolution, biological and cultural, in order to explain evidence of cultural progress without changes in related human body structures. Cultural progress depends on two factors, man's genetically determined physical structures (including the brain) and tradition. Weismann defends tradition, but his tradition would give no comfort to Miss Glasgow's contemporaries, for it also continually changes. Tradition here has absolutely no connection with hereditary germ plasma; it is a symbolic construct, the "entire growth of culture, the development of language, of the sciences, . . . and of every kind of art." Each generation may start "from the acquirements of the preceding one," and "with the same powers," climb to more advanced civilization. Thus in cultural evolution, though not in biological, there takes place what Lamarck called the transmission of *acquired* characteristics—which makes for very rapid change. This was a revolutionary scientific position, one which remains at the base of all modern social reform, for it means cultural diffusions across class and racial boundaries are the rule and not the exception.[5] It is this sort of transmission which shapes Christopher Blake in the second half of *The Deliverance*, where his conceptual environment, his education by Maria Fletcher, is infinitely more important than his blood, his race, his ancestry, or his natural, social, or economic milieu. He discovers, as a colleague of Weismann noted, that "by means of language and of social institutions we inherit the acquired experience, not of our ancestors only, but of other races [and classes] in the same sense of 'inheritance' in which we talk of people inheriting land or furniture or railway shares. . . . Indeed, might we not define civilization in general as the sum of those contrivances which enable human beings to advance independently of hered-

4 See Mackintosh, *From Comte to Benjamin Kidd*, 125–31.
5 Weismann, *Essays Upon Heredity*, iii, 36, 47, 65–69.

ity?" [6] Thus the advocates of change had usurped the very words with which southern aristocrats conjured awe and fear for the holiness of tradition: heredity, human beings, social institutions, inheritance, even civilization. And they had turned all the values upside down.

The conservatives resisted by destroying the process by which knowledge was transmitted for a generation; they put the public debt above the public schools and denied an education to blacks and poor whites, the groups who would profit most from change. Good families were expected to provide for themselves. But in *The Deliverance*, the fallen aristocrat, Christopher Blake, grows up illiterate. This, Miss Glasgow implies, is solely the fault of northern intervention (7). Actually the refusal to tax railroads, bondholders, property holders, and manufacturers to support education was a policy of the conservative Funders who controlled Virginia during the "Redemption" from Reconstruction.[7] The Jeffersonian concept of public education, which makes many assumptions supported by Weismann, was ironically dismissed by politicians as a carpetbag measure. As Miss Glasgow so powerfully symbolizes in *The Deliverance*, the South, in it resistance to change had, perhaps unwittingly, taken steps to become a closed society, equipped with its own newspapers, textbooks, and agreed-upon subjects of conversation, topics which tolerated, as Miss Glasgow observed, no stimulation to those parts of the brain that initiate change or disrespect for authority.[8]

In light of her knowledge of Darwin, Bagehot, Weismann, and of the intent revealed in her preface, it is understandable that Miss Glasgow would exercise great care, in portraying Blake in *The Deliverance*, to assign only those characteristics to heredity which are, from the point of view of moral character, strictly neutral or ambiguous. From Blake's father's family come his most striking physical traits, light hair, great size, and a classic brow offset by a salient jaw suggestive of "sheer brutality" (11, 13, 54)—which com-

[6] D. G. Ritchie, *Darwinism and Politics* (London, 1891), 100–101, quoted in Weismann, 51n.
[7] Woodward, *Origins of the New South*, 61–64, 92–94, 398–400.
[8] Coulter, *The South During Reconstruction*, 328–29.

bine to form a physical type popular at the time in works by Jack London and Frank Norris. Psychological traits shared by Blake and his father might have either hereditary or environmental sources; they include a tendency to bully, a dry throat, an aversion to the use of tobacco, a few scholarly interests, and a tendency toward mental instability which shows up in his father's mental breakdown following the war and in Blake's capacity for hatred and his fixed idea of revenge (7, 8, 12, 202, 331, 383). As it turns out, however, the intensity of his hatred may owe more to rural isolation and daily intimacy with the strong forces of the earth (125, 241), for Christopher, potentially a hedonist, finds himself in a situation where there is only one pleasure upon which he can glut himself—hatred for Bill Fletcher (156). Biologically, temperamentally, Blake simply embodies a force which "might serve equally the agencies of good or evil" (384).

What tips the scale from one to the other is vision. This is a novel of vision or, in Frederick McDowell's words, of psychology rather than sociology. There are three separate conceptual environments or mental sets which work upon Blake's neutral energy; these are embodied in three characters who keep up a chorus-like commentary upon the action. The Calvinistic outlook, important in *The Descendant*, is here assigned to a comical local merchant, Susan Spade, who distrusts human nature (especially in a man), believes in a wrathful deity that intervenes in the affairs of men (usually to punish), and takes great pride in her own moral righteousness (368, 474). Susan's influence on Blake is slight; it is likely that the self-disgust he feels when he sees the result of his project to corrupt Will Fletcher owes something to the image of man he acquired, along with his whiskey, in the back room of the Spades' store (331–32). More important to Christopher's behavior are the conceptual environments centering about his mother and her brother, Tucker Corbin.

Mrs. Blake is one of the most powerful embodiments Miss Glasgow ever found for two important interrelated themes: the sheltered life and evasive idealism. Although the old woman's condition, autistic blindness, is perfectly recognizable, in the behavioral psychology of the period, as an aggravated state of traumatic hysteria,[9] it is more interesting as a symbol for the postwar frame of mind of the South and as an example of the fascinating mental state which Marx calls "false consciousness," William James "willed belief," Henry James "self-deception," and Sartre "bad faith." As such, Mrs. Blake and her daughter Cynthia are two aspects of the same personality—the first passive, the other active. Unable to tolerate the uncertainty and change necessitated by the war's destruction of the material foundations of class and longing for the stone-like impenetrability made possible by the passionately fixed idea of being an aristocrat (Walter Page called the aristocrats "mummies" or "ghosts"), Mrs. Blake simply *will not see* the unpleasant truths: that the South lost the war, that slavery was an unforgivable crime against man and, perhaps, the God of the Episcopal Church, that the Blakes are no longer a great family, that the slaves have scattered to the winds, that her polite manners and gentle views of love and life count for nothing in a flimsy cabin where the staples are cornbread, bacon, and back-breaking work. To maintain this massive, impenetrable ideal, it is necessary for all Mrs. Blake's children, who are but products of her influence, to conspire *with* her. It is Cynthia especially who is the conscious architect and chief defender of the family's illusion (95); she has sacrificed "everything," become a sadly grotesque martyr to their cause. At the same time, her sacrifice itself is selfishness, for she had had nothing in her past life to renounce, while her chosen position gives her considerable power (96, 102, 119).

With Mrs. Blake's false situation established as credible, Miss Glasgow quietly proceeds to tick off one by one the characteristics of evasive idealism. Some are amusing, others insidious. Evasive idealists have an optimistic concept of the world (70), worship heroics (159), maintain stern class distinctions (117), thrive on nostalgia for antebellum balls and graces (54, 103), and repress the uncomplimentary traits of their ancestors (112). They seriously believe that since all free Negroes are failures and rebellious, blacks are better

[9] Cf. Bailey, *Accident and Injury*, 296–97; Cf. Bailey's later article, "The Wishful Self," 115–21.

off as slaves (477). Governed by abstract laws, "principles," and living upon lies (74), the evasive idealist remains ignorant of change and therefore unable to make new adaptations (58–59). The most pernicious aspect of this mental state, which is at the core of all genteel southern ideology, is that it founds itself upon an ideal, an absolute, which easily becomes the unchallengeable "good end" that justifies questionable tactics, including the sacrifice of other people. In Mrs. Blake's words, the ability to be a gentleman "embraces all morality and a good deal of religion" (479)—to which we need only contrast Miss Glasgow's apothegm that a reasonable doubt (in any area) is the "safety valve of civilization." It is Cynthia's ability to create faith in the ideal of Mrs. Blake's sheltered condition that allows her to maintain an incestuous tyranny over all family loyalty and affection (119). The parallels between Cynthia's use of her mother's situation and post-Reconstruction southern politicians' use of the masses' ideals—purity of southern women and the absolute holiness of southern soil—to fight racial and economic reforms are too close to spell out.

The most important and insidious consequence of faith in Mrs. Blake is the distorted passion of Christopher's early life. It is Cynthia again who transforms their mother's false position into the uncompromising family honor, pride, and rigid dignity Christopher feels he must avenge, for she clings desperately to memories "of the past grandeur, the old Blake power of rule" which he, like his twin sister Lila, is too young to have known (109, 112, 117, 118, 244, 431). It is Cynthia who transfers to Chris her class's strong sense of private property and the belief that prolonged occupancy is the origin of individual claims to the earth (25, 88). She also first paints Fletcher as the sole destroyer of their wasteful, alcoholic father, creates in Chris a hatred, "deep-rooted like an instinct," of the usurper, and makes that passion "an article in the religious creed the child had learned" (88, 95). Having listened obediently to her instruction, Chris sometimes visits the old Blake graveyard, to pillow his head on his father's grave and dream of revenge (90). Cynthia has almost complete control over his mental development through Book III.

Tucker Corbin is near Chris in these early years, but the old man's view of life cannot compete with the solidarity of intent created in his nephew by his niece. Tucker's vision—and he has matured into a man of vision, not a man of action—dissolves the class conflict stressed by the other Blakes (aside from Lila) and the man-against-man, man-against-nature conflicts assumed by Susan Spade. Whereas Cynthia's sense of time is dominated by past power, Chris's by future revenge, and Susan Spade's by future reward, Tucker alone lives in the present. Only half a man (he lost an arm and a leg in the war), he nevertheless is the only member of the family with eyes to see: the earth's green, the sky's blues, the metamorphoses of clouds, the commotion of wrens (106–107). Unlike his sister, he does not evade the difficult past; he accepts it in order to transcend it, for, to him, "happiness is not so much in what comes as in the way you take it" (107). A lady-killer before the war, Tucker *acquired* his mature vision in the abyss, during an encounter with death, "the hardest knock that life could give" (295). Both Tucker and his sister are "half-dead," but for Mrs. Blake the living part is that which dwells on the past within; for her brother it is the part which contemplates the present without. He has found that the mind which dwells upon itself must be morose, for in its egoism it misses the amazing transformations of nature and lacks "the sympathy which projects itself into states of feeling other than its own" (111). Atoned, mentally and physically, to both the beauty and brutality of elemental forces, Tucker Corbin has become a saint of the things of nature.

It is only through the influence of Maria Fletcher that Blake grows into Tucker's vision of things. And, like Tucker and Blake, Maria is herself an illustration of the novel's theme, that "environment more than inheritance determines character," especially the environmental force of extreme suffering. Before her marriage, she gives the appearance of grace and quiet elegance, but, to a well-bred observer like the attorney Carraway (Miss Glasgow's distorting "reflector" in the opening chapters), her poise is patently inauthentic, acquired, not hers by family right but through a northern education at a "high-and-mighty boarding-school" (27). To Carraway, who does not often rise above his own "old-fashioned loyalty to a strong class prejudice," Maria is "a dressed-up doll-baby" with "all the natural thing squeezed out of her" (27, 36). But Miss Glasgow, who remains a limited essentialist for all her emphasis on environment, takes care that Carraway see in Maria, even at the beginning, "the making of a woman . . . after all" (67, 505).

It requires six years of a wretched marriage—with a womanizer who loses his mind before dying in an asylum under his wife's care— and a return to rural life to open up Maria's nature and develop her second skin (240, 251, 356, 361). Like Tucker, she has had the abyss experience: "I went down into hell, . . . and I came out—clean. I saw evil such as I had never heard of; I went close to it, I even touched it, . . . and I was like a person in a dream" (435). She returns to Virginia with her eyes open, able for the first time to see its desolate red roads, luxuriant tobacco fields, primitive, ignorant people, and wild countryside as her true heritage, mirroring the defiant vital force she herself incarnates (357–58). This ability to find value in what she once turned her back on derives from her change of outlook; she has decided that, despite the blindness of events, "one must believe that there is a purpose in it [experience], . . . or one would go mad over the mystery of things" (390). But purpose is often an "ideal we put into" things, a passionate commitment of "our heart's blood" to otherwise dry, inanimate objects of faith and doubt (391–93). In short, as Kant argued and William James implied, the beauty, meaning, and purpose of things exist, perhaps, only in the observer's mind. Although the essence of *things* is beyond experience, the soul of *men* is, in this novel, a visible light. Maria's own fervent spirit, which is said to show radiant in her face (339, 352–53), becomes the key to an elaborate chain of light images representing the force that draws Christopher out of his morose inner darkness.

Near the end of *The Battle-Ground*, a beaten Dan Montjoy looked up and saw Betty Ambler "coming toward him with a lamp shining in her hand." Maria Fletcher is another Betty, one who has time to spread her healing light before the novel in which she appears ends. Initially, fire images in *The Deliverance* are associated with the burning lust for revenge about which Blake circles blind as a moth (322–23). But even before Maria's return, Blake's hatred has run its course, his volition is unstable, he feels alienated from his family and the earth by his unnatural passion with which he is weary unto death (196, 199–200, 253, 337); he simply is unable, nonetheless, to stop the process he has initiated in turning Will against his grandfather. After a single encounter with Maria, however, he begins to awaken from his dark deluded past: "His whole life was shattered into pieces by the event of a single instant. Something stronger than himself had shaken the foundations of his nature, and he was not the man that he had been before. He was like one born blind, who, when his eyes are opened, is ignorant that the light which dazzles him is merely the shining of the sun" (348). It would be tedious to describe in detail how this light of love and reality grows, or the stages through which Blake's comprehension of natural delights expands, or the ways in which his heroics during a smallpox outbreak, his false confession, and his eclipse in prison work to strip away his old skin and expiate past crimes. Miss Glasgow herself might have foreshortened the last two books of the novel, for the success of such internal processes is finally asserted rather than shown. Here it will suffice to say that Maria's function in this slow upward movement is to redirect, nourish, and give new impetus to the great emotional power Blake formerly squandered on hatred, so that after his prison nadir he awakes at last to the knowledge that experience has "altered . . . the vision through which he [has] grown to regard the world"; the sun, the sky, a spouting fountain produce in him "a recognition . . . of the abundant physical beauty of the earth" (538). Vision is the ultimate boon, the sign of atonement of the inner and outer worlds.

As mentioned earlier, *The Deliverance* is much less interesting from the sociological point of view than from the psychological one exploring the way social structures are internalized as psychic blindspots. Neither Fletcher nor Blake is an especially faithful copy of his historical counterpart. Historians tell us that very little land redistribution followed the Civil War although some plantations were sold for taxes. It is true, however, that where plantations changed hands they remained virtually intact as does the Blake place. Although one of the fastest rising self-made men in Virginia, Fletcher is too recognizable as a type-character from French literature (Rabelais for comical vulgarity and Molière for miserliness) to offend many of the postwar southern new rich. No attention is paid to the oppressive sharecrop system through which men like Fletcher usually built their fortunes by doubling as the village merchant and banker and taking liens against their own tenants' crops in exchange for food, clothing and other necessities sold on credit.[10] There are several references to Virginia's bad rural roads and to its failure to innovate the processing of tobacco—but only in passing. Although some feeling for the growing of tobacco is created, it comes across more as a ritual tied to the seasons than an industry. Blacks, often the dominant theme of postwar southern thought, are scarcely alluded to in this novel, although the point is driven in that they still respect their former masters and feel only contempt for lower-class whites (7, 9, 18, 20, 41).

Nonaristocratic whites receive relatively close attention, for the novel is a variation on the "reconciliation theme" popularized in this period by Thomas Nelson Page and Joel Chandler Harris, a variation in which the conflict to be resolved involves classes rather than regions. To see how Miss Glasgow has shifted the emphasis, one need only compare Harris' short story, "The Old Bascom Place," from his 1891 collection, *Balaam and His Master*; there, an uprooted aristocratic family reclaims its old plantation in 1876 when the planter's daughter weds the industrious New York stater who bought the place during Reconstruction. Miss Glasgow's focus on the class struggle seems less a fairy tale than Harris' subject. Not only must Blake transcend the pernicious distortions of his own class, but Maria must rise above the vulgarities of the environment created by her father. The image projected of Fletcher's class (which seems to include any white man not born an aristocrat) is reasonably complex in that it embodies both good and bad qualities. Some lower-class whites are scraggy tobacco chewers; most have weak grammar, crude manners, and poor taste in furniture. Some of their women are vain, impractical, and promiscuous; others are

10 Buck, *The Road to Reunion*, 147.

valued only for appearances and working abilities before marriage and after marriage are tied to joyless tasks which allow no time for such impractical activities as lovemaking. But the nonaristocrat's most dangerous characteristic is the way his ideas suffer from having worked their way down the socioeconomic ladder; in the South, the poor white unconsciously worships the aristocrat's values (487, 535). Unable, therefore, to turn against his oppressor, he can only *transcend* his own class by imitating his "betters." Thus we find Jim Weatherly, the handsome, handy yeoman who weds Blake's adaptable sister, Lila, learning to speak with precision and to scrape and bow, cavalier-fashion, at Mrs. Blake's throne (263, 272). Although Susan Spade claims that the poor are simply the victims of God's equitable judgment (a position that Adam Smith, Malthus, Spencer, or a Presbyterian industrialist might be comfortable with), the novel demonstrates that, allowing for individual temperaments, the lower classes, as much as the aristocrats, are "plastic matter for the mark of circumstances" (180). Indeed, Blake comes to feel that someone like Maria possesses even higher possibilities than the aristocrats of his family because, unlike the "ghosts" and "mummies," her defiant vital force has not been weakened by "old claims and old customs" (413).

In one important sense, *The Deliverance* is the thematic as well as chronological sequel to *The Battle-Ground*. Christopher Blake begins where Dan Montjoy ends, as an aristocrat bereft by the war of the tradition which protected his class. More importantly, however, Miss Glasgow's fifth novel is a culmination and extension of all her previous interests in the conflict between human nature and civilization. Like Michael Akershem, Christopher's early experiences produce in him a dominant attitude of conflict, a sense that his ego must be defended against others. But unlike Akershem, Blake's later experiences deliver him from this attitude of conflict. Like Anthony Algarcife, Christopher passes through a crisis of identity in which he is alienated from others, feels disgust for himself, and loses his formerly vital passions; like Algarcife, those passions are revived through the love of a woman. In Algarcife's case, his environment remains hostile even after the restoration of emotion; Blake, however, comes to terms with his surroundings. In Algarcife's case, the descriptions of psychological transformations often seem to be analysis for the sake of analysis; in Blake's case, the analysis is generally subsumed by the drama. As with Nick Burr, Christopher Blake's story begins in poverty and ignorance. In contrast to Burr, Blake begins with the heritage of a great family behind him; it becomes his chief burden. Again unlike Burr, he ends in poverty and relative ignorance. Blake, nevertheless, achieves a state of grace which Burr never found. Blake's deliverance comes from without: whereas Burr's beloved, blue-blooded Eugenia Battle, married one of her kind, Maria Fletcher, daughter of a coarse upstart, waits patiently for Blake.

Although personal disappointment soon led Miss Glasgow to renounce the "part that romantic love plays in the triumph over revenge" in *The Deliverance* (*Measure,* 34)—in retrospect, its success seemed more a hypothetical possibility than a probability—it cannot be denied that the power she ascribes in this novel to love was true to her vision of human possibilities in 1903. Love, or one of the deceptive passions associated with it, had brought the same conversion of her consciousness as occurs with Tucker Corbin, Maria Fletcher, and Christopher Blake. Miss Glasgow must have reasoned that after writing four largely critical and negative novels she had earned the privilege of a modest affirmation, without at the same time opening herself to the charge of having joined the "uplift" or "evasive idealism" school of fiction. As readers and critics, we speak constantly about the need for the expression of love, especially in Faulkner and the southern context in general, to redeem modern man from his estranged condition; yet when we see love used to restructure the mental set of Christopher Blake, we remain incredulous. Rightly so. The excess sentimentality pervading this and many other southern novels seems only one more distorted outlet for a powerful but ideologically blocked emotional force which might be more naturally expressed as open love between the races and/or sexes. A single mouth-to-mouth kiss between a fallen aristocrat and a beautiful girl *risen* from the lower classes (436) does not go very beyond sentimental wish-fulfillment. For all its criticism of evasive idealism, *The Deliverance* seems, in light of the true psychological problem of the modern South, to be a call for the reconciliation of all southern whites under the banner of a modified aristocratic ideal with the black man playing the familiar role of excluded scapegoat. The veils of bad faith are exceedingly numerous and adhesive. They are much easier to detect today than in Miss Glasgow's time; we should perhaps be grateful for the direction she moved in, rather than judge too harshly the place at which she arrived by 1904.

One of the traditional functions of creative literature (sometimes neglected in realism) is to generate nonexisting possibilities, desirable goals for further exploration. Tucker Corbin embodies such a goal. In later denying the triumph of passion over the past, it is significant that Miss Glasgow did not deny Corbin's peculiar state of grace. Tucker is the first of a series of her characters, "saints of the things of nature," or mystical materialists, who manage to remove themselves from the Malthusian–Darwinian universe—not by constructing an artificial, sheltering garden of tradition—but by absorbing conflict, by passing through the abyss and becoming reconciled in the process to the brutality and beauty of natural forces. He and his spiritual kin in *The Deliverance* are the first of Ellen Glasgow's saintly failures: men (and, less often, women) who succeed in dissolving the attitude of conflict otherwise dominant in life—at least in the universe of her novels. Because the book gave so artful expression to her most important earlier themes—especially the problems of determinism and the sheltered life—while skillfully anticipating, in Tucker Corbin, her later ones, *The Deliverance* remained Miss Glasgow's best and strongest novel, at least, until *The Miller of Old Church* (1911), *Virginia* (1913), and, perhaps, until *Barren Ground* (1925).

SUSPENSION OF THE EXILE

The success of *The Deliverance* was threefold: good sales, good reviews, and new acquaintances for Miss Glasgow. The book profited from two popular trends: historical romance and novels of professions or commodities. It carried the subtitle, *A Romance of the Virginia Tobacco Fields*, thus suggesting an association with Frank Norris's romantic "Epic of the Wheat," including *The Octopus* (1901) and his posthumous *The Pit* (1903), which was Doubleday, Page and Company's first big seller. Page advertised Miss Glasgow's novel glowingly, and from January to March it led most booksellers' lists. It sold over one hundred thousand copies by December, sufficient to earn second place for 1904—behind Winston Churchill's *The Crossing*.

Northern reviewers responded warmly. For example, Edward Marsh of the *Bookman* commended Miss Glasgow's restraint in keeping tobacco in the background rather than allowing the commodity to dominate characters as Marsh felt Norris had allowed wheat to do in *The Octopus* and James Lane Allen had permitted hemp to do in *The Reign of Law*. Marsh also liked her use of humor to resist sentiment and melodrama. Eckert Goodman, in *Current Literature*, judged her the equal of George Eliot and thought her characters the most convincing ever created by a woman novelist. Only the *Nation* and the *Lamp* were unfavorable—chiefly because Mrs. Blake's fixation in the past seemed implausible to them.[11]

With *The Deliverance*, a number of southern critics began taking Miss Glasgow seriously. The previous summer, John B. Henneman in the *Sewanee Review* had praised the "growing intellectual power" of her novels but seemed to regret that, like the analytic school of New England, she borrowed her impulse from foreign sources— he mentions George Eliot, Tolstoy, Zola, and Ibsen—rather than from the local color and dialect tradition of the South, which he considered more truly American than the international naturalism or realism of James and Howells.[12] John Ormond, a year later in the *South Atlantic Quarterly*, was extremely critical of the southern tradition that Henneman had praised. Ormond saw two major

11 *Bookman* (New York), XIX (March, 1904), 73–74; *Current Literature*, XXVI (March, 1904), 315–16; *Nation*, LXXVIII (March 24, 1904), 234–35; *The Lamp*, XXVIII (February, 1904), 70. These reviews have been epitomized in Kelly, "Struggle for Recognition," 54–64.

12 John B. Henneman, "The National Element in Southern Literature," *Sewanee Review*, XI (July, 1903), 345–66.

trends in southern fiction since the Civil War: the Negro-dialect writers, Joel Chandler Harris and Thomas Nelson Page, who dealt only with good, happy Negroes under ideal conditions, and writers like James Lane Allen who treated the old southern planter class after the Civil War with great idealism and loyalty but with no critical insight. Ormond thought both formulas exhausted and that neither represented "truly the condition of Southern society since the war. . . . Starting out, as they do, to exalt the old planter in the days of his adversity they give a false color to existing Southern life; for it is true that most of the people who are doing things in the South today are not the sons of the old planters, but those who represent the old middle classes. The leading professional men, business men, financiers, and politicians of the new time are from this class." For this reason, Ormond especially admired the work of Miss Glasgow: she, "of all the living Southern novelists, has perhaps the strongest grasp on actual life. Her sympathies are human and her observation seems to have been many-sided. Her faculty of portrayal is excellent." Although Ormond thought Miss Glasgow's originality less than striking in *The Deliverance*—for Christopher Blake seemed to follow the formula for the regulation southerner of fiction—still "all things considered," he found "abundant genius in the book." [13] Archibald Henderson, reviewing *The Deliverance* for the *Sewanee Review*, agreed with Ormond; Miss Glasgow was preëminent among novelists of the New South for her blend of art, story, charm, introspection, and rigid self-examination. Henderson found the book strong in masculine appeal and especially commendable for its "mastery of a tremendous moral, ethical and social problem." [14]

All the English reviews of *The Deliverance* were complimentary, but lacked penetrating analysis. The *Spectator* went so far as to call Christopher Blake one of the "more striking" characters ever drawn in American fiction. By 1904 Miss Glasgow seems to have become— with Frank Norris and Mary Wilkins—one of the three most popu-

[13] John R. Ormond, "Some Recent Products of the New School of Southern Fiction," *South Atlantic Quarterly*, III (July, 1904), 285–89.

[14] Archibald Henderson, "Recent Novels of Note," *Sewanee Review*, XII (October, 1904), 456–64; epitomized by Kelly, "Struggle for Recognition," 67–69.

lar American authors with the relatively small English reading audience.[15]

In one sense, *The Deliverance* proved a point for Miss Glasgow: that she need not subserve regional piety in order to hold her head up among successful southern writers. Thus, in the spring of 1904, with her book high on the sales lists, she had no qualms about opening a friendship with Mary Johnston, a fellow Virginian whose historical novel, *To Have and To Hold*, was one of the greatest financial successes of the period.[16] Apparently through Cary McCormack,[17] Miss Glasgow began an exchange of letters with Miss Johnston, addressing her as "my dear fellow-craftsman," expressing the wish to know her better, but warning, "Yes, I dare say we are different in many ways—it will be interesting, don't you think, to learn how different. And the main thing, perhaps we both have." [18] The differences between the two novelists were indeed large. Miss Johnston, whose photographs reveal a petite, delicate, thin, fair beauty given to full-length white organdy dresses and

15 This, at least, was the opinion of Chalmers Roberts writing in Walter Page's magazine, *World's Work*, VIII (October, 1904), 5430. His article—as well as the review in *Spectator*, XCII (April 2, 1904), 539—is discussed by Kelly, "Struggle for Recognition," 70–71.

16 Spiller *et al.*, *Literary History of the United States*, 1119.

17 Cary McCormack seems to have become—perhaps through Coralie Johnston—an ardent friend of Mary Johnston before Ellen Glasgow knew her. Mrs. McCormack's letters to Miss Johnston suggest that the novelist was deeply worried about Cary's various illnesses. The letters reveal both the fervor of Cary's affection for Miss Johnston and Cary's worries about her own mental condition. She speaks of "the queer hitch in my brain," of mental and physical depressions, of being "devoid of nervous force," and of "forgetting always the words I want to say." Or, again, Cary writes, "Oh my beloved Mary, there is never a memory of you that is not dear & honour-'able—dear to me & honourable to you. . . . I have always seen, felt & clung to the big, broad woman you are—& you have helped me. I have missed you sorely—& I yearn for you. . . . I have been & I fear I am very ailing—as soon as a nurse can be gotten I believe they intend putting me to bed for rest & care. . . . You will read between the lines all my poor heart wants to say & my feeble brain may not. . . . I put my hungering spirit arms about you. . . . I shall think clearer soon." Mary Johnston Collection, Alderman. Such insight into Mrs. McCormack's condition throws light forward on Miss Glasgow's emotions during the next two years; it suggests that Miss Glasgow's sense of anguish was not totally egocentric and that there were sound psychological reasons for her wishing to find a life of her own. As dear as her sister was to Miss Glasgow, Cary is one likely model for the parasitic—often tyrannous—invalids that people her novels.

18 March 22, 1904, *Letters*, 43–44.

wide-brimmed white organdy hats, came close to the ideal of the Victorian southern lady. Her early novels reveal more of the conventional romance of the period than do Miss Glasgow's, although in this period she seems to have been moving towards the intellectual rebellion which mars her later books. Miss Glasgow's own intellectual preferences had so changed by 1904 that during the next three or four years the two writers became rather good friends and exchanged frequent visits, during which they would sit in Miss Glasgow's study or Miss Johnston's parlor to drink tea and discuss art, Italy, Eastern or Idealistic philosophies, and modern novels, including such popular romances as Robert Hichens' *The Garden of Allah*, about a monk who, finding the monastery intolerable, leaves it to face the world, a situation remarkably close to that of Miss Glasgow's next novel. Occasionally they would refer to one another's fiction, though this subject seems not to have been a very comfortable one.[19] Through Mary Johnston, Miss Glasgow came to know the popular English-American actress, Eleanor Robson, who eventually married New York financier August Belmont. Another of Miss Glasgow's Virginian friends at this time was Amélie Rives, once a *cause célèbre* for her sensually "scandalous" novel, *The Quick or the Dead?* (1888), but now the author of popular romances like Miss Johnston's and the wife of Prince Pierre Troubetskoy, Russian portrait painter.[20]

Like her new acquaintances, Miss Glasgow preferred to spend as few summers as possible in Richmond and as many as possible abroad. In 1904 she and her two sisters, Rebe and Cary, wished to visit central Europe. As Cary McCormack wrote Miss Johnston, they would sail on the *Kaiser Wilhelm der Grosse*, July 19, for Bremen and go directly to Langenschwalbach, an iron bath near Wiesbaden. The bath, Mrs. McCormack went on, "was highly recommended to Ellen—and the Doctor tells me, too, now that it will be the making of me. We shall probably be there three weeks. Then

---

[19] See "Mary Johnston, Her Book and Her's Alone," an unpublished diary, December, 1906 to May, 1907, in Mary Johnston Collection, Alderman. Hereinafter cited as "Her Book."

[20] *Letters*, 46, 47.

trot about a bit to supple our iron frames. Nuremburg, Munich, Vienna, Prague, Dresden, etc. and sail the 3rd of September from Bremen on the *Grosser Kurfürst*. Hardly breathing space! . . . We have not the time for England." [21] As it developed, however, Cary fell ill and spent a totally discouraging summer with her father and other Richmonders at White Sulphur Springs in West Virginia. In the middle of August she would journey northward—apparently for medical treatment. Meanwhile, Miss Glasgow and her younger sister continued with their trip. But Miss Glasgow was seasick throughout the voyage and spent a good while in her cabin while Rebe made new friends. As in the previous year, B. probably accompanied or arranged to meet Miss Glasgow (in which case they would have had only a comfortable run from Munich to return to Mürren and the Jungfrau). But the wheel seems already to have turned. Her good fortune, it is likely, had already passed its peak. The two travelers, as Cary noticed from her sister's letters, seemed "tolerably cheerful but not hilarious." [22]

21 July 15, 1904, Mary Johnston Collection, Alderman.
22 Cary McCormack to Mary Johnston, July 27, 1904, in *ibid.*

Chapter VIII

Alternative to Realism, 1904–1906

The Wheel of Life

If, as Kant suggests, the fascination of the science of metaphysics, by which he meant the problems of "God, Freedom (of will) and Immortality," is an unavoidable, dispositional malady of the human mind,[1] then perhaps it was inevitable that Ellen Glasgow would sooner or later pass through the intellectual phase into which she plunged headlong after *The Deliverance*. If Kant is right, Miss Glasgow's growing preoccupation with transcendental options should be attributed to human nature and not to such personal circumstances as her decreased happiness after the summer of 1904. Perhaps she did, as she later said, turn to philosophy "as the ancient decreed pursuit of the highest good"—and not, as many have, for consolation.[2] Whatever the causes, it is clear that, during the next year, her interest in metaphysics increased while her joy in living declined proportionately, and that her former devotion to Darwinism and the new sciences was eclipsed by this growing fascination with older philosophic points of view.

During the latter half of 1904 Miss Glasgow experienced a kind of death of the spirit. As she wrote Mary Johnston two years later, "For a year I was so dead that I couldn't feel even when I was hurt because of some curious emotional anaesthesia, and . . . I had to

---

1 Immanuel Kant, *Critique of Pure Reason* (New York, 1900), 5, 13.
2 *Woman*, 171.

fight—fight, a sleepless battle night and day, not for my reason but for my very soul." [3] Letters from this period show Miss Glasgow was upset by her sister's illness and by her own problem with hearing. These worries certainly contributed to her loss of spirit, but comparison of the letters, her novel of the period, and her later autobiography suggests that the major cause was some unspecified crisis in her relationship with B.

At any rate, by February 1905, her letters to Mary Johnston were heavy with transcendental speculations and occasional quotations from Eastern thought. She spoke of Miss Johnston in the same way she had described Maria Fletcher: "There are moments when one seems almost to see the soul of one's friend shining through the delicate flesh." Then—in a comment which suggests that she had already looked seriously, though with some doubt, into the "perennial philosophy" (perhaps as expressed by the *Upanishads* or even Spinoza)—she gives the radiance in Miss Johnston the name the supreme pantheist would have: "The people I love best, I love for their spiritual quality, for it shows me God, somehow, and I hunger for him even when I am least positive of his being underneath us all." She felt that she and her friend were guided by the same spirit and that though they might not be headed down the same path, they would, as the Buddhist proverb assures, "come out upon the mountains" and "see the self-same sun." She felt that while her friend was well-disciplined, she herself had become a puppet of her impulses: "Mine so often carry me breathlessly away." [4]

In February, her major impulse drew her back to New York. It may have been during this visit that she wrote Miss Johnston that she and Rebe had been seeing "doctors, publishers and dressmakers" for three weeks—then added a note on her current frame of mind and its relation to intellectual interests: "It has been quite cold, damp and disagreeable . . . and the city seems so full of people, of compressed humanity, that it makes it hard to believe that the world isn't rushing entirely to matter. I find it very harassing to one's philosophic vision and in order to compose my soul I have

[3] September 15, 1906, *Letters*, 55.
[4] February 3, 1905, *ibid.*, 46.

been reading Spinoza and Plotinus." [5] Shortly afterwards, her major responsibility drove her suddenly back to Richmond. Cary's doctor had found her illness grave enough to necessitate a "very serious operation . . . to prolong her life." [6] Afterwards Miss Glasgow wrote to Mary Johnston, "It has been a hard winter in many ways—I don't complain of the cold for I love it—but I have worked like a driven slave and accomplished little.[7] Cary has succumbed at last and[,] after her operation[,] is overruled by a trained nurse." Then she added a few words about her personal outlook: "From a person of inordinate desires and 'spacious dreams,' I have brought my existence down to the contemplation of the concrete fact—I look neither before nor after, for if I did I'd stand perfectly still and shriek!" But her reading remained a potpourri of the romantic and the realistic, chiefly the former. She mentioned *The Garden of Allah* by Robert Hichens, the poetry of Christina Rossetti, and ("Strange Combination!") Balzac and Anthony Trollope. "In my Buick," she added before closing, "is *The Imitation of Christ* and *The Bhagavad-Gita.* Are you mystic enough, I wonder, to care for these?" [8] Miss Glasgow had herself come a good way from the lame translations of German scientists that once pleasured her.

By the last week of March, with her sister looking "at least fifteen years younger . . . and more cheerful and less nervous" than during the five years before her operation, Miss Glasgow was planning ahead for two trips. First, in mid-April she would travel to Charlottesville, stopping at Castle Hill for a visit with Amélie Rives and Troubetskoy. Then, for the summer, she had in mind a return

[5] Undated letter (addressed from 10 West 30th Street, New York), in Mary Johnston Collection, Alderman.

[6] Ellen Glasgow to Arthur Graham Glasgow, March 27, 1905, *Letters*, 47. Mrs. McCormack was forty-two years old at this time.

[7] Probably Miss Glasgow meant she was working on *The Wheel of Life*, which was under way by March 1905; cf. *Letters*, 48.

[8] Undated letter ("Sunday. Midnight"), in Mary Johnston Collection, Alderman. (From the stationery and by comparison with a letter from Ellen Glasgow to Arthur Graham Glasgow, March 27, 1905, *Letters*, 47, it can be dated as March 12, 1905.) One cryptic comment from this letter may have some bearing on Miss Glasgow's relationship with B.; referring to a note from Miss Johnston, she says, "Yes, I remember her Miss Malcolm distinctly, and it was juicy about Mr. Bell. What a small place our planet is, after all."

with Rebe to Germany, this time apparently for medical reasons. As she wrote her brother Arthur, her purpose would be to consult "Dr. Isadore Müller, who is said to be the first living aurist. It may be that he can do nothing for me, but my ears interfere so with my enjoyment of life that I should like to feel that I have done all in my power to make them hearable.[9] Dr. Müller is at Carlsbad for three months every summer, and we intend to go directly there." She regretted that her passage would not allow her to stop in England to see her brother.[10] On July 6 she and Rebe sailed directly for Bremen, at which time her reading seems to have centered about Spinoza and the question of the power of will.[11]

It was during this 1905 trip to Europe that Miss Glasgow came out of her year of emotional anaesthesia. She has left at least three accounts of this "awakening of myself," as she called it. The least embroidered record was in a letter written to Mary Johnston a year afterwards. After a brief description of her period of spiritual death, she said: "Then at the end of a year—at Mürren[12] last summer I came out triumphant, and for three whole months it was as if I walked on light, not air. I was like one who had come out of a dark prison into the presence of God and saw and knew him, and cared for nothing in the way of pain that had gone before the vision." She had, she wrote in a statement resembling Maria Fletcher's description of her own nadir, sunk so far down in suffering that she "saw at the end of her road the mouth of hell," but then had managed to turn and struggle back to life.[13] Elsewhere, she admitted that the sacred books of the East had brought her back.[14]

[9] Dr. H. Holbrook Curtis (1856–1920) seems to have been the American specialist in whom she placed most confidence. *The Deliverance* bears the following dedication: "To Dr. H. Holbrook Curtis, With Appreciation of His Skill and Gratitude for His Sympathy."

[10] March 27, 1905, *Letters*, 47–48; de Graffenried, *Scrap Book*, 203.

[11] *Letters*, 44–45, 47–48. The first of these two letters seems to refer to the trip of 1905, which began on July 6—not, as Rouse suggests, to the trip of 1904, which started on July 19.

[12] The place-name is not completely legible. Rouse, following Miss Glasgow's account in *Woman*, has chosen "Mürren." The word, however, is probably "Blumental." I have left it "Mürren," because Blumen-tal is within sight of Mürren, and "Mürren" has associations with Miss Glasgow's earlier life.

[13] September 15, 1906, *Letters*, 55–56.

[14] Ellen Glasgow to Walter Hines Page, Christmas, 1905, *Letters*, 50.

A second account of this awakening appears in Miss Glasgow's autobiography. Here the catalyst for the experience was a letter she received from B., while she was at the Kurhaus Mürren, saying that he had delayed an operation too long and now had "only a few weeks at worst, a few months at best." Here her deliverance from the sense of pain took the form of a mystic vision:

Many days later (I cannot be more exact concerning the time) I went up on the hillside, and lay down in the grass, where a high wind was blowing. Could I never escape from death? Or was it life that would not cease its hostilities? If only I could lose myself in nothing or everything! If only I could become a part of the grass and the wind and the spirit that moved round them, and in them. I thought of the mystics, who had attained Divine consciousness through a surrender of the agonized self. By giving up, by yielding the sense of separateness, by extinguishing the innermost core of identity. I tried with all my strength to find absorption in the Power people called God, or in the vast hollowness of the universe. . . . Then, after long effort, I sank into an effortless peace. Lying there, in that golden August light, I knew, or felt, or beheld, a union deeper than knowledge, deeper than sense, deeper than vision. Light streamed through me, after anguish, and for one instant of awareness, if but for that one instant, I felt pure ecstasy. In a single blinding flash of illumination, I knew blessedness. I was a part of the spirit that moved in the light and the wind and the grass. I was—or felt I was—in communion with reality, with ultimate being. . . . There was no thought, there was only blissful recognition, in that timeless awakening. . . . Then the moment sped on; the illumination flashed by me; the wind raced through the grass; the golden light shone and faded. . . . The vision was gone, and neither vision nor spirit ever returned.

Gone, too, was B.; he died, her autobiography asserts, before she sailed for America and she learned of it from a paper she saw on an European train. According to this version, the period of seeming anaesthesia succeeded rather than preceded the awakening (*Woman*, 165–67).

A third account is the fictionalized one which forms the thematic climax of *The Wheel of Life*. This version will be discussed below;

all that is needed here is a general comment on its similarities to
the other two. As a full mystic vision, it parallels the passage in the
autobiography. Otherwise, it resembles the brief description in the
letter to Miss Johnston. It comes as a deliverance from a period of
death-in-life. Moreover, it is not brought on by the physical death
of the heroine's lover, but by the death of his spiritual possibilities.
Perhaps, in relation to these events, Miss Glasgow used the word
"death" in an Eastern sense, to suggest the death of the inner man—
of that "spark of divinity" which, according to Eastern thought, illumines the man who has discovered Truth.[15] Finally, the fictionalized account, like the letter, shows less skepticism regarding the
vision than the autobiography. Writing thirty or so years afterwards, Miss Glasgow weighed the encounter critically, as her bal-
anced phrases show. Had she gone through phenomenal reality to
commune: with "nothing or everything"? with "God, or . . . the
vast hollowness of the universe"? "with the Absolute, or with Absolute Nothingness"? Was the experience an intuition of ultimate
being, or "a fantasy of tortured nerves"? In her letter and novel
she thought she knew the answer. Thirty years later she was not
certain.

An important aspect of her account in the autobiography is
that it throws into confusion our working hypothesis, based on
Joseph Collins' suggestion, that "P. B.," Pearce Bailey, was the man
Miss Glasgow loved, for he did not die in 1905. Perhaps the word,
"death," must again be given an Eastern slant so that it was not
Bailey's body that Miss Glasgow considered dead in 1905 but certain "higher qualities" that she thought she had once detected in
the man. If our hypothesis is still viable, we can now make some
conjectures regarding the nature of Miss Glasgow's relationship
with Bailey. We should push its beginning back to at least 1896 or

15 Cf. Miss Glasgow's use of the word "dead" in her novel of the period: The
heroine says, "I used to think that people only died when they were put in coffins,
but I know now that you can be dead and yet move and walk about and even laugh
and pretend to be like all the rest—some of whom are dead also. . . . One instant I
was quite alive—as alive as you are now—and the next I was as dead as if I had been
buried centuries ago." Ellen Glasgow, The Wheel of Life (New York, 1906), 454.
Hereinafter cited as Wheel or simply by page.

1897 and suppose that after a period of estrangement around 1899 (Bailey married Edith Lawrence Black of New York in November 1899), Miss Glasgow and Bailey knew one another well again between 1901 and 1905. An estrangement must then have followed which lasted perhaps until about 1914, by which time Mrs. Bailey was dead. The then renewed relationship lacked passion, on Miss Glasgow's part, and probably fell to pieces well before Bailey's death in February, 1922. Afterwards, she was free to give fictional expression to their excruciating affair in *Barren Ground* (1925). Admittedly, there are many gaps in this hypothesis; much remains to be done with the whole episode.

It is clear, however, that by the end of 1905 Ellen Glasgow had become an enthusiast of metaphysics and mysticism, and a devotee of living. Christmas caught her at the Glen Springs in Watkins, in the western part of New York State. Cary, as Miss Glasgow wrote Walter Page, was improved but still had "a long weary road to pull up." Miss Glasgow herself was taking pleasure from "the lovely Glen in its drapery of ice." Having apparently seen the manuscript of her new book, Page warned her against the intellectual line she now was following. Her response to his advice was one of complete assurance:

> In my leisure hours, . . . I have been diverting myself with Schopenhauer who is decidedly more interesting than fiction besides being a better training for the muscles of the intellect. Alas, my dear friend, you are speaking with your political intelligence when you counsel me not to "take metaphysics seriously." If there is one subject upon earth which a human being can take seriously with dignity it is the soul of man—and what is metaphysics except the science of the soul?

Then she informed Page that she had made a major departure from her past intellectual outlook: "I am a born sceptic, you know, but in my first period, at the time I first knew you—in my materialistic and pessimistic days, I could not so much as tolerate any philosophizing that was not hitched fast to the concrete fact." If this statement explains why Plato had made no profound impression on her when she read him many years earlier (*Woman*, 172), then the comment which followed repeats the cause for her change of view regarding metaphysics in general: "I suppose I am doomed to pass through as many intellectual phases as are possible to this planet, but the truth remains that in the roughest place in my life, I was brought back to some kind of acceptance and reconciliation wholly through an interest in the most abstruse and transcendental metaphysics in existence which is that of the sacred books of the East— But there! I didn't mean to deliver you a lecture." [16]

Like many of her contemporaries in a decade when, as H. Stuart Hughes has shown, important American and European intellectuals were revolting against the mechanistic, materialistic, and naïvely progressive aspects of positivism, Ellen Glasgow found it relatively simple to synthesize the older metaphysics with her earlier devotion to evolutionary thought. Unlike many of her contemporaries, however, her concern for transcendental options followed, rather than preceded, a thorough exposure to the sciences of phenomenal reality.[17] The former was, therefore, a secondary interest for Miss Glasgow (from the point of view of her entire life), although at the time it seems to have eclipsed other intellectual concerns. Evidence presented above shows that by the publication of *The Wheel of Life* Miss Glasgow had studied: writings of the Hindus and Buddhists (especially *The Bhagavad-Gita*), the Neoplatonic *Enneads* of Plotinus, the mystical *Imitation of Christ* attributed to Thomas à Kempis, the theistic monism (or pantheism) of Spinoza, and an old favorite, Schopenhauer's very Eastern speculations regarding the Will, Maya (illusion), and Nirvana (extinction). (To these transcendentalists, other sources suggest we should add her continuing interest in the Stoics, especially Marcus Aurelius.) The drift of her reading is apparent. In *The Wheel of Life* she drew on it to give a metaphysical dimension to the notion of sympathy she formerly had grounded in natural science and personal experience.

In the long run, however, Miss Glasgow decided there was a good deal of literary truth to Page's warning about the effect metaphysics

16 Ellen Glasgow to Walter Hines Page, Christmas, 1905, *Letters*, 49–50.

17 By "contemporaries" I mean the majority of the poets discussed by Frederick W. Conner, in *Cosmic Optimism*, especially vii–viii.

might have on her fiction. For although *The Wheel of Life* managed, perhaps inadvertently, to add a further dimension to her grasp of the conflict between civilization and biology, the book which followed two years later did not; the latter *(The Ancient Law)* is the most abstruse novel she ever wrote.

ALTERNATIVES: PUPPETS AND SAINTS

The Wheel of Life is at once the most and least realistic of Ellen Glasgow's early novels, if by realism one means fidelity to the material surfaces of life. It embodies a gain in realism through its fidelity to personal experience. As Miss Glasgow later confessed, it is the most autobiographical of her novels: "the only one . . . that was taken directly from experience." [18] The street scenes, the luxury apartments and clothing, the physical descriptions of characters, the attack on romantic love, the frank treatment of sexual desire, including adultery—all these are palpable and convincing. Ultimately, however, the novel rests not on such material foundations but in a transcendental vision which permeates the book's abstract and exhaustive analyses of motives and supports the mystic experience in which it culminates. Nevertheless, the novel advances Miss Glasgow's theory of temperament and nurture, illustrates an important connection between the themes of the sheltered life and evasive idealism, and sets a few realistic limits to her conception of sympathy as a social force.

In her sixth novel Miss Glasgow recoiled from her defense of romantic love in *The Deliverance* by employing an antiromantic plot. In the popular romantic plot (infatuation, obstructed love, and reconciliation), the obstacles to love represent illusion while the reconciliation of the lovers is reality. In *The Wheel of Life* the opposite is the case. Indeed, the romantic hero (Arnold Kemper) functions as the villain, while Roger Adams, whom the narrator calls the hero, is an unromantic man of vision and remains peripheral to the central action. A third person, Laura Wilde, is the central character. The opening chapters, set during a snowy winter,

[18] Ellen Glasgow to Bessie Zaban Jones, April 18, 1938, *Letters*, 238.

find Laura Wilde leading a cloistral life in a Gramercy Park brownstone. At thirty she has made a quiet but highly respected reputation as a poet. Her chief literary friend is Roger Adams, who edits
the *International Review* and whose admiration for Laura's work
blends, at times, with his affection for her person, despite his own
marriage. Laura's confidante and friend since schoolgirl days, Gerty
Bridewell, introduces Laura to Arnold Kemper. The introduction
comes at a time when Laura is troubled by the impulse to quit her
shelter in order to find what her imagination tells her is "life."
Kemper, divorced ten years earlier, has just ended a three-year affair with the celebrated soprano, Madame Jennie Alta. Much of the
book consists of an analysis of Laura's mental and emotional states
in her relations with Kemper—analysis that tends to overwhelm
any sense of drama. The story reveals the consequence of Laura's
fitting her ideal of "life," like a mask, on Kemper and then pur-
suing this illusion though it leads her dangerously near the abyss'
edge. Meanwhile, Adams waits near at hand with (literally) saintly
patience, although his personal tragedies, including the death of
his wife, are so dramatic that they too seem, at times, to overshadow
the major action.

Three-fifths of the way through the novel, Laura and Kemper
become engaged, an agreement characterized by bad faith for both
parties, for he privately believes that love is only an emotion, that
it is therefore transient, and that men are "not born monogamous,"
while Laura, for her part, spends a spring and summer trying to
throttle suspicions regarding his good faith. The crisis follows the
autumnal reappearance of Madame Alta when Laura discovers that
the presence of the singer requires greater dissimulation and self-
deception than she will force herself to practice. Only days before
their wedding (set for December 19), in a confrontation over Madame Alta, Laura confesses that she has no faith in Kemper, and sends
him away.

Then Laura tries to escape into the city or, perhaps, into death.
She disappears for three days, returns, and spends six months in a
state of spiritual death, until in June, in the mountains, she experiences a mystic vision during which her dead soul takes new life. She

returns to the city to lose herself in aiding the socially deprived. On Christmas Eve, she meets Kemper at the Bridewell's house and discovers she is unmoved. When she leaves, she finds Adams outside—and finds, too, she is pleased he is waiting for her.

Thematically the novel is a contrast between the two basic character types—types which Carl Jung calls introverted and extroverted. Although Jung's formulation is more recent than the novel, it will help us understand an autobiographical situation that Ellen Glasgow felt herself too near to grasp completely. In the novel there are static paradigms for each of the types—Perry Bridewell for the extroverted and Roger Adams for the introverted—with other characters moving between, or representing combinations of the two attitudes. Laura Wilde is the character in whom the two attitudes war most bitterly.

At the start Laura is excessively introverted. Her "enclosed," "shielded" life in the brownstone of her ancient eccentric, if not neurotic, bachelor uncle and spinsterish aunt has made her an idealist who sees others through a distorting ideal image and for whom external reality is colored by a conventual vision (53, 76, 96). Innocent of the guises of society, she permits the free expression for her radiant energy. Having concentrated always upon the imaginary otherworld of poetry and ideas, she has the sense that she is in control of her own fate (272). Her poetry, however, remains unpopular because it is too contemplative, too much a "cloistral vision of an unrealized world"—or, as she later puts it, "pretty lies" (52, 167, 464). The subjective elements dominate all her interests.

The case could be made that Laura's guarded Gramercy Park address—an "old brown house hidden in creepers"—is actually "One West Main Street, Richmond," imaginatively transplanted for dramatic tightness. Even the ménage is familiar, for droll Percival shares with sententious Horace Payne many of the avuncular duties performed in *The Deliverance* by Tucker Corbin, and sheltered Aunt Angela falls under the dominion of the past as did Mrs. Blake. But the southern influence in Laura's life is more concretely explained through her mother, who just after the war married a northern soldier and entered New York society. The pattern was a

familiar one in this period, especially in the nineties when inter-
marriage gave "New York's best society a distinctly southern blend"
and the wealthy from both regions mingled freely at Newport, the
White Sulphur, Saratoga, and Bar Harbor, the most prestigious re-
sorts in the land.[19] Life seemed to be imitating artistic fantasy, for
this, of course, was the formula for bringing the nation together
again dreamed up in the eighties by T. N. Page, J. C. Harris, and
company. Miss Glasgow turns fantasy back into reality by introducing a tragic element into the pattern: the intersectional union
leads to the suicide of Laura's mother; of a self-conserving defensive
attitude, she wants the impossible: to possess her husband totally,
to protect him against all external claims (24–26). This failure of
the centripetal emotions of a southern woman to accept the centrif-
ugal drives of a northern male foreshadows Laura's unhappiness.

The weakness that exposes Laura to suffering is her inability to
be solidly "southern" and introverted. Jung's theory suggests that
because every individual possesses both extroverted and introverted
tendencies, a rhythmical alternation of the two attitudes should
ideally occur. Usually, however, one or the other movement dominates the whole conscious personality forcing the opposite tendency to seek an unconscious compensatory development so that a
consciously introverted person, like Laura, is unconsciously extroverted—and vice versa. Since personalities run thus by contraries,
introverted Laura finds external objects, which she consciously
deprecates, taking on a strange and terrifying because irrepressible
attraction. When she meets Arnold Kemper, a strong-willed masculine part of her longs to be free, like a man, to "live" (90). And
as their relationship grows, she feels developing within her a new
identity, perhaps a new temperament, for which "external objects
of fortune, to which she had always believed herself to be indifferent," are "endowed at the moment with an extraordinary and unreal value" (258–59). At times she senses within herself a "dual
nature" which questions the suitability, for her, of Kemper's extroverted way of life. At other times the bad faith of her romantic fervor allows her to repress altogether her former values, especially her

[19] Woodward, *Origins of the New South*, 148–50.

critical detachment from the life of sensual impulse (282, 319). But before she awakes from the hypnotic effect of things, she plunges deep into the pleasure-seeking ways of Arnold Kemper, the Bridewells, and "New York's best society."

As a representative of the extroverted attitude, Kemper is too complicated to be a pure type, for something in him that once led him to write a novel now causes him to regard a platonic love affair with Laura as somehow finer than his usual "fleshly" ones (219). But dominant in his temperament are qualities which have made him financially successful as an importer of French cars, owner of the controlling shares in a southern railroad, and director of a life insurance company (155, 160, 162). These qualities are variously described as a powerful magnetic nervous vigor, as the ability to "concentrate his whole being upon a single instant, to apply himself with enthusiasm to the thing [immediately] beneath his eyes" (whether a woman or a business deal), and as a cruel impetuous egoism (12, 162, 399, 406–407). In Kemper, there is a great deal of his distant cousin, Perry Bridewell, whom Miss Glasgow uses to mirror Kemper when all his guises are dropped; it is a resemblance between the two in a portrait that aids Laura's awakening (406–407). An embodiment, like Kemper, of the moods and rush of city streets, Bridewell is a man of imposing animal splendor, supremely and brutally selfish with the means and time to follow his bodily impulses (5, 7, 64, 291). Since it is assumed by all that males are nonmonogamous, a condition they blame on biology, adultery is frankly accepted as the convention of their class (156, 219). Accustomed to finding their personal world in the eyes of mistresses, Bridewell and Kemper are often mere puppets of a woman's fickle tastes—especially Bridewell (277–78).

Indeed, the most searching charge Miss Glasgow brings against the lords of the city and their consorts is that their pursuit of a plethora of external objects robs them of freedom. When she read *The Thoughts of the Emperor Marcus Aurelius* in 1899 and 1903, she scribbled "Thou shalt renounce!" by the following passage, which she also underscored: "Neither is . . . the receiving of impressions by the appearances of things, nor being moved by desires as puppets by strings . . . a thing to be valued. . . . What then is worth being valued? . . . This, in my opinion: to move thyself and to restrain thyself in conformity to thy proper constitution, to which end both all employments and arts lead." [20] But Laura Wilde's destiny is her temperament and, in leaving her guarded tower to pursue a chimera, she has surrendered to an inversion of temperament. During her breakdown, she comes to feel that self-control is impossible; in a clear echo of Marcus Aurelius, she tells Adams: "Nobody can help anything. . . . We're all drawn by wires like puppets, and the strongest wire pulls us in the direction in which we are meant to go. . . . There is no soul, no aspiration, no motive for good or evil, for we're every one worked by wires while we are pretending to move ourselves" (454). Along the way from excessive introversion to helpless extroversion, she has passed through the situation of Gerty Bridewell, the circle of hell where wives compete with their husband's mistresses by trying to maintain the pretty surfaces for which they were married (401–404). Formerly free of social deceptions, she learns to dissemble her dislike for Kemper's old mistress, to deceive herself into believing she is happy when she knows happiness is always just ahead, and even to lie outright to Kemper (348, 356, 409–12). She comes to agree with Gerty that the goal of life is the discovery of oblivion: "Call it by what name you will—religion, dissipation, morphia—what we are all trying to do is to intoxicate ourselves into forgetting that life is life" (352); "all society, all occupations, all amusements," Gerty's clothes, Kemper's sensuality are "so many unsuccessful attempts to escape" from one's own personality (425). The most extreme embodiment of the urban pattern Laura has embraced emerges in helpless Connie Adams, a cynical dyed blond with large, innocent, blank eyes, whose love of pleasing sensations must remain forever frustrated because she lacks the energy, money, and social position to support the flutter of her indiscretions (48, 339). To compensate she falls back on the "frequent use of stimulants"; her plunge includes alcoholism, narcotic hallucinations, hysteria, adultery, seeming nymphomania, and a merciful death while undergoing surgery to escape impulsive de-

20 Tutwiler, *Ellen Glasgow's Library*, 12.

sire (51, 175, 232, 253, 333–39). If Laura fails to descend this far into the abyss, it is chiefly because she receives support from Connie's husband, Roger.

When Laura renounces or is stripped of all her worldly objects, in traditional mystic fashion there comes to her the ultimate boon, a glimpse of Absolute Being, a vision to which Adams has climbed through years of suffering. Their shared state of spiritual grace is actually a paradox which dissolves the conflict between introverted and extroverted attitudes by subsuming the latter within the former and making the significance of objects a function of subjectivity or vision. The narrator spells out the nature of this paradox in passages analyzing the thoughts and emotions of Adams.

The key to Adams' philosophy, self-renunciation, blends three austere ingredients: a residual childhood Puritanism, Stoicism, and mystical idealism. His near-fatal bout with a lung disease as a student and his miserable affectionless marriage to a drug addict combined with an unprofitable career as magazine editor[21] have developed in Adams "a resolute will to endure as well as to resist" (47). But putting up with Connie is his most instructive trial, for it forces him to search for a meaning to justify suffering (145). In giving up all things that lie outside himself, he finds himself for the first time "willing as God willed" (287). Then through compassion for Connie, which demands absolutely nothing of her in return, he gains himself—a spark of divinity within, which he thinks of as his soul. He has achieved what the narrator calls "that ultimate essence of knowledge which enables a man to recognise himself when he encounters the stranger in the street," for, at this level of vision, the personal passes suddenly into the permanent universal conscious-

---

21 The relation between Adams and Walter Page presents an interesting problem. Adams' *International Review* suggests two publications Page edited—the *Forum* and the *World's Work*. But little is said of Adams' magazine. Adams, however, does, at one point, rush somewhere for an appointment and interview "with a famous Russian revolutionist who had promised him an article for the *Review*" (136). This recalls the somewhat controversial series, "The Memoirs of a Revolutionist" by Prince Peter Kropotkin, which Page secured in 1897, while Kropotkin was in Boston, for a third publication he edited, the *Atlantic Monthly*. Burton J. Hendrick, *The Life and Letters of Walter H. Page*, I, 61. However, the essential Adams, the mystic and saint, bears little resemblance to the seemingly very practical-minded Page.

ness so that the spark which illumines Adams dwells in all men
(288, 293); all men are brothers in suffering. Thus, in his moment
of greatest adversity immediately prior to Connie's death, he is able
to transcend pain, for the "I" is "not more evident to his illumined
consciousness" than is the "Thou"; his mind is fixed upon the
Absolute he thinks of as God (344–45).

Every character in the novel other than Adams hangs helplessly
upon the wheel of life, which in Hindu philosophy is a wheel of
torture, the terrible wheel of death and rebirth, temporalized here
as the cycle of impulsive desire, pursuit of illusory pleasure, grati-
fication, satiety, spiritual death, and psychological renewal. Laura's
mystic experience in the Adirondacks seems to free her also from
the cycle, for it resembles that of Adams—but is presumably of a
lower level since the narrator speaks of "his deeper vision" and
"her mere vague instinct for light" (474). Whereas he encounters
the Absolute in other human beings, the vehicle of her vision comes
from the vegetable kingdom: still in great emotional shock, Laura
manages to hypnotize herself by focusing all her attention upon a
small blue flower "until there was revealed to her, while she looked,
not only the outward semblance, but *the essence of the flower which
was its soul.* And this essence of the flower came suddenly in contact
with the dead soul within her bosom, while she felt again the energy
which is life flowing through her body" (468–69, italics added). Immediately, by the "divine miracle of resurrection," she is reborn to
a larger, fuller life than either she led before. Laura's "ecstasy"
closely resembles the ecstacies described by Plotinus in the *Enneads*,
as well as those of Eastern mysticism, which Miss Glasgow linked
with Neoplatonism.[22] Her little blue flower is perhaps an offspring
of the blue cornflower, the symbol for ultimate value and ideal
being popular in German romanticism after Novalis.

The metaphysical foundation of compassion, then, according to
Adams' deeper vision, is the awareness that every man—indeed,
every animal, plant, and object—is inhabited by, or is a manifestation of, divinity: the universal mind or spirit. It is to this spark of

22 Tutwiler, *Ellen Glasgow's Library*, 23.

divinity in the other that one responds when one is compassionate. On the other hand, it is this highest possibility of the other that one offends when, in a social context, one acts sadistically or selfishly. Because that which determines one's own worth is also that which determines the other's ultimate worth, there exists a ground for sacrificial action. But, by the same token, there is no reason for Laura (to take the example at hand) to sacrifice herself to gratify Kemper in his pursuit of superficial pleasures (393). Ultimately, the value of this ethic depends on one's ability to accept its metaphysical base, which itself depends on one's electing to give such not uncommon experiences the very special names the two saints of *The Wheel of Life* choose.

Since Ellen Glasgow herself later chose to disown this novel and its metaphysics, it seems more than fair to offer a psychological explanation for what occurred both to Laura and, presumably, her creator. According to the Jungian analysis, the individual who has assumed either the introverted or extroverted attitude has three options when he enters a phase of life in which the repressed attitude becomes demonically demanding; he may radically embrace his unconscious personality, or he may stiffen into a fanatical, even regressive defense of his old attitude, or he may strive to retain his "former values together with a recognition of their opposites." [23] The latter solution, though preferable, is not totally satisfactory, for the individual who tries it loses the stone-like impenetrability mankind desires, by becoming totally aware of the potential for error, falsehood, uncertainty, and hate in either attitude he may assume. Ellen Glasgow, like Laura Wilde, grew to womanhood shielded (imperfectly, to be sure) by the romantic idealism of the southern set of mind. In rebellion, she embraced the opposite of lightheaded southern womanhood by accepting the mechanistic materialism of Darwinian philosophy, a phase of personal development which led perhaps to her impulsive and, presumably, sensual affair with B. When the affair ended in disillusionment, she re-

[23] C. G. Jung, "The Personal Unconscious and the Super-personal or Collective Unconscious," *Two Essays in Analytical Psychology* (London, 1928), reprinted in *Classics in Psychology*, ed. Thorne Shipley (New York, 1961), 729. See also: Patrick Mullahy, *Oedipus: Myth and Complex* (New York, 1955), 155–58.

coiled, not only from sensuality in love, but from materialistic monism as well. The idealistic third phase into which she and Laura pass seems a more effective synthesis of opposites than it actually is. It seems to acknowledge the values of extroversion by emphasizing the necessity of encounter with other people (Connie, the poor) and with external objects (the city, the sun, the sky, the flower). But it, instead, avoids the ambiguities and anxieties of a truly synthetic attitude by translating objects and people into categories of subjectivity or introversion—all life is a manifestation of consciousness, God's consciousness, in which man participates (474). In truth, the third phase for Miss Glasgow was simply a regressive defense of her sheltered first and, as such, little more than idealistic self-deception.

But whatever the worth of the metaphysical revelations described in *The Wheel of Life*, the novel managed to advance many of Miss Glasgow's older themes through its minor characters and situations. First, Laura's conversion offers a further demonstration of the idea developed in *The Deliverance*, that subsequent experiences can radically undo the consequences, at least at a psychological level, of an individual's heredity and early nurture, for Laura's vision separates her both from the eccentric Wildes of Gramercy Park and from Arnold Kemper. The effect, if not the means, resembles that of Christopher Blake's renewal.

Second, Miss Glasgow seems in her handling of several situations in *The Wheel of Life* to take a critical view of specific aspects of sympathy. For example, there is Mrs. Trent, a widow who has recently come from Virginia to New York to keep house for her son, a young playwright. She is accustomed to a perfectly provincial life which includes such patterns as her own twenty-five years of mourning for a husband killed during a fox hunt (56). Mrs. Trent tries, unfortunately, to transplant her provincial customs in a city apartment building. When she notices a doctor coming out of an apartment, she hurries with a glass of chicken jelly to inquire who is sick, but the shocked woman who opens the door is more rude than grateful. Mrs. Trent's son suggests that she not waste her jelly in the future, and her social instinct is frustrated: the thing she misses most about living in the city is visiting the sick (59–60). Occasionally, Mrs. Trent's pity incapacitates her for the give-and-take of urban living. When she calls the manager of her building about an inoperative radiator and he begins to complain about his own troubles, she hasn't the heart "to say anything about the heating" (201). A more pernicious perversion of compassion occurs in the behavior of Laura's bachelor uncle, Percival Wilde, who at eighty-two has begun to recover the pleasures of his childhood. Because his mind no longer equals his heart, his efforts to help others are usually received by the beneficiaries with timidity or anxiety: "His soul was overflowing with humanity, and he spent sleepless nights evolving innocent pleasures for those about him, but his excess of goodness invariably resulted in producing petty annoyances if not serious inconveniences" (21). In one curious episode, this droll old gentleman purchases a live white rabbit that happens to catch his eye as a gift for his old-maidish sister, a sufferer from all sorts of allergies. When he discovers that his sister has no use for a live white rabbit, he generously volunteers to care for it himself (28, 99–100). It is difficult to say whether this incident parodies enlightened self-interest (i.e., doing for others what you want them to do for you) or indicates that the old man lacks sufficient self-interest.

A third advance in Miss Glasgow's central themes turns up in the character and situation of Percival Wilde's sister: the first of Miss Glasgow's "Angelas." Angela Wilde has managed to live for forty years on a single indiscretion: "Unmarried she had yielded herself to a lover, and afterward when the full scandal had burst upon her head, though she had not then reached the fulfillment of a singularly charming beauty, she had condemned herself to the life of a solitary prisoner within four walls" (23). Angela thus leads an exaggerated form of the sheltered life. Her situation depends upon a moribund social tradition which places the ideal of feminine chastity above the natural well-being of any particular woman. Percival, in his simple-minded idealism, accepts the tradition wholeheartedly and evades the consequence for Angela. Laura accuses him of being responsible for Angela's condition: "Don't you see that by encouraging her as you did in her foolish attitude, you have given her past power over her for life and death. It is wrong—it is ignoble to bow down and worship anything—man, woman, child, or event, as she bows down and worships her trouble." To these charges, Percival can still answer, after Angela has spent forty years without seeing a male other than her brother, "Ah, Laura, would you have her face the world again?" (23–24). Although Angela's older, worldly sister, Rosa Payne, handles Angela's condition with verbal irony, which goes completely above the recluse's head, the fallen "beauty" has become "in the end at once the shame and the romance of her family" (23).

Angela's sheltered life originated, of course, in the chivalric ideal of woman, an invention, Miss Glasgow's later novels demonstrate, of males who desired to guarantee and protect the sanctity of their own bedrooms while they were busy in their neighbor's. Angela, however, has managed to subvert this original purpose. In forty years she has succeeded in transforming her trauma into a workable hypochondria replete with headaches, allergies, and exacerbatable nerves. As an invalid, she manages to prey upon the compassion of her family and, thereby, to tyrannize them.[24] There is some justice in this reversal in as much as her brother, whom she most complains about, is a masculine believer in the ideal which first required her to withdraw into her conventual room. There is less justice, however, in the way she uses her softhearted sister, Sophy Bleeker, and in the atmosphere Angela's sheltered existence creates for her young niece Laura (30, 32). The "Angelas" of Miss Glasgow's later novels—Angela Gay of *The Miller of Old Church* (1911), Angelica Blackburn of *The Builders* (1919), Eva Birdsong of *The Sheltered Life* (1932), and Lavinia Timberlake of *In This Our Life* (1941)—would more fully illustrate the causal connections between the moribund chivalric tradition (especially in its Victorian south-

[24] The theme of the tyrannical female invalid is not original with Miss Glasgow. It figured prominently, for example, in Strindberg's dramas—consider *The Father* (1886). Miss Glasgow's predatory women may stand as a bridge between Strindberg's and Tennessee Williams'. Miss Glasgow, however, because she was a novelist, seems to have been able to look more closely at the manner in which this feminine type is created by the unrealistic view of woman so central to chivalry. There is no allusion in her novels to the rather amusing "envy," or sense of organic inferiority, which Williams, following Freud, sees as the reason some females wish to mutilate males psychologically.

ern form), evasive idealism, the sheltered life, feminine invalidism, and commonplace feminine tyranny through the solicitation
of sympathy.

There is little else, however, in *The Wheel of Life* that reminds
the reader of the main body of Ellen Glasgow's fiction. This novel,
for example, dissects the social hypocrisy of the Bridewell-Kemper
circle precisely and with dead seriousness whereas her later novels
of manners would approach such deceits with the lofty irony closely
associated with her name.[25] Furthermore, Laura and Adams, having passed through the abyss, transcend phenomenal reality to encounter the Absolute, eternal universal consciousness; they come
from their mystic visions motivated by universal compassion. We
have seen that Anthony Algarcife, having passed through a similar abyss and having had the real world pulled from under him,
found nothing in the nothingness beyond; Algarcife came from
his confrontation with the void indifferent to himself and others.
Similarly, the heroine of Miss Glasgow's later masterwork, *Barren
Ground* (1925), descended into the abyss and learned that there is
nothing beyond the earth and beyond the will of an individual to
endure the plagues of the earth and to make it bloom beneath his
hand.[26]

It might be suggested that Miss Glasgow in *The Wheel of Life*
simply reached the conclusion expressed by a modern zoologist
when he found the following view of things helpful: The universe
as *known* is nature and, therefore, the proper subject for natural
science; the universe as *felt* is God and, therefore, belongs to poets,
philosophers, theologians, and men of faith.[27] This, however, does
not go far enough, for in *The Wheel of Life* Miss Glasgow is affirm-
ing beyond the idea expressed by the zoologist; she is asserting the
priority of Mind or Spirit (*Logos, Nous, Aum*) relative to Matter,

[25] See, for example, Majl Ewing, "The Civilized Uses of Irony: Ellen Glasgow,"
English Studies in Honor of James Southall Wilson, ed. Fredson T. Bowers (Charlottesville, 1951), 81–91.

[26] Figuratively speaking, of course. The earth represents all of nature and cultivation stands for all interactions between man and nature in which he makes active
use of its resources, including applied sciences and modern technology.

[27] A paraphrase of William E. Ritter, *Charles Darwin and the Golden Rule* (New
York, 1954), 353.

its priority both in time and value. This factor, it seems, takes the intended meaning of *The Wheel of Life* entirely out of the world of positivistic science—the Darwinian world. The idea of compassion expressed here has little resemblance to the social instincts Darwin spoke of, though their visible results might be the same. There can be, for example, little tension between self-preservation and sacrificial compassion, or much concern about the conflict between civilization and human nature, when the final judge of all actions is not the survival of the species, but the eternal universal consciousness, to which the individual knows he will eventually return, no matter what he has done in this life. Having had a foretaste of the eternal universal, the young lady, who, like Laura Wilde, once thought the customs of society frustrated the demands of her nature, simply renounces the nonmonogamous males of this world and awaits the rewards of the other.

Thus, in *The Wheel of Life*, Miss Glasgow took a (for her) new intellectual option and pursued it as far as she then knew how. In doing so, she dissolved, as even *The Deliverance* had not, the sense of conflict which dominated her past novels, the products of her "materialistic and pessimistic days." The questions the new book raised remained the same; she still wondered, for example, how a character endowed with great energies, sympathies, and determination might react to a major change of environment. But the answers she now found for these questions sprang from another dimension of being. There were hints regarding this new direction as early as Betty Ambler's animistic view of nature in *The Battle-Ground*, but there the beliefs which emerge as *the* Truth of *The Wheel of Life* were still only intellectual possibilities. It would be a mistake, however, to assume that Miss Glasgow had in any sense become an orthodox Christian. In the first place, Christianity would not accept her view that the Godhead is present in every aspect of the created world. In the second place, with the exception of St. Francis of Assisi, Miss Glasgow found nothing Christlike about Christians.[28]

28 St. Francis was one alone, while the robust Franciscan friars who would force a "small skeleton of a horse" to drag them up the steep hill to the Church of Assisi were a multitude (*Woman*, 175).

But she had moved closer, readers of 1906 probably supposed, to the religious views held by the majority of her American contemporaries.[29] And before she returned to the mainstream of her lifelong intellectual development, a position to which the phenomenal reality of Darwinian science had been and would again be of major importance, she would go even farther into the abstruse metaphysics about which *The Wheel of Life* turns.

THE LIMITS OF BELIEF

Whatever its internal problems, *The Wheel of Life*, published in January, 1906, arrived in a literary context which guaranteed poor reviews but good sales. First, the success of *The Deliverance* had conditioned a good number of critics to expect a certain type of novel from Ellen Glasgow—well-written psychological drama in a southern setting. Taken as a whole, her new novel satisfied no part of this expectation, for its psychological analysis lacks drama, it is set in New York, and the two worlds represented by Adams and Kemper are too diverse, it seems, to exist in one novel without a good deal more subordination of one or the other than Miss Glasgow yet could provide, probably because she lacked distance from the emotions she was dealing with. Second, *The Wheel of Life* appeared within months of Edith Wharton's well-done satire of New York society, *The House of Mirth*. Although not at all the same sort of book in its ultimate intention, Miss Glasgow's novel did deal with New York society, and was not as relaxed, unfortunately,

29 It would also be a mistake to suppose that the point of view represented in *The Wheel of Life* is a synthesis of ideas she collected from her exposure to nineteenth-century literature, as Frederick P. W. McDowell has suggested. McDowell detects signs of Arnold's God-as-impersonal-ethical-force, Browning's "gospel of effort," Tennyson's struggle between the lower and higher nature of man, Carlyle's or George Eliot's view that renunciation leads "to the highest beatitude," Meredith's "gospel of a necessary proportion between the senses and the soul," and Emerson's "self-reliance and the absorption of the individual by the Oversoul"—*Ellen Glasgow and the Ironic Art of Fiction* (Madison, 1960), 83. Granted, McDowell's purpose is probably to suggest the excessive intellectual ambition in this book, but his rhetoric clouds the fact that parallels to these so-called nineteenth-century ideas are stated much simpler either in Marcus Aurelius, the *Bhagavad-Gita*, Plotinus, or Spinoza—books Miss Glasgow was reading as she planned and wrote the novel.

as Mrs. Wharton's in those passages where they were most alike, a
weakness the critics were quick to note. The northern reviewers
disapproved of the similarities of the two novels, for although Mrs.
Wharton's book had not been published until the fall of 1905 there
was always the fact—useful to those who wished to make a case for
influence—that chapters of *The House of Mirth* had begun appearing in *Scribner's Magazine* the previous January. Only an old
friend, Louise Collier Willcox, thought *The Wheel of Life* had
more force and life than Edith Wharton's novel. Of the other critics who liked it, none gave a full explanation for his opinion. Gordon Pryor Rice of the New York *Times*, however, compared Adams'
renunciation with that in *The Resurrection* (1899) by Tolstoy.
Mary Moss in the *Bookman* criticized the author's knowledge of
New Yorkers. Southern reviewers were equally disappointed. The
general criticisms were that there are too many characters without
a center of interest, and that the characterizations are too labored
(for example, there are redundancies in the portrayal of Laura).
The critics encouraged her to stick to the South.[30]

The factors which worried the critics encouraged the buyers.
Those who liked *The Deliverance* rushed out expecting more of
the same. Readers responsible for the current burst of popularity
of stories dealing with social life, of which *The House of Mirth* was
one of a number, did the same. In April, *The Wheel of Life* led the
sales list, and three months out of the year it placed in the leading
six.[31] For 1906 it finished in tenth place—just behind Mrs. Wharton's book.[32] Nevertheless, Miss Glasgow later regarded the book,
"from every point of view, as a failure" (*Woman*, 171).

For the time, however, she continued the struggle which had produced *The Wheel of Life*, the dead-end search to find somewhere
in all the philosophies of the world "an antidote to experience, a
way out" of herself (*Woman*, 171). In August she and Rebe were

---

[30] *Literary Digest*, XXXII (March 31, 1906), 284–85; *New York Times Saturday
Review of Books*, January 21, 1906, p. 32; and *Bookman* (New York), XXIII (March,
1906), 91–93. These and other reviews are epitomized in Kelly, "Struggle for Recognition," 81–85.

[31] "Chronicle and Comment," *Bookman* (New York), XXIV (January, 1907), 438.

[32] Kelly, "Struggle for Recognition," 81–85.

back in the Adirondacks, having taken a cottage at Hurricane Lodge in Essex County, New York. From mysticism and Neoplatonism she had turned, by now, to modern idealism. But in "the eccentric whirl of a summer hotel," she had given herself over to the *dolce far niente*: Kant and Bradley stood half read on her desk, and for a month she had not dared open her "best beloved Fichte." When she wished to advise Mary Johnston to stay well, she drew on the *Upanishads* rather than the idealists: "You must . . . keep always with me in this 'small old path . . . difficult to tread as the keen edge of a razor.' " She drew also upon Eastern sentiments to express to Miss Johnston her nonattachment and her strange contentment; during the last year she had been happy, she then felt, for the first time in her life: "I who have all these things, [comparative health and strength to work and play and wander about the earth and make friends and enemies if I choose], . . . possess so little of the natural happy instinct for life that today at thirty-two, I could lie down quietly and give it up and pass on to one of the thousand lives I see beyond." For she was happy "not in the outward shadow part of me, but in my soul which is clear and radiant out of a long darkness." This mixture of joy and indifference to living resulted in a similar indifference to her work; she had spent the "summer staring (with newly sharpened pencils beside me) at a spotless sheet of paper." [33]

The loss of B., whether through death or disenchantment, changed her view of the Adirondacks, where they had probably been together a good deal after the summer of 1902. Now these mountains held no more illusions for her, and her "four years dream of a camp" there had "been washed away in rain." For this reason, she and Rebe soon packed for Montreal and Quebec to spend September and early October. From Chateau Frontenac in Quebec, Miss Glasgow wrote Miss Johnston a self-analysis that demonstrates the extent to which certain themes of her novels since the morose portrait of Christopher Blake in *The Deliverance* were products of her efforts to work out personal problems for herself, often, perhaps, by intuition alone: "I was born with a terrible bur-

[33] Ellen Glasgow to Mary Johnston, August 15, 1906, *Letters*, 52–54.

den of melancholy—of too much introspection—but for a whole
year, for the first time in my life, I have not known a single instant
of the old depression. I am perfectly willing to die, but I can say
now, as I never could before, that I am equally willing to live until
I come to where my road turns again." She had, she felt, been delivered from the individuated self, and to convey this idea to Miss
Johnston she drew an analogy between her own philosophy and
that of Whitman: "The sense of eternity—of immortality that is not
a personal immortality has brought to me not only reconciliation,
but the kind of joy that is like the rush down from the battle of the
senses. I have come at last into what Whitman calls 'the me myself,'
that is behind and above it all." [34] This is one of her earliest favorable references to an American writer other than Poe, Lanier, and
Henry James, and an indication how well her outlook had, by an
independent route, aligned itself with the main transcendental
currents of American thought.

The seemingly ultimate step along this road had been taken by
December, 1906, the month of Rebe's wedding. In October, Miss
Glasgow had returned to Richmond to renew the teas with Mary
Johnston, where the conversation ranged from Marcus Aurelius,
Neoplatonists, Kant, Schopenhauer, and "speculative philosophy
in general" to the national literary tradition represented by Irving,
Thoreau, Alcott, Emerson, and Mark Twain.[35] On December 5,
Rebe married Carrington C. Tutwiler of Philadelphia, formerly
of Lexington, Virginia. The visiting minister presiding over the
small ceremony, at which Ellen and Cary both appeared white and
worn, was the latest of Miss Glasgow's suitors, Frank Ilsley Paradise.
The following Sunday, Miss Glasgow and Miss Johnston attended
services in St. Paul's Episcopal Church, Richmond, for a taste of
the sort of sermon members of Grace Episcopal Church in Medford, Massachusetts, were accustomed to hear from Paradise, their
rector.[36]

During the week that followed, Miss Glasgow showed Richmond

---

[34] Ellen Glasgow to Mary Johnston, August 15 and September 15, 1906, *Letters*,
52–57.

[35] Entries for November 10, 11, 24, 1906, in "Mary Johnston, Her Book and Her's
Alone," an unpublished diary in the Mary Johnston Collection, Alderman.

[36] Entries for November 12, December 2, 5, 9, 1906, "Her Book," Alderman.

to Paradise, whom she had known as an abruptly outspoken vaca-
tioner like herself, at Hurricane Lodge in Essex County. Photographs suggest a man of dark reflection. Born in Boston (1859) and
educated at Yale (A.B., 1888),[37] he seems to have had two interests
in Richmond: Miss Glasgow and the condition of the Negroes. On
the Wednesday following her sister's marriage, Miss Glasgow and
he were joined by Mary Johnston and Miss Glasgow's long-time
friend, Carrie Coleman,[38] for a visit to a Richmond tobacco factory,
because she wished Paradise, in Miss Johnston's words, "to see and
hear the negroes." The diary kept by Miss Johnston, whose novels
belong to the Harris-Page tradition, describes the visit with touches
reminiscent of the then popular image of good antebellum blacks
living happily on the plantations. Since the war the plantation, we
see, has become the factory. She uncovers the elements of local
color: the Negroes "smiling, rolling their eyes," their singing, the
"Rembrandtesque" arrangement of browns and reds in the people,
the interior, the weed itself.[39] Surely Paradise and Miss Glasgow
saw deeper than the local color; it is likely that his philanthropic
idealism and advice that she try to get out of herself influenced the
social concern of her next novel, *The Ancient Law* (1908), which
treats factory conditions—among white workers in the Virginia tex-
tile industry. One wonders, however, if hers was not the stronger
influence, one pulling Paradise down to earth, when she invited

[37] Paradise had his B. D. (1890) from Berkeley Divinity School in New Haven. He
had served churches in Milford, Conn. (1890–93), and East Greenwich, R. I. (1893–
94). For four years, 1894–98, he was dean of a church in New Orleans. His connections with the Medford church lasted from 1898 to 1915. Then, after a four-year
hiatus, he became acting rector of the American Church of the Holy Trinity, the
Cathedral of Paris, from 1919 to 1920. Paradise was married twice—once, before he
met Miss Glasgow, to Caroline Wilder Fellowes, and again, in 1915, to an English
woman, Dorothy Pyman. He had had three sons and one daughter by his first wife
and would have two daughters by his second. He wrote books on Jesus Christ, on
Lincoln and Mazzini as champions of democracy, and on political relations between
America and England. He died in 1926, still somewhat smitten with Miss Glasgow if
his 1925 letters to her are any indication. See *Who Was Who in America, 1897–1942*
(Chicago, 1942), I, 933, and F. I. Paradise to Ellen Glasgow, August 2 and October 17,
1925, in Glasgow Collection, Alderman. Photograph referred to is in Glasgow Collection also.

[38] Later Mrs. Frank Duke, and Miss Glasgow's traveling companion after Rebe's
marriage took the latter to Philadelphia and after illness and, shortly, death ended
Cary McCormack's voyages with her sister.

[39] Entry for December 12, 1906, "Her Book," Alderman.

him to One West Main Street to dine on eight courses: raw oysters, sweetbreads, pheasants, salad, ham, ice cream, sherry and champagne.[40]

Miss Glasgow's romance with Paradise would eventually involve an engagement which lasted three years although she considered it "honestly and frankly experimental." As described in her autobiography, it supplied everything her love for B. had lacked: "Not only freedom from other ties, but intellectual congeniality, poetic sympathy, and companionship which was natural and easy, without the slightest sting of suspicion or selfishness." It lacked only "the sudden light in the heart," the madness she believed to be "the essence of falling in love." Although she felt sincere gratitude for the great love Paradise brought, there still lived, planted in the nerves of her memory, the vibrations caused by B., and a faint whisper of that old emotion "would start awake at a touch or a breath from the past" (*Woman*, 178–79). Under Paradise's guidance, she discovered she could love (after a fashion), she could worship; but she could not believe. She lacked the faith to go the entire mystic way—lacked the spiritual wings for the "flight of the alone to the Alone" (*Woman*, 172, 176).

This realization that mysticism did not suit her mind would mark a turning point for Miss Glasgow, when it came, near the end of the decade—a turning backward to her basic commitment to a rational, if not a positivistic, conception of what is. She would return too to the themes and problems explored in her earlier novels—hereditary and environmental determinism, instinctual drives, evasive idealism, the sheltered life—and discover that they, the true center of her interest, deserved greater development. Indeed, it may be said that by 1906 Ellen Glasgow had both found herself, as a woman and a writer, and then lost what she had found. The way back would be a halting one—accomplished perhaps only with the 1913 publication of *Virginia*. In the meantime, Ellen Glasgow would be divided against herself both intellectually and emotionally, and her work would suffer from the conflict.

[40] Ellen Glasgow to Mrs. Cabell Tutwiler, December 14, 1906, Ellen Glasgow Collection, University of Florida Library.

Conclusions and Continuations
The Novel of Possibilities

Ellen Glasgow's motives for later returning to the realistic out-look cannot have been as dramatic as the causes—visible in retro-spect between the lines of her life—of her original interest in crit-ical realism and the "new sciences" as tools to help understand the post-Reconstruction South. In most general terms, she initially found the Darwinian world view credible because it was strenu-ous; it stressed conflict and struggle as essential aspects of the human condition.

To a young woman born in a region recently torn by the most violent sort of conflict and raised by parents of diametrically op-posed temperaments, such catchwords as the "struggle for survival" had the clear ring of truth about them. The tragic deaths, within the same eight months, of both her mother and her mentor, George Walter McCormack, confirmed her acceptance of the modern scien-tific view, for their sad fates impressed upon her the necessity each man faces of struggling unceasingly in a universe where nothing is guaranteed; these twin disasters taught her that there is no certain justice in the natural order of things, no benevolent deity taking care that the best prosper—there are, instead, only chance and the necessity of struggle. In later life she would come to every important personal problem—the effort to find good publishers, the search for health, and her relations with the nonmonogamous males of the species—with this attitude that assumes conflict from the start.

Darwin appealed also to the skeptical quality of her mind. Although educated at home, she received the same diet of romance and idealism offered her contemporaries in small private schools; she, however, could not square these evasive views of life with the world she saw about her. Several early experiences—with her father's hard-shell Calvinism, with the evangelism of Dwight L. Moody, with postwar southern chauvinism, and with a divided family—created a vacuum of values, by alienating her from the trinity of middle-class verities conjured by the slogan, "God, Country, and Motherhood." Darwinian theory later filled that emptiness. Evolutionary theory, simply as a controversial philosophy, appealed also to her spirit of rebellion. Darwin and other scientists seemed, moreover, to provide a kind of verified, or verifiable, truth to replace the assertions and dogmas of religion and of idealistic writers. Perhaps most surprisingly (considering the time and the place), Darwin and the new sciences were accessible, thanks to the interest Walter McCormack, young lawyer, radical thinker, Reform politician, brother-in-law, took in her intellectual development.

In her early twenties, Darwinism became the master lens through which she studied both her region and the world at large, and remained so, although from time to time other pieces were added to her instrument of vision. When she tried at seventy to epitomize the unifying subject of the social history she had initiated four decades earlier with *The Voice of the People*, she returned to a theme she had come near articulating as early as 1935, but now she expressed it in Darwinian terms as a conflict between cultural environment and heredity; she wrote her literary confidant, James Branch Cabell: "I meant by social history the customs, habits, manners, and general outer envelope human nature had assumed in a special place and period. My place happened to be Virginia, and my period covered the years from 1850 to the present time. But the inner substance of my work has been universal human nature—or so I have always believed. . . . My major theme is the conflict of human beings and human nature, of civilization with biology." [1]

1 October 28, 1943, James Branch Cabell Collection, Alderman. Also: Ellen Glasgow to Allen Tate, April 3, 1933, and Ellen Glasgow to Miss Forbes, December 3, 1935, *Letters*, 134, 203.

Although this is an inference long after the fact based on many years of introspection and rethinking the motives of her own novels, a study of the books from first to last reveals that, for the most part, it is a true statement.

The protagonist of *The Descendant*, her first novel, finds himself in conflict with society because his egoism or instinct of self-preservation limits him to behavior of a half-savage kind. Her second protagonist, in *Phases of an Inferior Planet*, falls into conflict with civilization because social conventions prevent his obeying his own highly developed social instincts. Following her second novel, Miss Glasgow became interested in the ways rigid attitudes of social class pervert human nature. By *The Deliverance*, her fifth novel, she had found that such perversions can, in certain cases, be overcome with human compassion. In her sixth novel, *The Wheel of Life*, she looked once more at the highly endowed social innocent in conflict with the conventions of a sick society; in the latter work, the social innocent refuses to adjust and withdraws—seemingly into another world.

Evolutionary theory also stimulated Ellen Glasgow's interest in the problem of strict determinism as embodied in the conflict between Nature and Nurture. In her first three novels, an irreversible determinism seems in effect: the exercise of individual will is ultimately futile, though in itself admirable. By *The Deliverance* she had decided that a radical change in environmental forces could significantly change a character's patterns of conduct, if the original behavior was a result of class conditioning. This new view of determinism followed Miss Glasgow's personal conversion of outlook caused by love and, perhaps, literary success. In her next novel, *The Wheel of Life*, she showed that determinism might be transcended completely through the mystical view of life.

Ellen Glasgow's early interest in the connection between the sheltered life and evasive idealism was an extension of the distinction made by Darwin's chief advocate, Thomas Huxley, between the savage state of nature and the artificial state of human civilization. Miss Glasgow realized that the sheltering traditions and institutions of man's society often permit him to forget the abyss of savagery over which his civilization is suspended. This evasion, though nobly motivated, is potentially dangerous. In *Phases of an Inferior Planet*, the protagonist withdraws from the savage struggle for life into the shelter of the church, where he carries on a completely hypocritical ministry. In her next three novels Miss Glasgow was primarily concerned with the unreal world created by the sheltering tradition of the Virginia aristocracy; the false position of Mrs. Blake in *The Deliverance* was the most powerful early representation of the pernicious aspects of the sheltered life. In *The Wheel of Life*, the author used Angela Wilde to illustrate the manner in which the sheltered life may produce feminine invalidism and, consequently, the tyrannical female.

Two additional problems that Miss Glasgow's early works borrowed from Darwinian theory were: (1) an understanding of the pernicious effects a character's uncritical acceptance of hereditary determinism might have on his behavior, and (2) a concern about the dangers of certain forms of sympathy, especially excessive family feeling and compassion untempered by intelligence.

Although three of these first six novels have New York settings and deal critically with urban manners and social situations, all touch forcefully on problems closely associated with the South: its rigid class attitudes, its often inflexible belief in hereditary determinism, its blind defense of traditional order and feminine fragility, its uncritical elevation of sentiment and family feeling above reason. In addition, these early books dramatize the way the South oppresses poor whites, the religious outlooks dominant in the region, the South's defense of slavery, both the aristocratic obsession with revenge and the vulgarity of the new rich after Reconstruction, the defeat of reform politics by conservative forces in Virginia, and the inability of the protected "southern mind" to adjust effectively to the sensual attraction of a great commercial city. The major southern issue that escaped full-blown critical treatment in Miss Glasgow's early works—prior to *Virginia* (1913)—is the exploitation of blacks. (That she could remain in Richmond while George Washington Cable, who had dealt significantly with race in Louisiana, had been forced to retreat to Massachusetts tells us more about the ultimate base of the southern outlook, one deeper than all the talk about agrarianism, stability, and states' rights, than it does about differences between Richmond and New Orleans.) In writing as honestly as she knew how about those aspects of the southern system which jarred her moral sense, Miss Glasgow by 1906 had already touched on most of the supporting themes of her career (though she had not yet formulated the exact phrases to tag on them): the "sheltered life," "evasive idealism," the "vein of iron" (will to live), "family feeling," "saints of the things of nature," all are present under other names.

Indeed, it is likely that every book she ever wrote—with the exception of one product of her mystical and idealistic period, *The Ancient Law* (1908)—would reward the sort of biocultural analysis pursued in the present study. For example, in *The Miller of Old Church* (1911), the last book written in the "rather curious blend of romance and realism" that Ellen Glasgow called her "earlier manner," [2] the general thrust of the drama, and of human nature, is to bring together the passionate, sometime lovers, Molly Merryweather and Abel Revercomb, between whom blood and society place innumerable barriers. At the start, Molly's blood seems the chief obstacle, for she is the illegitimate offspring of an aristocratic "soldier of fortune," Jonathan Gay, and his overseer's daughter. To Abel's joyless Calvinistic mother, Molly's coquetry "proves" that she has inherited the sin of her parents; she is damned in the eyes of others for the same reasons as Michael Akershem.[3] Other passages suggest, however, that her flirting and fickleness express a temperamental impulsiveness inherited from her father's family (67). But her cruel teasing of suitors is also in part the product of environment, for her mother, with understandable vengeance, taught the girl to hate all men before she was ten (60). In her mistreatment of Abel there is as well an element of feminine perversity (the Wife of Bath's "queynte fantasye") which causes her always to want what she cannot have and to discover, once she has attained a goal, that she no

---

[2] *Measure*, 129.
[3] Ellen Glasgow, *The Miller of Old Church* (Garden City, 1911), 7, 53, 167. Hereinafter cited by page only.

longer desires it (68, 255, 305, 404). This perversity derives in part no doubt from the unconscious sense of personal unworthiness forced upon Molly, and on women in general, by a traditionally male-dominated culture, a feeling which causes them to believe unwittingly that there must be something second-rate about anyone who loves them. But perversity is also, in this novel, a mode of disobedience through which one tastes freedom (313, 315). In time, however, Molly discovers that the wish to keep free through perversity is itself determined by the romantic illusion that one might, through remaining free, "travel a certain distance . . . and pass the boundary of the commonplace and come into the country of adventure"; instead she finds "life is all just the same everywhere" (363–64). When Molly receives an inheritance from her father's will (symbolic of the past attempting to control the future) and moves into the Gay mansion, she is swayed temporarily by class attitudes associated with fine clothes (252), but sees later that such refinements are totally superficial (333). It is her perverse and automatic defiance of all social pressures that keeps her free of the snob attitudes and the aristocratic sweetness in which the Gays attempt to smother her (317, 326, 332–33). In the end, the narrator sees Molly's behavior as the complex product of a richly woven web of forces (278, 405). This interest in the *over*determination of Molly's attitudes and actions marks a breakthrough for Ellen Glasgow from the simple positivism of her earlier novels where character was too often the arithmetic product of instinct and environment.

The same growth toward complexity of motivation, however, does not mark Miss Glasgow's handling of Jonathan Gay and Abel Revercomb, her chief male characters in *The Miller of Old Church*. The younger Jonathan Gay, the disorganized, overripe nephew of Molly's father, seems little more than the present avatar of his philandering uncle and of their class's irresponsible impulsiveness. Blood and environment cannot be distinguished in young Jonathan's case since they exert parallel influences; his mother's shielded invalidism, for example, provides the same convenient alibi for his irresponsibility, in not acknowledging the way he has compromised Blossom Revercomb, that it furnished his uncle after he exploited Molly's mother (370, 410, 426).

If Jonathan also repeats the simple sensual impulsiveness of Perry Bridewell and Arnold Kemper of *The Wheel of Life* (but without the latter's drive), Abel Revercomb is as uncomplicated as Nick Burr of *The Voice of the People*. Like Jonathan (and the Reverend Mr. Orlando Mullen, who seems to have been modeled on F. I. Paradise), Abel is heavily dominated by his mother (166). His father was paralyzed, under the antebellum system, into poor-white shiftlessness by the necessity of competing with free black labor (48). Economic changes following the war, however, set free in Abel the great passionate drive his mother's family, the Hawtreys, had formerly drained off through their religious fanaticism (47, 206). This freedom and emotional force combine in Abel with the Hawtrey hardness, "impregnable self-esteem" and "iron will"—nourished through the generations on humorless Calvinism (116, 290)— to make young Abel, a miller, the fastest-rising self-made man and foremost citizen of the region around Bottom's Ordinary (16–17). Later, when Abel begins to study political economics in order to formulate a social philosophy suitable for the "enlightened and instructed proletariat" he intends to lead to political power, he is fully aware that he is free to create himself as he wishes to be (275–77).

The chief obstacle to Abel's freedom is that his drive toward self-advancement must compete, for his great emotional energy, with his social instinct. Through the first two-thirds of the novel he squanders his passion uselessly chasing elusive Molly to make her his bride. In the final third, his emotional force expresses itself as the sympathy he wastes upon Judy Hatch; he marries Judy, a plain, brainless girl, as a second choice, without knowing she is foolishly in love with the naïve minister, Orlando Mullen (259, 272, 360). Their marriage, based upon pity rather than love, becomes a burden to his political career (388). In this relationship, Ellen Glasgow amplified a theme she had touched on in *The Wheel of Life*: that certain forms of compassion untempered by critical intelligence are pernicious.

Parallel dangers of excessive family feeling emerge from the somewhat static portraits *The Miller* provides of two sisters, Mrs. Angela Gay (young Jonathan's mother) and Kesiah Blount. For the

ladies of the Gay house, the protective garden has been brought
inside: the tapestried furniture of the long drawing room is "all in
soft rose, a little faded from age" (73). As Mrs. Gay reminds Jonathan, only once in their lives has Kesiah had the perversity to go off
the lawn of the house without a gentleman to protect her (74). Mrs.
Gay comes gracefully, as she withers, into the powers which are
hers by right of female invalidism, and, by force of will, maintains
her illusions about her beloved brother-in-law's responsibility for
Molly's birth: "Oh, be careful, I am so sensitive. Remember that I
am a poor frail creature, and do not hurt me. Let me remain still
in my charmed circle where I have always lived, and where no unpleasant reality has ever entered" (77). Like old Mrs. Blake of *The
Deliverance*, she is almost physically destroyed by the shock that
ends her evasive idealism: her brother-in-law's will making his guilt
general knowledge (190, 220). Kesiah Blount, on the other hand,
lacks Angela's grace for submitting to the sexual double standard
of the sheltered life. As a girl, Kesiah had shown a gift for self-
expression not included among possibilities allowed her sex: she
wished to be a painter, and "rebelled fiercely . . . against nature,
against the universe, against the fundamental injustice" of her lot.
But the rebellion was crushed, and her gift withered "away in the
hothouse air that surrounded her." Although she seems an austere
saint, her buried emotional forces rage on as an active resentment
and consuming self-criticism, which have turned her into something
very much like an Andersonian grotesque (73, 75, 79–80, 229–30).

The natural saint of *The Miller* is Reuben Merryweather, Molly's grandfather. The grace with which Reuben accepts death furnishes the most sublime passage in any of Miss Glasgow's earlier
novels, a lyrical description of despair and death showing them to
be natural phases in the undivided movement of life (222–28). But
his general philosophy of resignation is more appropriate for a
lower-class role under the rigidly structured antebellum system than
for the New Men who emerge in the more fluid postwar situation.
As overseer of Jordan's Journey, Reuben reverenced his employer,
old Jonathan Gay, under whom he had also served as a soldier
(34–35). Forced by the loss of a leg in the war into a position of

idleness, humility, and sacrifice (185–86, 248), Reuben accepts both
the social and natural orders as God-ordained (216, 223–24), sub-
mits without resentment to the evils of slavery and ignorantly remains loyal to the corrupter of his own daughter (34–35). Although
some elements indicate he has achieved a profound wisdom of the
heart (215), it is the vision with which old men await death—not
that with which young men create themselves or re-create society.
For the latter ends, the hardness and arrogance of Abel's mother's
Calvinism provide a more useful starting point. The critical limits
Ellen Glasgow places on the validity of Reuben's vision indicate
the distance she had traveled, by 1911, back toward realism and
away from the materialistic mysticism which characterized Tucker
Corbin (*The Deliverance*), Laura Wilde, and Roger Adams (*The
Wheel of Life*). The next book would move farther in the same
direction.

In *Virginia* (1913), her first novel to eschew a superimposed romantic plot, Ellen Glasgow effectively broadened the significance of
the sheltered life beyond the southern situation. Although *Virginia*
chronicles the dull commonplace life of a southern lady between
1884 and 1912, it would be a mistake to confuse the novel's significance with its subject. Miss Glasgow has not "used the millstone to
crush a butterfly," as Joyce is accused of doing in the Nausicaa
episode of *Ulysses*. A novel must be about "something," and a dramatic novel must be about something relatively small since it works
synecdochically, not kaleidoscopically: it dramatizes the part and
makes it stand for the whole, rather than squander intensity attempting to show the whole. Virginia is a southern girl, to be sure.
But Virginia is also a state, a condition of the body, and, most important, a state of mind. Timid Virginia, not rebellious Eve, is the
fitting female companion of the American Adam. Published in the
year when idealism was proclaimed the official mental stance of
the nation in the person of President Woodrow Wilson and on
the eve of that great orgy of romantic idealism which became World
War I, *Virginia*, an anatomy of the virgin mind, was perhaps the
best informed and least mitigated fictional assault on American innocence since Melville's *Benito Cereno*. Within the limits of one

character's life and town, it manages to suggest something of the sexual, familial, artistic, racial, and economic tragedies of a nation of people who innocently assume that idealism is a moral position and forget that, at base, it is an ontological commitment which they lack the courage or (in Dinwiddie, at least) the intelligence to examine.

As anatomized in *Virginia*, the major motive for evasive idealism is the desire to avoid the immediate pains of ugly realities, either by simply refusing to see them[4] or by deflecting attention to another subject (41). No thought is given by the characters to the eventual anguish of disillusionment should glaring reality ever force itself through the "quivering rosy light" of adolescent desire, for that shock is one of the ugly actualities to be evaded. The primary axiom, or rationalization, supporting the idealistic state of mind in *Virginia* is the Providential alibi, that since the benevolent God of the Episcopal Church is in his heaven, all things happen for the best (67). This is a principle mindlessly subscribed to, at some point, by every important character, except the family of Cyrus Treadwell. Cyrus, however, imitates his own Scotch-Irish God in making certain always to be numbered among the oppressors of society rather than the economically oppressed, a pious imitation which enables him, like his neighbors, to avoid the unpleasant sense that he is responsible for economic and social realities (75). It is through Virginia Pendleton's mind that Ellen Glasgow explores the causes, the nature, and ultimate disaster of viewing life through a single, unquestioned, unchanging set of mind, especially through the veil of idealistic false consciousness.

Virginia's evasive idealism is overdetermined through the parallel influences of nurture ("The System" of Chapter One) and nature ("Her Inheritance" of Chapter Two). It would not be fair to summarize Miss Glasgow's exquisitely damning analysis of female education in Dinwiddie, but the dominant symbols associated with Priscilla Batte's Academy for Young Ladies are a solitary bud on a microphylla rosebush, a canary in a wire cage, and Miss Batte's "cameo brooch bearing the helmeted profile of Pallas Athene"

4 Ellen Glasgow, *Virginia* (Garden City, 1913), 35. Hereinafter cited by page only.

(3–5), suggesting the delicacy, imprisonment, and power for which she prepares young southern womanhood. Since pretty Virginia is "cut out for happiness," it is Miss Batte's function to make certain that she is thoroughly educated in "ignorance of anything that could possibly be useful to her," and that her reasoning faculties are paralyzed "so completely that all danger of mental 'unsettling' or even movement" is "eliminated from her future" (22–25). Virginia's mother, a professional beneficiary from other peoples' charity (41–42), is so much the product of the same educational system that it is difficult to determine whether she makes any uniquely personal contribution to her daughter's character at all. By precept and example, humorless Mrs. Pendleton, like the system, teaches Virginia to accept the Pauline and Prayer Book dogma of woman's inferiority (200), to assume all things are for the best (67), to look upon the oppressed situation of the blacks without seeing it as a problem (47), to efface herself and suffer with a smile (42–43), and to regard the world outside Dinwiddie with the most provincial fear imaginable (199).

Virginia's father, a mild, easy-going Episcopal clergyman who has allowed his own garden to be overrun by bleeding hearts and honeysuckle, teaches Virginia to live on humility, patience, and illusions, especially the illusions that all men (except Yankees and scalawags) are honest, that all women (even New England Abolitionists) are virtuous, that antebellum Virginia was perfection attained, and that the present state of things falls little short of that high condition (23, 26, 30, 35–36, 202). A master of the idealistic art of whitewashing actuality, Gabriel Pendleton demonstrates for his daughter in his own person how "ladies" can manipulate a man who takes the sentimental view of women (60, 251). That Gabriel was cut out for a bolder role is evident from his fond memories of savage years spent as a Confederate soldier, the "four happiest years" of his life, and in the atavistic pleasure he feels while sacrificing his life to save a young black from being lynched (76, 381). But all except the seed of this natural savage instinct to struggle has been tamed out of Gabriel by his wife and by the artificially mannered system of Dinwiddie life, so that sacrifice is his dominant instinct.

Had Virginia married someone with her father's commitment to self-sacrifice and his sentimental regard for feminine virtue, her life might have been less pathetic. With her family background and education, she is prepared ("programmed" would be the precise word if it were not anachronistic) for two functions: to attract a husband and then to have, and care for, their children (203–204, 227). No other reality need ever concern her. When at twenty, the great life force begins to stir Virginia, a passionate and fervently imaginative creature, she will not see it as a sexual instinct but as a power calling her to a special and glorious destiny, marriage (32–33, 52, 154–55, 158–59). Only after she is well along in her career as wife and mother does she learn that, as the delicate product of a long tradition of sexual selection, the strongest drive left her is neither the sexual nor the maternal instinct but the desire to sacrifice herself for someone—anyone—who needs her (5, 139, 279). Before she is forty-five, however, Virginia's children and husband discover other centers for their attention: no one at all needs her any longer. At this point when it is most important for her to do so, she lacks the natural instinct to compete for their attention and the flexibility to adjust to their new world views; these faculties have been smothered in her (217–18, 336, 481, 487, 494, 522). Virginia has outlived her world and her usefulness (443).

The husband, however, that Virginia selects, Oliver Treadwell, is prepared for success, not sacrifice. If she belongs, like the rose in her hair, to tradition, he belongs, like the new machines of the era, to change (5, 15). He cannot commit himself to the traditional view of women, nor to any position for very long, for the dominant facets of his character are an impetuous energy and a dedication adaptable to the interest at hand, both traits inherited, it appears, from his Treadwell ancestors (32, 122, 125). In several ways, Oliver resembles his uncle, Cyrus Treadwell, a leader of the new industrial South (64). Both view their projects through the great innocent "illusion of success," a veil which enables Cyrus, operating in tobacco, railroads, cotton, and lumber, to make theft seem honest and falsehood seem truth, much as it permits Oliver—who had earlier attempted to create a realistic drama that the country was too idealistic to accept—to console himself a bit with the financial and sexual rewards of serving up "theatrical wedding-cake" and "sugar plums" for an adolescent nation (64–65, 105, 403–404, 475). But Oliver, aware that he is pandering to a sentimental audience, never achieves that total complacency about his success which dulls Cyrus' brain into impenetrable certainty; Oliver considers himself a failure by his own aesthetic criteria (81, 85, 392, 479). Neither is Oliver as cold-blooded and soulless in dealing with women as Cyrus: the richest man in Dinwiddie, Cyrus reduces his aristocratically born wife to a grotesque invalid who must raise squab and sell her family's silver to obtain household money (112–13, 165–66); he is so skilled at evasion that he can completely close out of consciousness his responsibility as a capitalist for the deplorable economic and social conditions of workmen, farmers, and blacks—especially his obligation to Mandy, his wife's light-skinned washerwoman with whom he conceived a son he will neither acknowledge (hardly even to himself) nor support (81–82, 171–75, 365–68). (If Miss Glasgow's autobiography is accurate, it is plain that she modeled Cyrus after stolid aspects of her father's character.) At bottom, however, Oliver views the world, like his uncle, through the veil of "indomitable egoism" which guarantees that he will always "get the thing he wants most"—certainly from a wife who sees life, at its best, as an endless array of possible sacrifices (207, 217, 456). It is with a show of anguish that Oliver sacrifices Virginia, but sacrifice her he does—as Cyrus sacrificed his wife and Mandy—to pursue with minimal pain the things he most desires (490).

In *Virginia*, all Ellen Glasgow's major themes are skillfully integrated into the critique of evasive idealism as the mode by which the naïve or sheltered individual symbolically constructs his world. Virginia's conflict between an artificially nurtured duty to sacrifice self and a natural instinct to struggle for self is described as one between "principle" and "passion" or between "law" and "life"—terminology closely approximating the novelist's later categories, "civilization" and "biology" (488, 514). The dangers of excessive sympathy and family feeling supply the pathos that surrounds the female characters, while the actions of Oliver, Cyrus, and Susan

Treadwell spring most often from the opposite Darwinian instinct, self-interest. There are, however, no saints of natural things in *Virginia*, for the philosophy of acceptance which characterized Tucker Corbin, Roger Adams, and Reuben Merryweather becomes here only one more evasion paving the way for destructive self-sacrifice: it is the upward thrust of the life force during the spring that carries Virginia blithely to her sacrificial marriage with Oliver, and Gabriel blindly to his doomed intervention in a lynching (154–55, 158–59, 372–81). In the fallen world of Dinwiddie, the nearest person to a saint is ironically the poor sempstress, Miss Willy Whitlow, who remains alone, independent, buoyant, and harmless because she approaches her situation without illusions, without power over others, and with a will to struggle (91–92, 97, 207, 454).

More than any Glasgow novel before *The Romantic Comedians*, *Virginia* must be read with a constant knife-sharp alertness to the critical levels: almost every page is scintillant with hard, repellent irony. There are emotionally soft passages, for Miss Glasgow, like Oliver Treadwell, knew how to catch her audience in "the kind of thing they like," but she also knew, as Oliver did not, how to undercut such sentiment. For Ellen Glasgow, these soft passages are the novelist's strategy equivalent to a quarterback's "trap play"; the ironic reversal following each passage turns the unwary, sentimental reader, who is most likely an evasive American idealist, into the very object of the book's satire. The intellectual hardness that informs most of this novel makes the "pathos and irony" of post-World War I American fiction—say, of Hemingway's *The Sun Also Rises* and *A Farewell to Arms*, which also dramatize the dangers of sentiment and sacrifice—seem (after allowances are made for veils of ironically soft and hard styles) a little like Byronic *Weltschmerz*. Not only is *Virginia* one of Ellen Glasgow's four or five best novels—with *Barren Ground, The Romantic Comedians, They Stooped to Folly*, and *The Sheltered Life*—but its publication in 1913 must be counted one of the major events to occur in American fiction during the decade and half which passed between the appearance of James's *The Golden Bowl* (1904) and Anderson's *Winesburg, Ohio* (1919).

Viewed in terms of the biocultural themes around which Ellen Glasgow built her first six novels, the works of her major period (1925–41) would be of special interest, for there the original problems and possibilities are brought to an exceptionally high level of technical mastery and thematic clarity. For example, the conflict between human nature and civilization is brilliantly expressed in the rebellion Jenny Blair Archbald stages in the name of "being alive," against the world of *Little Women*, the garden shelter created by the Victorian ideal of the lady; Jenny's story *(The Sheltered Life)* receives additional poignance from her return to the shelter created by chivalry's false image of woman—after her surrender to romantic impulse causes the tragic death of George Birdsong. Dorinda Oakley's life *(Barren Ground)* embodies a conflict between Nature and Nurture; for Dorinda begins as a rather ineffective, impulsive creature but emerges, after a period of suffering and a change of environment, as a courageous (if stubborn) woman capable not only of endurance, but of re-creating her former environment more to her liking. The connection between evasive idealism and the sheltered life is deftly treated in *The Sheltered Life*, where General Archbald, limited by an idealized view of the female, tries to protect Jenny Blair Archbald and Eva Birdsong from realities they must face in order to avoid a warped state of mind. Lavinia Timberlake *(In This Our Life)* is one of the grotesque invalids the sheltered life makes of women; during twelve years of hypochondria she succeeds in tyrannizing her family as she never could in good health: she uses invalidism to prey upon the sympathies of her husband, who has disliked her for thirty years.

This recurrence of themes and problems with significant variations throughout Ellen Glasgow's career suggests an important dimension of her theory of realistic fiction. For her the novel was not simple mimesis, the imitation of life generally assumed of realism; as she often insisted, "the novel is experience illuminated by imagination." [5] Simple mimesis is the imitation of past and present experience; to this, imaginative illumination may add a future dimension extrapolated from forces set in motion by present and past

[5] Ellen Glasgow to Allen Tate, September 22, 1932, *Letters,* 124.

experience. In this way, Miss Glasgow felt herself able to explore such possibilities as the presence of an Akershem or a Burr in Virginia, or the romance of a Blake and a Fletcher, of a Laura Wilde and an Arnold Kemper, even when they did not yet exist or, at least, were not commonplace. All her novels might be regarded as parts of a continuing experiment to discover the kinds of human behavior possible when characters endowed with carefully specified instincts or temperament are placed in given environments. The sort of experimental novel she seems to have written under the influence of Darwinism differs from fiction influenced by other views of reality in that it is a novel of human possibilities rather than a novel of ideological imperatives. She is more interested in the "possible" (the "can be") than in the political, religious, or moral "imperative" (the "must be"). The "possible" is, of course, a compromise between things as they are or have been, and things as the unique human capacity for projection into the future imagines they might be; the "imperative" simply refuses to make that compromise with things as they are and, therefore, remains forever lost in things as they might be. The novel of possibilities looks out upon an open universe;[6] the novel of ideological imperatives looks to a universe hemmed in by dogma.

Beyond commonplace success and failure, four general possibilities for human conduct especially interested Ellen Glasgow in her later novels: the individual may, according to these recurring patterns, confront the beauty and brutality of his life with evasion, irony, an attitude of conflict, or an intuition of the essential unity of man and nature. General Archbald and George Birdsong (*The Sheltered Life*) are her most interestingly portrayed practitioners of evasion, and illustrate the vanity of the great tradition running from Adam, through St. Paul and courtly romance, to the Victorian

---

[6] Cf. Northrop Frye on art as "workable hypothesis, imitating human action" and the "events of a fiction" as "not real but hypothetical events," in *Anatomy of Criticism*, 84–85, 113; as well as the "possibilism" of William James discussed in Gay Wilson Allen, "William James's Determined Free Will," *Essays on Determinism in American Literature*, ed. Sydney J. Krause (Kent, Ohio, 1964), 69–71; and Mark Schorer's discussion of D. H. Lawrence's use of the novel as an "imaginative test of theoretical abstraction" in "Introduction," *Lady Chatterley's Lover* (New York, 1959), 12, 21.

period. Archbald evades the truth about the sexual desires that "ladies" have in order that the world might have objects suitable for its admiration; in doing so, he believes he has the best interests of women at heart. Birdsong idealizes women for his own selfish reasons; with white women on a pedestal and safely out of the way, he may visit his mulatto mistress with relatively little compunction.

In her major period (after 1925), Ellen Glasgow seems often to have looked to irony as the attitude by which an individual can best remove the sting from reality. Irony does not involve the self-deception of evasive idealism: the character who lives by irony does not turn his back on reality; he simply destroys its power to inflict pain by placing a buffer zone—usually a zone of humor; otherwise, one in which everything has a double meaning—between his vulnerable self and the offending truth. Miss Glasgow's greatest fictional ironists are Edmonia Bredalbane *(The Romantic Comedians)* and Mrs. Dalrymple *(They Stooped to Folly)*, two ripe, opulent, international adventuresses, each with her own collection of husbands and lovers, who are able to return to their home town only because their own shells of irony fend off the pernicious gossip that keeps neighbors safely within narrower patterns of conduct. The fact that Miss Glasgow's novels after *They Stooped to Folly* do not contain an important character blessed with the vein of irony seems to indicate that during the middle 1930's she decided certain realities are too painful and powerful to be repelled with humor or a doubleness of vision.

Because irony does not succeed and evasion is, of itself, unsound, the major attitudes that a character in Miss Glasgow's novels may assume towards existence are the sense of conflict and the sense of unity. The hero of Miss Glasgow's first novel, Michael Akershem, was notable for his extraordinary determination and his sense that he was involved in a gigantic struggle of all against all—of man against man, and man against nature. The outlook of Akershem persists in Miss Glasgow's later novels, but with an important modification. It dominates the lives of Dorinda Oakley *(Barren Ground)*, Ada Fincastle *(Vein of Iron)*, and Roy Timberlake *(In This Our Life)*. Miss Glasgow's later heroines—unlike Akershem, for whom

the struggle meant sudden outbursts of violence—are all characterized by a vein of iron, or fortitude, which enables them to endure
the desperation of commonplace living. One wonders whether she
ever came to realize that the conflict-attitude dominant in these perhaps autobiographical characters is considered a symptom of neuro-
sis by modern psychologists.[7]

Miss Glasgow's final two novels, *In This Our Life* and the recently published *Beyond Defeat*, make it clear that, though she
admired her heroines endowed with the vein of iron, she favored
her heroes blessed in addition with the "vein of gold," an intuition
of the essential unity of man and nature. Her first "saint of the
things of nature" was Tucker Corbin *(The Deliverance)*; her last
was Asa Timberlake *(In This Our Life* and *Beyond Defeat)*. The
important difference between Corbin and Timberlake is the role
that volition plays in their ascending to a state of natural grace.
Physical suffering and trauma gave Corbin the vision to revere the
beauty and brutality of nature; he remains, thereafter, a passive
spectator. Timberlake, by contrast, finds himself caught between
his natural desires and his family feeling. In a time of economic
depression, he believes he must work in a tobacco factory to fulfill
all his responsibilities to his family before he can leave them and
join his "great companion" (Kate Oliver) at Hunter's Fare, a sus-
taining rural environment with Jeffersonian overtones, the only
place where he feels he comes alive.[8] In order to achieve his goal he
must will to pursue a course of progressive adaptation to things as
they are. It is Timberlake's view that there is only one success, a
minimal one, without which the word "success" has no significance:
to live in unity with man and nature. Because critics—even while
awarding her the Pulitzer Prize for *In This Our Life*—failed to
understand the success of a failure like Asa Timberlake, Miss Glasgow wrote the sequel, *Beyond Defeat*; there the vein of gold in Asa
is clearly contrasted with the vein of iron in his daughter, Roy

[7] Alfred Adler, "New Leading Principles for the Practice of Individual-Psychology"
and "Individual Psychology, its Assumptions and its Results," *The Practice and
Theory of Individual Psychology* (London, 1955 [1923]), in *Classics in Psychology*,
ed. Thorne Shipley (New York, 1961), 687–714, especially 711n.

[8] Ellen Glasgow, *In This Our Life* (New York, 1941), 173–75, 372–75.

Timberlake. In the sequel, Roy comes to see that her father's sense of unity embodies greater wisdom than her own sense of conflict.[9]

The two basic possibilities described by Ellen Glasgow's novels, the two visions through which man may realistically comprehend his position in the universe—with a sense of universal conflict or an intuition of unity—are as important to modern thought as they were in the period of the debate over Darwinism at the end of the nineteenth century and the beginning of the twentieth. William Barrett, in his important study of the most influential intellectual movement since World War II, *Irrational Man* (1958), has demonstrated that the basic difference between two modern leaders of this movement, Martin Heidegger and Jean-Paul Sartre, may be reduced to this distinction in attitudes. Sartre cannot transcend conflict; his "Being-for-itself" (consciousness) finds itself "irremediably opposed to the Other" and alienated from "Being-in-itself" (nonconscious being). By contrast, Heidegger's Field Theory of Being dissolves the Cartesian gulf between subject and object, between mind and body. Man exists as *Dasein* (Being-in-the-World); he does not find himself wholly within himself, but outside himself "tuned" to the mood *(Stimmung)* of his surroundings. Because man *is* this mood, he is intimately united with his surroundings—whether the things of nature or the things made by man. "Because man stands in this context, this open space of Being, he may communicate with other men." In thus dissolving the gulfs between man and things, between man and man, Heidegger also dissolves the *necessity*, though not the probability, of conflict.[10]

This comparison is not, of course, an effort to put Ellen Glasgow forward as an early American existentialist; only to show the extent

9 Cf. Ellen Glasgow, *A Certain Measure*, 253–54; *Beyond Defeat: An Epilogue to an Era*, ed. Luther Gore (Charlottesville, 1966), 125–28; Parent, *Ellen Glasgow*, 345–46, 514. Miss Parent, while noticing the author's fondness for Asa, finds him lacking in admirable qualities, chiefly, I assume, because she does not place him in his proper context—with Tucker Corbin and Miss Glasgow's other saints of natural things, Reuben Merryweather *(The Miller of Old Church)* and John Fincastle *(Vein of Iron)*; the latter, because he is intellectually committed to idealism, would require discriminating attention.

10 William Barrett, *Irrational Man, A Study in Existential Philosophy* (New York, 1962), 224, also 217–24, 248–50, 257–58. Werner Brock, "An Account of *Being and Time*," in Martin Heidegger, *Existence and Being* (Chicago, 1949), 14–15.

to which an analysis of her fiction from the biocultural point of view brings one to its inner substance and universal qualities, that the central possibilities it describes are still lively issues, and that Miss Glasgow's conception of man and man's struggle with his civilization deserves the searching attention of readers other than professional scholars.[11] That she defined "human nature" (as Darwin did) in terms of a tension between two basic instincts—self-interest, which leads to an attitude of conflict, and sympathy, which may lead to a sense of unity—whereas influential modern thinkers deny the existence of "universal human nature" and prefer to speak instead of the "human condition," [12] is not as important as the fact that the same modern thinkers (Heidegger and Sartre) are still faced with the basic attitudes she insisted upon. If she leaned at the end more toward the possible unity of men and nature posited by Heidegger (whom one pictures comfortably rooted on a peak of the Black Forest Mountains)[13] than toward the sense of unending conflict described by Sartre (the champion of deracination, whom one imagines forever perched precariously on the edge of a bench in a bistro), it was probably because she had known the pleasure of the seasons, of the Swiss Alps, the Scottish lakes, and of Virginia's woods, hills, streams, sky, and blooming fields. Even though we, as modern readers, more easily understand Sartre's anguish than Heidegger's "letting Being be," there is enough of the former in Miss Glasgow's finest novels to hold our interest.

If the preoccupation of American fiction since the twenties with sensation ever gives way to an interest in novels of vision, then there is a hope that Miss Glasgow's books will in the future find friendlier critics and readers of greater understanding than they have in the past thirty years. Such will be the case, however, only if coming

11 See William W. Kelly, "Introduction," *Ellen Glasgow: A Bibliography* (Charlottesville, 1964), xxxi.

12 Jean-Paul Sartre, "Existentialism," *Existentialism and Human Emotions* (New York, 1957), 14–39, especially 14–15, 38. Interest in "universal human nature" declined after William McDougall's concept, the "human instinct," fell from intellectual favor in the late twenties; Shipley, *Classics in Psychology*, 1336.

13 Stefan Schimanski, "Foreward," Heidegger, *Existence and Being*.

critics are more interested in a novel of possibilities than one of ideology, and only if future readers come to the books they read with spirit of open inquiry rather than a rage for order at any cost or a nostalgia for religious, political, social, and philosophic orthodoxy.

Selected Bibliography

The thoroughness of William W. Kelly's recent *Ellen Glasgow: A Bibliography* (301 pp.) makes it unnecessary for scholars to list all ephemeral materials related to Ellen Glasgow. The following bibliography includes manuscript collections consulted, items cited in this book, materials that have appreciably influenced my understanding of the early period of Ellen Glasgow's life, and a few titles not included by Kelly.

The bibliography is in two sections: Manuscript Collections; and Books, Pamphlets, Articles, and Newspapers.

MANUSCRIPT COLLECTIONS CONSULTED

MAJOR GLASGOW COLLECTIONS

The Ellen Glasgow Collection in Alderman Library, University of Virginia.
The Ellen Glasgow Collection, University of Florida Library.

OTHER MANUSCRIPT COLLECTIONS

The James Branch Cabell Collection in Alderman Library, University of Virginia.
The Margaret May Dashiell Collection, University of North Carolina Library.
The Mary Johnston Collection in Alderman Library, University of Virginia.
The Howard Mumford Jones Collection, Harvard College Library.
The Charles H. Towne Collection, New York Public Library.

256 BIBLIOGRAPHY

The Carl Van Vechten Collection, Yale University Library.
The Robert W. Winston Collection, University of North Carolina Library.

BOOKS, PAMPHLETS, ARTICLES, AND NEWSPAPERS

Adams, J. Donald. "The Novels of Ellen Glasgow," *New York Times Book Review*, December 18, 1938, pp. 1, 14.
———. "Speaking of Books," *New York Times Book Review*, November 24, 1940, p. 2.
———. "Speaking of Books," *New York Times Book Review*, October 30, 1955, p. 2.
Ahnebrink, Lars. *The Beginnings of Naturalism in American Fiction.* New York, 1961.
American Booktrade Directory. New York, 1928.
Andrews, Matthew P. *Virginia: The Old Dominion.* New York, 1937.
[Anonymous]. "By a Richmond Girl," Richmond *Dispatch*, June 12, 1897, p. 2.
———. "Chronicle and Comment," *Bookman* (New York), V (July, 1897), 368–70.
———. "Chronicle and Comment," *Bookman* (New York), XX (January, 1905), 402–405.
———. "Chronicle and Comment," *Bookman* (New York), XXIV (January, 1907), 438, 441.
———. "Henry W. Anderson for Vice-President—The Foremost Anti-Sectionalist and Advocate of a More Perfect Union" [pamphlet supporting Anderson's candidacy for Republican vice-presidential nomination in 1929].
———. "Miss Ellen Glasgow," Baltimore *Sun*, April 19, 1903, p. 7.
———. "New Writer," *Bookman* (London), XIX (September, 1900), 167–68.
———. "Portrait," *The Critic*, XLIV (March, 1904), 200.
Auchincloss, Louis. *Pioneers and Caretakers: A Study of Nine American Women Novelists.* Minneapolis, 1965.
Auerbach, Erich. *Mimesis: The Representation of Reality in Western Literature.* New York, 1957.
Bailey, Pearce. *Accident and Injury, Their Relations to Diseases of the Nervous System.* New York, 1899.
———. "Change of Masters," *Harper's Magazine*, CXXVIII (October, 1913), 752–59.
———. "The Wishful Self," *Scribner's Magazine*, LVIII (July, 1915), 115–21.

Barrett, William. *Irrational Man, A Study in Existential Philosophy.* New York, 1962.

Becker, Allen W. "Ellen Glasgow and the Southern Literary Tradition," *Modern Fiction Studies,* V (Winter, 1959–60), 295–303.

Book Buyer, XIV (July, 1897), 564–65.

Bookman (New York), XXII (February, 1906), 554.

Bookman (New York), XL (January, 1915), 478.

Brickell, Herschel. "Miss Glasgow and Mr. Marquand," *Virginia Quarterly Review,* XVII (Summer, 1941), 405–17.

Bridges, J. Malcolm. *Richmond, Capital of Virginia: Approaches to its History.* Richmond, 1938.

Briney, Martha M. "Ellen Glasgow: Social Critic," (Ph.D. dissertation, Michigan State University, 1956), *Dissertation Abstracts,* XVII (1957), 1334.

Brooks, Van Wyck. "Ellen Glasgow, 1874–1945," *Commemorative Tributes at the American Academy of Arts and Letters, 1942–1951.* New York, 1951.

Bruce, Kathleen. *Virginia Iron Manufacture in the Slave Era.* New York, 1939.

Buck, Paul H. *The Road to Reunion.* Boston, 1937.

Burke, Kenneth. *Permanence and Change: An Anatomy of Purpose.* New York, 1965.

Cabell, James Branch. *As I Remember It.* New York, 1955.

————. *Let Me Lie.* New York, 1947.

————. "Two Sides of the Shielded," *New York Herald–Tribune Books,* April 20, 1930, pp. 1, 6.

Canby, Henry Seidel. "Ellen Glasgow: A Personal Memory," *Saturday Review of Literature,* XXVIII (December 22, 1945), 13.

————. "Ellen Glasgow: Ironic Tragedian," *Saturday Review of Literature,* XVIII (September 10, 1938), 3–4, 14.

————. "SRL Award to Ellen Glasgow," *Saturday Review of Literature,* XXIII (April 5, 1941), 10.

Cargill, Oscar. *Intellectual America, Ideas on the March.* New York, 1941.

Cash, W. J. *The Mind of the South.* Garden City, New York, 1956.

Chamberlin, T. C., ed. *Fifty Years of Darwinism, Modern Aspects of Evolution.* New York, 1909.

Charleston *News and Courier,* June 18, 19, 20, 1894.

Chase, Richard. "Letters to the Establishment," *New Republic,* CXXXVIII (March 10, 1958), 18–19.

Chesterman, Evan R. "Her Views of Life," Richmond *Dispatch,* November 30, 1898, p. 5.

Clark, Emily. "Appreciation of Ellen Glasgow and Her Work," *Virginia Quarterly Review*, V (April, 1929), 182–91.

———. "A Week-end at Mr. Jefferson's University," *New York Herald-Tribune Books*, November 8, 1931, pp. 1, 2.

Clemons, Harry. *Notes on the Professors for Whom the University of Virginia Halls and Residence Houses Are Named.* Charlottesville, 1961.

Collins, Joseph. *Taking the Literary Pulse: Psychological Studies of Life and Letters.* New York, 1924.

Colvert, James B. "Agent and Author: Ellen Glasgow's Letters to Paul Revere Reynolds," *Studies in Bibliography*, XIV (Charlottesville, 1961), 180.

Conner, Frederick W. *Cosmic Optimism: A Study of the Interpretation of Evolution by American Poets from Emerson to Robinson.* Gainesville, 1949.

Cooke, John E. *Surry of Eagle's-Nest.* New York, 1894.

Cooper, Frederic T. "Representative American Story Tellers: Ellen Glasgow," *Bookman* (New York), XXIX (August, 1909), 613–18.

Couch, W. T., ed. *Culture in the South.* Chapel Hill, 1935.

Coulter, E. Merton. *The South During Reconstruction, 1865–1877.* Baton Rouge, 1947.

Cowley, Malcolm. "Promise Paid," *New Republic*, CXIII (December 10, 1945), 805.

Crane, Stephen. *The Red Badge of Courage,* ed. R. W. Stallman. New York, 1960.

Dabbs, James McBride. *Who Speaks for the South?* New York, 1964.

Dabney, Virginius. *Liberalism in the South.* Chapel Hill, 1932.

Darwin, Charles. *The Origin of Species and The Descent of Man.* New York, The Modern Library, n.d.

———. *The Variation of Animals and Plants Under Domestication,* 2 vols. New York, 1897.

Davidson, Donald. "Another Woman Within," *New York Times Book Review,* January 19, 1958, pp. 7, 14.

———. "A Mirror for Artists," *I'll Take My Stand: The South and the Agrarian Tradition, By Twelve Southerners.* New York, 1930.

Dewey, John. "Evolution and Ethics," *Monist*, VIII (April, 1898), 321–41.

———. *The Influence of Darwin on Philosophy.* New York, 1910.

Dictionary of American Biography, 20 vols. New York, 1928–37.

Dictionary of National Biography, 2nd supp., 3 vols. London, 1912.

Dobzhansky, Theodosius. *Mankind Evolving: The Evolution of the Human Species.* New Haven, 1962.

Dollard, John. *Caste and Class in a Southern Town.* New York, 1957.

Dunbar, John R. "The Reception of European Naturalism in the United States: 1870–1900." Ph.D. dissertation, Harvard University, 1947.

Edel, Leon. "Postal Portrait," *Saturday Review of Literature,* XLI (January 18, 1958), 17.

Egly, William H. "Bibliography of Ellen Anderson Gholson Glasgow," *Bulletin of Bibliography,* XVII (September–December, 1940), 47–50.

Elias, Robert H. *Theodore Dreiser: Apostle of Nature.* New York, 1949.

Ewing, Majl. "The Civilized Uses of Irony: Ellen Glasgow," *English Studies in Honor of James Southall Wilson,* ed. Fredson T. Bowers, Charlottesville, 1951.

Fadiman, Clifton, ed. *I Believe.* New York, 1939.

Farrar, John. "Publisher's Eye View," *Saturday Review of Literature,* XXX (August 9, 1947), 11–12, 26.

Field, Louise M. *Ellen Glasgow: Novelist of the Old and the New South: An Appreciation.* Garden City, New York, 1923.

Flitch, J. E. C. *The National Gallery.* Boston, 1912.

Franklin, John Hope. *Reconstruction: After the Civil War.* Chicago, 1961.

Freeman, Douglas S. "Ellen Glasgow: Idealist," *Saturday Review of Literature,* XII (August 31, 1935), 11–12.

Freud, Sigmund. *A General Introduction to Psychoanalysis.* New York, 1953.

Frye, Northrop. *Anatomy of Criticism.* New York, 1966.

Garland, Hamlin. *Companions on the Trail: A Literary Chronicle.* New York, 1931.

———. *"The Descendant* and Its Author," *Book Buyer,* XV (August, 1897), 45–46.

———. *My Friendly Contemporaries.* New York, 1932.

———. *Roadside Meetings.* New York, 1930.

Geismar, Maxwell. *Rebels and Ancestors: The American Novel, 1890–1915.* Boston, 1953.

Giles, Barbara. "Character and Fate: The Novels of Ellen Glasgow," *Mainstream,* IX (September, 1956), 20–31.

"Glasgow Choice Urged for Years," New York *Times,* May 5, 1942, p. 14.

Glasgow, Ellen. "Agent and Author: Ellen Glasgow's Letters to Paul Revere Reynolds," *Studies in Bibliography,* XVI (1961), 177–96.

———. *The Ancient Law.* New York, 1908.

———. *Barren Ground.* Garden City, New York, 1925.

———. *The Battle-Ground.* New York, 1902.

_____. *Beyond Defeat: An Epilogue to an Era*, ed. Luther Y. Gore. Charlottesville, 1966.

_____. "The Biography of Manuel," *Saturday Review of Literature*, VI (June 7, 1930), 1108–1109.

_____. "Branch Cabell Still Clings to His Unbelief," *New York Herald-Tribune Books*, October 6, 1935, p. 7.

_____. *The Builders*. Garden City, New York, 1919.

_____. *A Certain Measure*. New York, 1943.

_____. *The Collected Stories of Ellen Glasgow*, ed. Richard K. Meeker. Baton Rouge, 1963.

_____. *The Deliverance*. New York, 1904.

_____. *The Descendant*. New York, 1897.

_____. "Elder and Younger Brother," *Saturday Review of Literature*, XV (January 23, 1937), 3–5.

_____. "Flush: Portrait of a Famous and Much-Loved Dog," *New York Herald-Tribune Books*, October 8, 1933, pp. 3, 21.

_____. *The Freeman and Other Poems*. New York, 1902.

_____. "George Santayana Writes a 'Novel,'" *New York Herald-Tribune Books*, February 2, 1936, pp. 1–2.

_____. "German Propaganda in America," New York *Times*, February 3, 1915, p. 10.

_____. "Heroes and Monsters," *Saturday Review of Literature*, XII (May 4, 1935), 3–4.

_____. *I Believe*, ed. Clifton Fadiman. New York, 1938.

_____. "Impressions of the Novel," *New York Herald-Tribune Books*, May 20, 1928, pp. 1, 5–6.

_____. *In This Our Life*. New York, 1941.

_____. *Letters of Ellen Glasgow*, ed. Blair Rouse. New York, 1958.

_____. *Life and Gabriella*. Garden City, New York, 1916.

_____. *The Miller of Old Church*. Garden City, New York, 1911.

_____. "Mr. Cabell as a Moralist," *New York Herald-Tribune Books*, November 2, 1924, pp. 1–2.

_____. "No Valid Reason Against Giving Votes to Women," New York *Times*, March 23, 1913, Sec. 6, p. 11.

_____. *One Man in His Time*. Garden City, New York, 1922.

_____. *Phases of an Inferior Planet*. New York, 1898.

_____. "'The Professional Instinct,': An Unpublished Short Story by Ellen Glasgow," *Western Humanities Review*, XVI (Autumn, 1962), 301–17.

_____. "Richmonders in Constantinople," Richmond *Dispatch*, April 23, 1899, p. 7.

_____. *The Romance of a Plain Man*. New York, 1909.

_____. *The Romantic Comedians*. Garden City, New York, 1926.

_____. *The Shadowy Third and Other Stories*. Garden City, New York, 1923.

_____. *The Sheltered Life*. Garden City, New York, 1932.

_____. "The Soul of Harlem," *Bookman* (New York), LXIV (December, 1926), 509–10.

_____. *They Stooped to Folly*. Garden City, New York, 1929.

_____. *Vein of Iron*. New York, 1935.

_____. *Virginia*. Garden City, New York, 1913.

_____. *The Voice of the People*. New York, 1900.

_____. "What I Believe," *The Nation*, CXXXVI (April 12, 1933), 404–406.

_____. *The Woman Within*. New York, 1954.

_____. *The Wheel of Life*. New York, 1906.

Gore, Luther Y. "Ellen Glasgow's 'Beyond Defeat': A Critical Edition." Ph.D. dissertation, University of Virginia, 1964.

de Graffenried, Thomas P., ed. *The de Graffenried Family Scrap Book*. Charlottesville, 1958.

_____. *History of the de Graffenried Family, from 1191 to 1925*. New York, 1925.

Hackett, Alice Payne. *Fifty Years of Best Sellers, 1895–1945*. New York, 1945.

Hall, Calvin S. *A Primer of Freudian Psychology*. New York, 1955.

Hartwick, Harry. *The Foreground of American Fiction*. New York, 1934.

Hatcher, Harlan. *Creating the Modern American Novel*. New York, 1935.

Hawkins, Richmond L. *Auguste Comte and the United States, 1816–1853*. Cambridge, 1936.

Heidegger, Martin. *Existence and Being*, intro. Werner Brock. Chicago, 1949.

Heilbroner, Robert L. *The Worldly Philosophers*. New York, 1961.

Hendrick, Burton J. *The Life and Letters of Walter H. Page*, 2 vols. New York, 1922.

_____. *The Training of an American: The Earlier Life and Letters of Walter H. Page, 1855–1913*. New York, 1928.

Henkin, Leo J. *Darwinism in the English Novel, 1860–1910: The Impact of Evolution on Victorian Fiction*. New York, 1940.

Henneman, John B. "The National Element in Southern Literature," *Sewanee Review*, XI (July, 1903), 345–66.

Herrick, Christine Terhune. "The Author of *The Descendant*," *The Critic*, XXX (June 5, 1897), 368–70.

Herron, Ima H. *The Small Town in American Literature.* Durham, 1939.

Hicks, Granville. *The Great Tradition.* New York, 1935.

Hierth, Harrison E. "Ellen Glasgow's Ideal of the Lady with Some Contrasts in Sidney Lanier, George W. Cable, and Mark Twain" (Ph.D. dissertation, University of Wisconsin, 1956), *Dissertation Abstracts,* XVI (1956), 2150.

Hill, Belle M. "The Flight from Love Motif in the Novels of Ellen Glasgow." Unpublished M. A. thesis, University of Virginia, 1957.

Himmelfarb, Gertrude. *Darwin and the Darwinian Revolution.* Gloucester, Mass., 1967.

Hofstadter, Richard. *Social Darwinism in American Thought.* Boston, 1955.

Holman, C. Hugh. "The Southerner as American Writer," *The Southerner as American,* ed. Charles G. Sellers. Chapel Hill, 1960.

————. *Three Modes of Modern Southern Fiction.* Athens, Ga., 1966.

Hubbell, Jay B. "Poe and the Southern Literary Tradition," *Texas Studies in Literature and Language,* II (Summer, 1960), 151–71.

————. *The South in American Literature.* Durham, 1954.

Hughes, H. Stuart. *Consciousness and Society: The Reorientation of European Social Thought, 1890–1930.* New York, 1958.

Huxley, Thomas H. *Evolution and Ethics, and Other Essays.* New York, 1896.

Hyman, Stanley Edgar. *The Tangled Bank: Darwin, Marx, Frazer, and Freud as Imaginative Writers.* New York, 1962.

The Impact of Darwinian Thought on American Life and Culture, Papers Read at the Texas Conference on American Studies. Austin, Texas, 1959.

James, William. *The Varieties of Religious Experience: A Study of Human Nature.* New York, 1961.

Jessup, Josephine L. *The Faith of Our Feminists: A Study in the Novels of Edith Wharton, Ellen Glasgow, Willa Cather.* New York, 1950.

Jones, Howard M. "Ellen Glasgow, Witty, Wise and Civilized," *New York Herald-Tribune Books,* July 24, 1938, pp. 1, 2.

————. "Is There a Southern Renaissance?" *Virginia Quarterly Review,* VI (April, 1930), 184–97.

————. "Mr. Lewis's America," *Virginia Quarterly Review,* VII (July, 1931), 427–32.

"Joseph Collins Foundation, 1951–1953" [Pamphlet published by Joseph Collins Foundation, New York, n.d.].

Kant, Immanuel. *Critique of Pure Reason.* New York, 1900.

Kauffmann, Stanley. "End of an Epoch?" *New Republic,* CLIII (October 16, 1965), 31–34.

Kazin, Alfred. *On Native Grounds*. Garden City, New York, 1956.

Kelly, William W. *Ellen Glasgow: A Bibliography*. Charlottesville, 1964.

_____, ed. " 'The Professional Instinct': An Unpublished Short Story by Ellen Glasgow," *Western Humanities Review*, XVI (Autumn, 1962), 301–17.

_____. "Struggle for Recognition: A Study of the Literary Reputation of Ellen Glasgow." Unpublished Ph.D. dissertation, Duke University, 1957.

Kidd, Benjamin. *Social Evolution*. New York, 1895.

Kilmer, Joyce. " 'Evasive Idealism' Handicaps Our Literature," *The New York Times Magazine*, March 5, 1916, Sec. 6, p. 10.

Krause, Sydney J., ed. *Essays on Determinism in American Literature*. Kent, Ohio, 1964.

Kropotkin, Peter. *Mutual Aid, A Factor of Evolution*. London, 1908.

Kunitz, Stanley J., and Howard Haycraft. *Twentieth Century Authors*. New York, 1942.

Lawrence, Margaret. *The School of Femininity*. New York, 1936.

Lecky, William E. H. *History of European Morals, From Augustus to Charlemagne*, 2 vols. London, 1882.

Le Hew, Anne. "The Rebel Motif in the Novels of Ellen Glasgow." Master's thesis, University of Virginia, 1955.

Leisy, Ernest E. *The American Historical Novel*. Norman, Okla., 1950.

"Letter Book of George Frederick Holmes," *Alumni Bulletin of the University of Virginia*, V (November, 1898), 74–77.

Lively, Robert A. *Fiction Fights the Civil War*. Chapel Hill, 1957.

Loggins, Vernon. *I Hear America: Literature in the United States since 1900*. New York, 1937.

Mackintosh, Robert. *From Comte to Benjamin Kidd: The Appeal to Biology or Evolution for Human Guidance*. New York, 1899.

Maine, Henry. *Ancient Law*. London, 1861.

Mann, Dorothea L., ed. *Ellen Glasgow*. Garden City, New York, 1927.

Mannheim, Karl. *Ideology and Utopia, An Introduction to the Sociology of Knowledge*. New York, 1959.

Marcosson, Isaac F. *Before I Forget: A Pilgrimage to the Past*. New York, 1959.

_____. "The Personal Ellen Glasgow," *Bookman* (New York), XXIX (August, 1909), 619–21.

Martino, Pierre. *Le Naturalisme Français*. Paris, 1923.

Marx, Leo. *The Machine in the Garden: Technology and the Pastoral Ideal in America*. New York, 1964.

McDowell, Frederick P. W. *Ellen Glasgow and the Ironic Art of Fiction*. Madison, 1960.

McIlwaine, Shields. *The Southern Poor-White from Lubberland to Tobacco Road.* Norman, Okla., 1939.

Mencken, H. L. "A Southern Skeptic," *American Mercury*, XXIX (August, 1933), 504–506.

Mims, Edwin. *The Advancing South: Stories of Progress and Reaction.* Garden City, New York, 1926.

————. "Southern Fiction After the War of Secession," *The South in the Building of the Nation*, ed. John B. Henneman. Richmond, 1909. Vol. VIII, pp. xlviii–lxiv.

Monroe, Nellie E. *The Novel and Society: A Critical Study of the Modern Novel.* Chapel Hill, 1941.

Morgan, C. Lloyd. *Emergent Evolution.* London, 1923.

Morgan, H. Wayne. *Writers in Transition, Seven Americans.* New York, 1963.

National Cyclopaedia of American Biography. New York, 1891–.

"Necrology," *Alumni Bulletin of the University of Virginia*, I (July, 1894), 35.

New York *Herald*, June 18, 19, 1894.

New York *Herald-Tribune*, April 26, 1935.

New York *Times*, June 19, 1894; February 25, 1896; April 26, 1925; January 2, June 23, 1929; June 19, 1932; April 26, June 16, 1935; January 1, 1937; May 1, June 7, December 19, 1938; February 1, May 5, 10, 1942; November 22, December 4, 1945.

Nietzsche, Friedrich. *The Birth of Tragedy and the Genealogy of Morals*, trans. Francis Golffing. New York, 1956.

Nordau, Max. *Degeneration.* New York, 1898.

Ormond, John R. "Some Recent Products of the New School of Southern Fiction," *South Atlantic Quarterly*, III (July, 1904), 285–89.

Overton, Grant. *The Women Who Make Our Novels.* New York, 1918.

Parent, Monique. *Ellen Glasgow, Romancière.* Paris, 1962.

Patterson, Daniel W. "Ellen Glasgow's Plan for a Social History of Virginia," *Modern Fiction Studies*, V (Winter, 1959–60), 353–60.

————. "Ellen Glasgow's Use of Virginia History," Ph.D. dissertation, University of North Carolina, 1959.

Perkins, Maxwell E. *Editor to Author: The Letters of Maxwell Perkins*, ed. John H. Wheelock. New York, 1950.

Persons, Stow, ed. *Evolutionary Thought in America.* New Haven, 1950.

Progressive Age, XXV (1907), 127, 567.

Quesenbery, W. D. "Ellen Glasgow: A Critical Bibliography," *Bulletin of Bibliography*, XXII (May–August, 1959), 201–206; XXII (September–December, 1959), 230–36.

Quinn, Arthur H. *American Fiction: An Historical and Critical Survey.* New York, 1936.

Ransom, John Crowe. "Modern with the Southern Accent," *Virginia Quarterly Review*, XI (April, 1935), 184–200.

Ravenel, Mrs. St. Julien. *Charleston: The Place and the People*. New York, 1927 [1906].

Richmond *Dispatch*, March 25, 1892; October 28, 1893; June 19, 20, 21, 1894; June 12, 1897; April 23, 1899.

Richmond *News Leader*, April 7, 1909.

Richmond *Times–Dispatch*, April 8, 1909; January 30, 1916; July 2, 1918.

[Riddell, Charlotte E. L.] or "Rainey Hawthorne." *Ruling Passion*. London, 1845.

Ritter, William E. *Charles Darwin and the Golden Rule*. New York, 1954.

Rouse, Blair. *Ellen Glasgow*. New York, 1962.

Rubin, Louis D., Jr. *Writers of the Modern South: The Faraway Country*. Seattle, 1966.

———. *No Place on Earth: Ellen Glasgow, James Branch Cabell, and Richmond-in-Virginia*. Austin, Texas, 1959.

———. "The Road to Yoknapatawpha: George W. Cable and 'John March, Southerner,'" *Virginia Quarterly Review*, XXXV (Winter, 1959), 118–32.

——— and Robert D. Jacobs, eds. *Southern Renascence: The Literature of the Modern South*. Baltimore, 1953.

Russell, Bertrand. *A History of Western Philosophy*. New York, 1945.

Rutherford, Mildred. *The South in History and Literature, A Handbook of Southern Authors from the Settlement of Jamestown, 1607 to Living Writers*. Atlanta, 1907.

Santas, Joan Foster. *Ellen Glasgow's American Dream*. Charlottesville, 1965.

Sartre, Jean-Paul. *Anti-Semite and Jew*. New York, 1965.

———. *Being and Nothingness, An Essay on Phenomenological Ontology*. New York, 1956.

———. *Existentialism and Human Emotions*. New York, 1957.

Savage, Minot J. "Natural Ethics," *North American Review*, CXXXIII (September, 1881), 237.

Schopenhauer, Arthur. *The Works of Schopenhauer*, ed. Will Durant and intro. Thomas Mann. New York, 1955.

Scott, William B. *The Theory of Evolution*. New York, 1917.

Sherman, Stuart P. "Ellen Glasgow: The Fighting Edge of Romance," *Critical Woodcuts*. New York, 1926.

Shipley, Thorne, ed. *Classics in Psychology*. New York, 1961.

Sidney, Philip Francis. *The Ruling Passion, A Comic Story of the Sixteenth Century*. Hull, 1821.

Simonini, R. C., ed. *Virginia in History and Tradition.* Farmville, Virginia, 1958.

Smith, Henry Nash. *Virgin Land: The American West as Symbol and Myth.* New York, 1959.

The Song of God: Bhagavad-Gita, trans. Swami Prabhavananda and Christopher Isherwood, and intro. Aldous Huxley. New York, 1951.

Spencer, Herbert. *The Study of Sociology.* New York, 1891.

Spiller, Robert E. *The Cycle of American Literature: An Essay in Historical Criticism.* New York, 1955.

_____ et al. *Literary History of the United States.* New York, 1953.

Steele, Oliver L. "Ellen Glasgow, Social History and the 'Virginia Edition,' " *Modern Fiction Studies,* VI (Summer, 1961), 173–76.

Sutherland, Alexander. *The Origin and Growth of the Moral Instinct,* 2 vols. London, 1898.

Sydnor, Charles S. *The Development of Southern Sectionalism, 1819–1848.* Baton Rouge, 1948.

Tate, Allen. "The New Provincialism: With an Epilogue on the Southern Novel," *Virginia Quarterly Review,* XXI (Spring, 1945), 262–72.

Tax, Sol, ed. *Evolution After Darwin: The University of Chicago Centennial,* 3 vols. Chicago, 1960.

Taylor, William R. *Cavalier and Yankee: The Old South and American National Character.* New York, 1961.

Turner, John M. "The Response of Major American Writers to Darwinism, 1859–1910." Ph.D. dissertation, Harvard University, 1944.

Tutwiler, Carrington C., Jr. *Ellen Glasgow's Library.* Charlottesville, 1967.

Van Auken, Sheldon. "The Southern Historical Novel in the Early Twentieth Century," *Journal of Southern History,* XIV (May, 1948), 171, 186.

Van Gelder, Robert. "An Interview with Miss Ellen Glasgow: A Major American Novelist Discusses Her Life and Work," *New York Times Book Review,* October 18, 1942, pp. 2, 32.

Villard, Léonie. "L'Oeuvre d'Ellen Glasgow, Romancière Américaine," *Revue Anglo–Américaine,* XI (December, 1933), 97–111.

Walcutt, Charles C. *American Literary Naturalism, A Divided Stream.* Minneapolis, 1956.

Weismann, August. *Essays Upon Heredity and Kindred Biological Problems,* 2 vols. Oxford, 1892.

Wellford, Clarence. "The Author of *The Descendant,*" *Harper's Bazar,* XXX (June 5, 1897), 458, 464.

Wells, Benjamin W. "Southern Literature of the Year," *Forum,* XXIX (March–August, 1900), 501–12.

Wermuth, Paul C. "Valley Vein," *Virginia Cavalcade*, VII (Winter, 1957), 13–16.

Wheeler, William M. *Emergent Evolution and the Development of Societies*. New York, 1928.

Whittle, Gilberta S. "The Brilliant Richmond Novelist," Richmond *Dispatch*. September 2, 1900, p. 2.

Who Was Who, 1897–1928, 2 vols. London, 1929–53.

Who Was Who in America, 1897–1960, 3 vols. Chicago, 1942–60.

Who Was Who in America: Historical Volume, 1607–1896. Chicago, 1963.

Willcox, Louise Collier. "Ellen Glasgow," Boston *Evening Transcript*, February 17, 1904, p. 17.

Williams, Wayne C. *William Jennings Bryan*. New York, 1936.

Wilson, Edmund. *Patriotic Gore: Studies in the Literature of the American Civil War*. New York, 1966.

Wilson, James S. "Ellen Glasgow: Ironic Idealist," *Virginia Quarterly Review*, XV (Winter, 1939), 121–26.

———. "Ellen Glasgow's Novels," *Virginia Quarterly Review*, IX (October, 1932), 595–600.

Woodward, C. Vann. *The Burden of Southern History*. Baton Rouge, 1960.

———. *Origins of the New South, 1877–1913*. Baton Rouge, 1951.

World's Work, XI (December, 1905), 69999.

Zola, Emile. *The Experimental Novel*. New York, 1894.

Zweig, Stefan. *Balzac*. New York, 1946.

Index